HIKING VIRGINIA

HELP US KEEP THIS GUIDE UP TO DATE

Every effort has been made by the authors and editors to make this guide as accurate and useful as possible. However, many things can change after a guide is published—regulations change, facilities come under new management, and so forth.

We would love to hear from you concerning your experiences with this guide and how you feel it could be improved and kept up to date. While we may not be able to respond to all comments and suggestions, we'll take them to heart, and we'll also make certain to share them with the authors. Please send your comments and suggestions to falcon editorial@rowman.com.

Thanks for your input!

HIKING VIRGINIA

A GUIDE TO THE STATE'S GREATEST HIKING ADVENTURES

FIFTH EDITION

Bill and Mary Burnham

FALCONGUIDES

ESSEX, CONNECTICUT

Between us, we have nearly twenty nieces and nephews, most of whom we have dragged hiking and camping at some point through the past 30 years. Several are featured in this edition as models, photographers, and subject matter. This fifth edition is dedicated to them, their future adventures, and to the memory of our nephew Josh.

FALCONGUIDES®

An imprint of Globe Pequot, the trade division of
The Rowman & Littlefield Publishing Group, Inc.
4501 Forbes Blvd., Ste. 200
Lanham, MD 20706
www.rowman.com

Falcon and FalconGuides are registered trademarks and Make Adventure Your Story is a trademark of The Rowman & Littlefield Publishing Group, Inc.

Distributed by NATIONAL BOOK NETWORK

Photos by Bill and Mary Burnham unless otherwise noted.
Maps by The Rowman & Littlefield Publishing Group, Inc.

British Library Cataloguing in Publication Information available

Library of Congress Cataloging-in-Publication Data available

ISSN 1547-3406
ISBN 978-1-4930-7565-2 (paper: alk. paper)
ISBN 978-1-4930-7566-9 (electronic)

♾™ The paper used in this publication meets the minimum requirements of American National Standard for Information Sciences—Permanence of Paper for Printed Library Materials, ANSI/NISO Z39.48-1992.

CONTENTS

THE HIKES

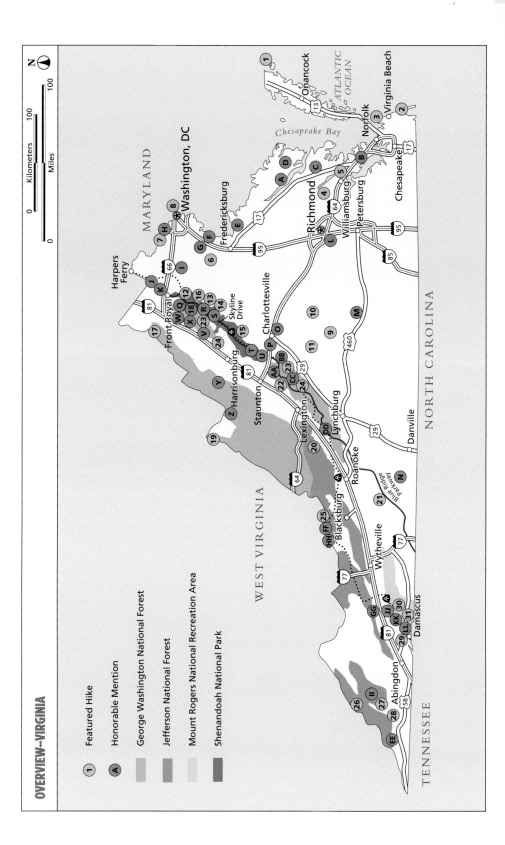

OVERVIEW—VIRGINIA

Featured Hike

Honorable Mention

George Washington National Forest

Jefferson National Forest

Mount Rogers National Recreation Area

Shenandoah National Park

MEET YOUR GUIDES

We began backpacking together while dating more than 30 years ago. Our first trip as a couple was in Shenandoah National Park (we can attest to the state slogan: Virginia truly is for Lovers!). *Hiking Virginia* was our very first book, the first edition published in 2001. Since then we've written numerous travel articles and several books about our state, the Old Dominion.

With this fifth edition, we crossed a major milestone: 30 years exploring and writing about Virginia. We are grateful you have trusted us to take you down the many and varied trails and backroads, blueways, and byways of Virginia.

In the last decade, we've added outdoor outfitting to our efforts, guiding people on winter kayak expeditions in the Florida Keys, Everglades, and Costa Rica, paddling and hiking in Virginia spring through fall.

Our home and kayak shop are located in Onancock on the Eastern Shore of Virginia, within easy reach of both sources of inspiration: ocean and mountains.

You can reach us and follow our adventures at www.burnhamguides.com or on Facebook. We'd love to hear about your adventures!

Falcon Guides by Bill and Mary Burnham:
Hiking Virginia
Best Hikes Near Washington, D.C.
Florida Keys Paddling Atlas
Kayaking for Everyone
Car Camping for Everyone

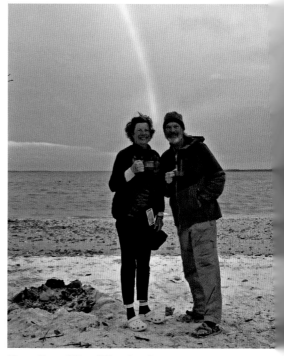

The authors, Bill and Mary Burnham.
DOM J. MANALO

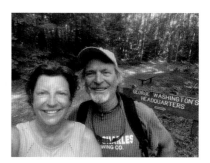

The authors in 2023

HOW TO USE THIS GUIDE

Take a close enough look and you'll find that this little guide contains just about everything you'll ever need to choose, plan for, enjoy, and survive a hike in Virginia. We've done everything but load your pack and tie up your bootlaces. Stuffed with useful Virginia-specific information, *Hiking Virginia* features thirty-one mapped and cued hikes, thirty-eight honorable mentions, thirty-three unique day hikes along the Appalachian Trail, and everything from advice on getting into shape to tips on getting the most out of hiking with your children or your dog. We've added accessible trails for people with disabilities, GPS coordinates for trailheads, and new color photographs. And you get the easy-to-understand color trail maps. With so much information, the only question you may have is: How do I sift through it all? Well, we answer that, too.

We've designed our guidebook to be highly visual, for quick reference and ease of use. What this means is that the most pertinent information rises quickly to the top, so you don't have to waste time poring through bulky hike descriptions to get mileage cues. They're set aside for you. Yet *Hiking Virginia* doesn't read like a laundry list. Take the time

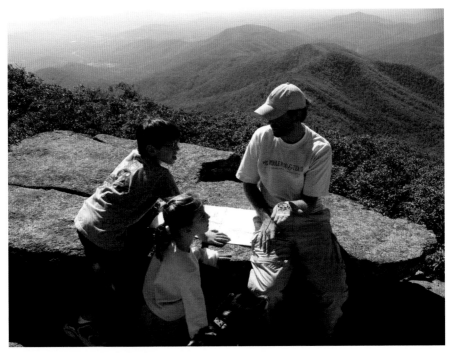

The author showing young hikers how to use a compass

to dive into a hike description, and you'll realize that this guide is not just a good source of information—it's a good read. Here's an outline of the book's major components.

To aid in quick decision making, we start each hike chapter with a short overview to give you a taste of the hiking adventure to follow. You'll learn about the trail terrain and what surprises the route has to offer. If your interest is piqued, read on; if it isn't, skip to the next hike.

The hike specifications that follow are fairly self-explanatory. Here you'll find the quick, nitty-gritty details of the hike: where the trailhead is located, hike distance, approximate hiking time, difficulty rating, type of trail terrain, land status, the nearest town, what other trail users you may encounter, if there's any accessibility for people with disabilities, whether it's pet-friendly, trail contacts (for updates on trail conditions), trail schedules, whether fees or permits are required, facilities and/or features at the hike venue, and available maps. Finding the trailhead provides dependable directions from a nearby city right down to where you'll want to park, with GPS coordinates.

The Hike is the meat of the chapter. Detailed and honest, it's our carefully researched impression of the trail. While it's impossible to cover everything, you can rest assured that we won't miss what's important. The Miles and Directions sections provide mileage cues to identify turns and trail name changes, as well as points of interest. The Hike Information section at the end of each hike is a hodgepodge of information. Here we'll tell you where to stay, what to eat, and what else to see while you're hiking in the area.

The Honorable Mentions for each section detail hikes that didn't make the cut. In many cases it's not because they aren't great hikes, but because we simply did not have the room. Be sure to read through these. A jewel might be lurking among them.

We don't want anyone to feel restricted to just the routes and trails that are mapped here. We hope you'll have an adventurous spirit and use this guide as a platform to dive into Virginia's backcountry and discover new routes for yourself. One of the simplest ways is to just turn the map upside down and hike the course in reverse. The change in perspective is often fantastic, and the hike should feel quite different. With this in mind, it'll be like getting two distinctly different hikes on each map.

For your own purposes, you may wish to copy the directions for the course onto a small sheet to help you while hiking, or photocopy the map and cue sheet to take with you. Otherwise, just slip the whole book in your backpack and take it all with you. Enjoy your time in the outdoors, and remember to pack out what you pack in. For more information about enjoying the outdoors responsibly, visit the Leave No Trace website at https://lnt.org.

NOTES ON MAPS

Topographic maps are essential companions to the activities in this guide. If the activity takes place on a National Geographic Trails Illustrated map, it will be noted. Continually setting the standard for accuracy, each Trails Illustrated topographic map is crafted in conjunction with local land managers and undergoes rigorous review and enhancement before being printed on waterproof, tear-resistant material. Trails Illustrated maps and information about their digital versions, which can be used on mobile GPS applications, can be found at www.natgeomaps.com.

BEFORE YOU HIT THE TRAIL

STATE OVERVIEW

Welcome to the fifth edition of *Hiking Virginia,* a book we first researched and hiked in the late 1990s before we had a GPS or a digital camera. Over 30 years of hiking, we've added new color photographs, GPS coordinates for the trailheads, and information for people with disabilities.

In our travels, we subscribe to the theory Richard Nelson eloquently expressed in *The Island Within:* "What makes a place special is the way it buries itself in the heart, not whether it is flat or rugged, rich or austere, wet or arid, gentle or harsh, warm or cold, wild or tame."

Our book is about more than destinations. It is about experiences set amid Virginia's natural beauty. More and more, people seek out culture and history where they travel. Walking, whether up a mountain or down a quaint city street, offers a traveler no better way of achieving this (admittedly, we're biased—we *love* hiking). A walk slows the world so sights, smells, and sounds may leave a mental imprint. *Hiking Virginia* is a trail of breadcrumbs you can use time and time again to enjoy Virginia's beautiful landscapes, rich history, and kind people.

Virginia lends itself to the foot traveler. Higher mountains and larger expanses of preserved land may be found elsewhere, but in Virginia, the best parts of many worlds exist. Flat, low-lying coastal areas enjoy temperate ocean breezes. The Piedmont unfolds westward, one gentle hill after another, up to the steep flank of the Blue Ridge, an ancient mountain range of billion-year-old granite and prehistoric lava flows. Beyond the Blue Ridge and great valley lies the Allegheny chain of mountains, with distinct valleys and

Hiking in Virginia ranges from sea level to mountaintop.

The authors, Mary and Bill Burnham, and Coco near mile-high Mount Rogers, the highest point in Virginia

ridges tending northeast-southwest. In the state's far southwest corner, the land rises to its highest peaks of nearly 6,000 feet.

In Virginia, hikers find endless possibilities. They might walk beneath the broad sky of a high-altitude meadow, inhale the spruce scents of a remnant boreal forest, delight in the natural richness of an Appalachian cove forest, walk along tidal marshes, or play in the ocean surf. The sun rises over an Atlantic barrier island, while hundreds of miles inland in a mountain valley, sunlight creeps, inch by inch, down a forested ridge until it alights on the deepest, coolest parts of the earth. From coast to mountain, Virginia beckons. Answer her call, find your place, and make it special.

Thank you for purchasing the fifth edition of *Hiking Virginia*.

VIRGINIA WEATHER

Virginia's climate is a seasonal mixed bag. In winter, storms arrive from the west. In fall, tropical weather arrives from the Atlantic or, occasionally, from the Gulf of Mexico. When severe enough, these tropical storms become hurricanes. During summer, warm air settles over the state, resulting in hot days punctured by thunderstorms. Late fall and winter are wet-weather seasons, while summer and early fall are generally dry.

Along the coast—the state's warmest region—the Atlantic winds exert a moderating influence on temperatures, making highs and lows less extreme. Back Bay Wildlife Refuge, a coastal barrier island, averages 86 degrees F in July. By contrast, the southern Piedmont city of Danville experiences an average temperature of 90 degrees F in July. Likewise, in winter, temperatures on the coast average above freezing. Inland, on the Piedmont, temperature averages dip to the mid-20s.

Weather can be extreme at Virginia's highest elevations.

Virginia's mountains and valleys produce wildly fluctuant temperatures and levels of precipitation. Virtually every state record—high and low temperature, high and low rainfall and snowfall—has occurred in the Blue Ridge Mountains and points west. Summer temperatures range from the mid-80s into the 90s. In winter, temperatures dip into the teens. Snow is common in the mountains, with average accumulations between 6 and 7 inches December through February.

When storms arrive from the west, the Allegheny Mountains cast a rain shadow over eastern mountain slopes and the Shenandoah Valley. When storms originate from the east, the Blue Ridge reverse the pattern, wringing moisture out on eastern slopes, leaving the western slopes and valleys dry. As a result, the Shenandoah Valley is the driest region of the state, averaging only 33 inches of rain annually. To the east, across the Blue Ridge, the city of Charlottesville averages 47 inches. And in far southwest Virginia, annual rainfall totals more than 60 inches.

Tropical storms and hurricanes deserve special mention in Virginia. They occur August through October and bring with them threats of high winds and flooding. A

Fog settles into the Blue Ridge Mountains. EDDIE FORT

hurricane is defined as a storm with sustained wind gusts of 74 mph, but a tropical storm can be as harrowing an experience. Hurricanes are often thought of as coastal weather events, but Virginia's worst 20th-century storm, Hurricane Camille in 1969, devastated Nelson County in the eastern Blue Ridge region.

VIRGINIA FLORA AND FAUNA

Virginia's forests are comprised primarily of broadleaf, deciduous trees. Under this forest blanket exist plant communities specially adapted to the state's varying climates.

Grasses, salt meadow hay, and hearty shrubs such as wax myrtle populate coastal fringes of Virginia. These are some of the most resilient plants in the world, able to withstand harsh winds and saltwater conditions. Inland from the beaches and dunes, lagoons mix a daily tidal wash with mainland runoff. Fish spawn here and crustaceans such as fiddler crab live out their early years on a nutrient-rich diet. On the mainland, forests of pines and oak typify the flat coastal region. In swampy areas, bald cypress and live oak are often draped with Spanish moss.

Besides cushioning a daily onslaught of waves and wind, the Atlantic barrier islands of Virginia support breeding and migratory birds. From Assateague to False Cape, the arrival and breeding of songbirds, raptors, shorebirds, and wading birds of all shapes and sizes mark every season. As many as 400,000 birds of prey, representing twelve species, have been observed at Kiptopeke State Park on the Eastern Shore during a single fall count.

Virginia's Piedmont has traditionally supported agriculture. By the 20th century, generations of farming left large swaths of barren land. Where forests returned, they are primarily black and white oak and Virginia and loblolly pine. In Virginia's state forests, oak and poplar are managed for harvest. Willow oak, river birch, hickory, and ash grow as well. Cumberland State Forest near Farmville marks the extreme western reach of the loblolly pine in Virginia. Turkey, fox, deer, raccoon, and squirrel populate these pockets of rejuvenated woodlands. Hunting has long been permitted, but state forests are a popular spot for hikers, horseback riders, mountain bikers, and campers as well.

The flowering dogwood is Virginia's state tree and flower.

Mountain laurel are common throughout Virginia's woodlands.

The Appalachian oak-hickory forest rises to dominance within the Blue Ridge. Hickory is the successor of the American chestnut. In the early 20th century, it was estimated one of every four trees in the Appalachians was a chestnut. Today, few grow taller than 6 feet before succumbing to the chestnut blight. In the absence of chestnuts, oaks have assumed primacy in Virginia's western regions. Chestnut oaks are found on dry, rocky ridges, while white and red oak populate mountain slopes. In the forest understory, scrub oak and chinquapins grow.

In moist pockets below 4,500 feet elevation, the Appalachian cove forest holds more than twenty species of trees—beech, sugar, maple, and yellow poplar noticeable among these. Stands of eastern hemlock once made for impressive viewing. However, damage from the invasive woolly adelgid is now widespread in Virginia. Evidence of its handiwork is especially striking in Shenandoah National Park, where entire stands of hemlock are defoliated and dying. Even so, quiet, cool pockets of this venerable evergreen may still be found along isolated mountain streams.

In the forest understory, dogwood and redbud bring colorful spring blossoms. Mountain laurel and rhododendron seem omnipresent on both dry, rocky ridges and in wet stream valleys. Wildflowers are profuse, from the common purple violets and white toothworts to the infrequently spotted Turk's cap lily. G. Richard Thompson Wildlife Management Area, on the eastern slope of the northern Blue Ridge, is thought to hold the largest population of trillium wildflowers in North America. At Mount Rogers and Laurel Fork, the state's highest elevations, spruce and fir trees indicate a remnant boreal forest more typical of Canada.

Deer have rebounded from overhunting and the habitat destruction of 100 years ago to rank as almost a nuisance throughout Virginia. Black bears are found primarily in the western regions of the state, but may be spotted in the Great Dismal Swamp in southeast Virginia. Otherwise, Virginia's forests support small-game wildlife. A hiker's footsteps may flush turkey or grouse from the woods. Raccoons and other nocturnal animals make hanging food a necessary part of any camping trip. Bobcats and coyotes are found statewide, but generally in larger areas of preserved forest.

The river systems of Virginia host a wide range of life, from the common brook trout to endangered freshwater mussels. The Clinch and Powell Rivers, flowing southwest to the Tennessee River, support a variety of the hard-shelled animals, many threatened or endangered due to sediment buildup and past toxic chemical spills. Salamanders and crayfish are present in Virginia's mountain streams.

Throughout Virginia, there are 210 species of freshwater fish. Wild trout streams range from Big and Little Wilson Creeks in Mount Rogers National Recreation Area to North Fork Moormans River in Shenandoah National Park. In the coastal regions, crabs, clams, and other crustaceans inhabit muddy flats in the James, York, Rappahannock, and Potomac Rivers. Seasonal runs of rockfish, sea bass, croaker, and other fish have made sport fishing a popular pastime in the Chesapeake Bay and Atlantic Ocean.

Photographing a turtle on the trail VANESSA KUBICK

Virginia has witnessed many successes under the federal Endangered Species Act, perhaps none as stirring as the return of a viable bald eagle population. Mason Neck Wildlife Refuge, Caledon State Park, and other preserves along the lower Potomac River are renowned nesting and viewing areas for this bird of prey. Likewise, on the James River between Richmond and Isle of Wight County, more than 300 bald eagles have been counted in summer months. Best viewing times in any location are June through August and November through January.

VIRGINIA WILDERNESS RESTRICTIONS/REGULATIONS

In northern and southeast Virginia, public lands fall under three broad categories: federal parks, forests, and refuges; state parks and forests; and municipal parks. Keep in mind that wildlife refuges exist for the benefit of animals, not humans. Sections may be closed off to the public during breeding seasons. Conversely, federal, state, and municipal parks exist for humans, a fact reflected in their sometimes crowded conditions.

Virginia's two national forests cover 1.8 million acres of mountain forestland. The George Washington National Forest stretches from north of Winchester to just south of Lexington and Covington. The adjacent Jefferson National Forest continues southwest to the Virginia-Tennessee border. Both are managed out of a single forest headquarters in Roanoke. While it is tempting to think the forests exist for hikers' enjoyment, they are in fact multiuse, with trails for horseback riders, cyclists, and all-terrain vehicles. Developed campgrounds and recreation areas are suitable for tents or motor homes. Hunting is permitted in season, and timber harvests are conducted regularly.

A National Forest Wilderness sign indicates the restrictions in these fragile areas.

Sharing the trail with equestrians in Mount Pleasant National Recreation Area

Virginia's national forests are divided into eight ranger districts, and each district is responsible for fire prevention, maintenance, and ecology within its boundary. Rangers and their assistants make excellent resources for hikers and can provide information on trails and weather. Contact information can be found here: www.fs.usda.gov/gwj. Mount Rogers National Recreation Area, which covers 117,000 acres of high mountain country in southwest Virginia, is a specially managed component of the national forest and was created in 1965 to serve the recreational needs of East Coast urban dwellers. Within it are 95 miles of trails for hikers, horseback riders, and cyclists.

Contained in Virginia's two national forests are twenty-four wilderness areas, which is an increase of seven since we wrote the first edition. The intent of wilderness is to allow land to return to a primitive state without interference from people. Motorized traffic and tools are not allowed, and trails may be unblazed and unmaintained. There are exceptions to every rule, however. In cases of emergencies, the Forest Service or local emergency company may use vehicles, helicopters, chainsaws, and other mechanical apparatus when responding in a wilderness area. Surprisingly, the wilderness designation does not automatically translate to remote. St. Mary's Wilderness Area, south of Staunton and Charlottesville, is blessed with an abundance of beautiful waterfalls; yet, because it's so easily accessed from I-81, it's more heavily used than some nonwilderness areas. That said, just as many of these areas feel truly remote. Many hikers have never heard of Beartown Wilderness, on the edge of Burke's Garden near Tazewell, or Kimberling Creek Wilderness, near Wytheville. For details, visit www.wilderness.net.

Shenandoah National Park is Virginia's—and one of the nation's—most visited parks. There is an entrance fee; annual passes are available. Most visitors simply cruise Skyline Drive, a beautiful highway with scenic views that traces the ridgeline of the Blue Ridge. (South of the park, the road continues as the Blue Ridge Parkway, a scenic highway that ends in Great Smoky Mountains National Park in Tennessee.) It is said that a majority of travelers on Skyline Drive stray no more than a half-mile from parking areas and pull-offs. Still, Shenandoah's backcountry receives a healthy number of visitors. Every hiker should be aware of the park's backcountry regulations, which govern issues from pets to fires to how to dispose of waste.

GETTING AROUND VIRGINIA

AREA CODES

Virginia currently has seven area codes: 276 serves southwest Virginia; 434 serves Charlottesville, Lynchburg, and central Virginia; 540 covers Roanoke and western and northern Virginia, excluding Arlington; 571 and 703 cover northern Virginia (Washington, DC's area code is 202); 757 serves Hampton Roads and the Eastern Shore; and 804 covers Richmond east to the Williamsburg area.

ROADS

For current information on statewide weather and road conditions and closures, call the Virginia Department of Transportation (VDOT) 24-hour Highway Helpline at (800) 367-7623 (TTY users, dial 711) or visit www.virginiadot.org/travel.

BY AIR

Major airports serving Virginia: Washington Dulles Airport (IAD) is 23 miles northwest of downtown Washington, DC. Ronald Reagan National Airport (DCA) is in nearby Alexandria, and Baltimore Washington International (BWI) is also convenient to northern Virginia. Richmond International Airport (RIC) is located 7 miles east of downtown Richmond. Norfolk International (ORF) and Newport News/Williamsburg International serve Hampton Roads.

Regional airports include Charlottesville, Roanoke, Lynchburg, Martinsville (Blue Ridge Airport), and Shenandoah Valley Airport (midway between Staunton and Harrisonburg).

BY TRAIN

Virginia is served by Amtrak. For information and/or reservations, visit them online at www.amtrak.com or call (800) 872-7245.

Virginia Railway Express (VRE) operates commuter rail service weekdays along two lines from Fredericksburg and Manassas to Union Station in Washington, DC. For more information, call (800) RIDE-VRE or visit www.vre.org. Washington Metro has bus and train service in the northern Virginia area: www.wmata.com.

BY BUS

Greyhound serves most larger towns and cities in Virginia along with Dulles Airport. For information and/or reservations, visit www.greyhound.com or call (800) 231-2222.

Always hike with a topographic map.

VISITOR INFORMATION

For visitor information or a travel guide, call the Virginia Tourism Corporation at (800) VISIT-VA or visit the website at www.virginia.org.

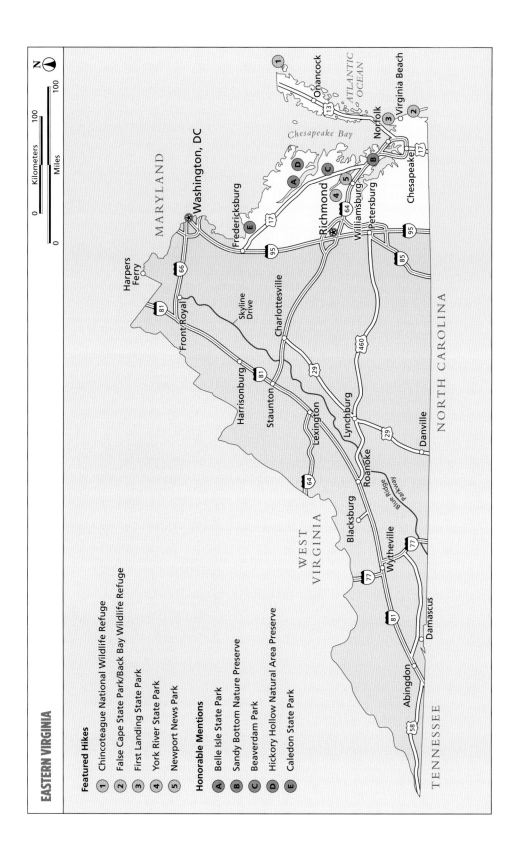

EASTERN VIRGINIA

Featured Hikes

1. Chincoteague National Wildlife Refuge
2. False Cape State Park/Back Bay Wildlife Refuge
3. First Landing State Park
4. York River State Park
5. Newport News Park

Honorable Mentions

A. Belle Isle State Park
B. Sandy Bottom Nature Preserve
C. Beaverdam Park
D. Hickory Hollow Natural Area Preserve
E. Caledon State Park

EASTERN VIRGINIA

Water, not the land, defines Virginia's eastern region. It washes up onto Atlantic barrier islands and rolls into the Chesapeake Bay, forming and shaping the coastline. It runs along a vast network of upland streams, molding river bluffs and carving small inlets and bays. It pours forth from western regions of the state, bursting into the estuarine lower reaches of the James, York, Rappahannock, and Potomac Rivers, giving shape to three large peninsulas that jut out into the Chesapeake Bay.

Over the long reach of geologic time, the influx and regress of water—sometimes gradual, sometimes dramatic—has been eastern Virginia's legacy. The Chesapeake Bay itself is the drowned mouth of the Susquehanna River. In glacial times, when the ocean levels dropped some 400 feet, what we know today as the Chesapeake Bay was a wide river valley. The coastline stood 60 miles out into the present-day ocean. The sand beaches and brackish lagoons of today were, millions of years ago, forests and freshwater ponds.

Images of colonial Virginia ring out in accounts written by early explorers. The English, seeking permanent settlement of North America, came ashore in Virginia Beach, present-day Cape Henry. After months at sea, they were awestruck by an abundance of trees, plants, and animals. They saw dense swamps with sheets of Spanish moss dangling from trees standing in knee-deep black water. Discarded oyster shells littered the beaches. Fish were abundant. Inland, the Algonquin Indians had cleared only a fraction of the forest for their crops. Trees were tall and thickly trunked, and sheltered an abundance of wildlife.

Eastern Virginia today harbors bits and pieces of this once-resplendent nature. Rare migratory birds winter over on Assateague Island. Endangered turtles live in the swamps of First Landing State Park. In the harsh beach and dune environments, piping plovers struggle against predators large and small. Behind barrier islands, marshes perform the critical job of filtering land runoff while supporting a nursery of fish and shellfish. In hidden, secluded spots, rare orchids bloom and old-growth trees spread their branches, inviting you to rest in their shade. Bald eagles nest and roost on stretches of the bay's major tributaries: the James, York, Rappahannock, and Potomac Rivers.

Wherever you choose to explore, bring a pair of waterproof boots. Because no matter where you hike in eastern Virginia, you're bound to hit water.

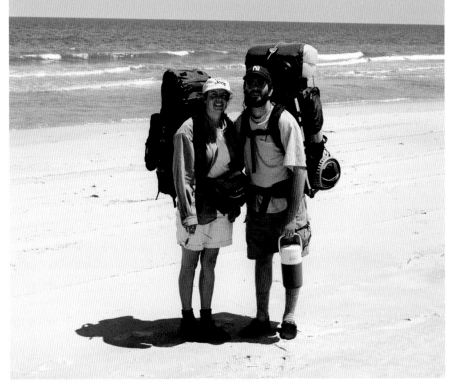
The authors on a Virginia beach in the early days!

THE HIKES
1. Chincoteague National Wildlife Refuge
2. False Cape State Park/Back Bay Wildlife Refuge
3. First Landing State Park
4. York River State Park
5. Newport News Park

HONORABLE MENTIONS
A. Belle Isle State Park
B. Sandy Bottom Nature Preserve
C. Beaverdam Park
D. Hickory Hollow Natural Area Preserve
E. Caledon State Park

1 CHINCOTEAGUE NATIONAL WILDLIFE REFUGE

Every spring and fall, millions of birds migrate between cold, northern environs and temperate and tropical homes in Central and South America. En route, their needs are simple: an occasional place to rest and food to nourish. Wildlife biologists at Chincoteague National Wildlife Refuge, on the southern tip of Assateague Island, have engineered a deluxe ornithological wayside for the winged travelers. Entire sections of beach are closed during nesting season for such species as the endangered piping plover and Wilson's plover. On small, man-made earthen mounds rising in the middle of bayside lagoons, waterfowl perch and feed, protected from predators. As the human hand tinkers with wildlife balance, real drama plays out in the daily life of birds and land animals—and it's on display for all to see.

Start: Wildlife Pond/Beachfront Loop: Herbert H. Bateman Educational Center on Beach Road; Beachfront Backpack: Toms Cove Visitor Center

Distance: Wildlife Pond/Beachfront Loop: 7.5-mile loop; Beachfront Backpack: 25.0 miles out and back

Hiking time: Wildlife Pond/Beachfront Loop: about 3 hours; Beachfront Backpack: about 10 hours

Difficulty: Wildlife Pond/Beachfront Loop is easy. Beachfront Backpack is moderate due to length. Between May and Sept, mosquitoes, greenhead flies, deerflies, and ticks make exploration of Chincoteague's interior shrub and maritime forest inadvisable, especially at dawn and dusk. Long-sleeved shirts, pants, and bug netting, plus bug spray, can alleviate this problem.

Trail surface: Wildlife Pond/Beachfront Loop: A network of paved roads, dirt roads, and sand jeep trails lead hikers to a wide ocean beach, maritime forest of oak and pine, low dunes, and saltwater marsh. Beachfront Backpack: Sand and surf along a wide ocean beach.

Land status: National wildlife refuge and national seashore

Nearest town: Chincoteague, VA

Other trail users: Cyclists, anglers, over-sand vehicles, horseback riders, and hunters (in season)

Accessibility: Fully half of the refuge's trails are paved, including the Wildlife Loop, Swan Cove Trail, and Black Duck Trail.

Canine compatibility: Dogs not permitted, not even in the car

Trail contact: Day hikes: Chincoteague National Wildlife Refuge, 8231 Beach Rd., Chincoteague; (757) 336-6122; www.fws.gov/refuge/chincoteague. Backcountry: Assateague Island National Seashore, Toms Cove Visitor Center (Virginia Ranger Station), (757) 336-6577, www.nps.gov/asis

Schedule: Chincoteague NWR is open daily, 5 a.m. to 10 p.m. May through Sept; 6 a.m. to 6 p.m. Nov through mid-Mar; 6 a.m. to 8 p.m. mid-Mar through Apr and Oct. The Toms Cove Visitor Center (national seashore) is open 9 a.m. to 4 p.m. daily. Portions of beaches and trails may be closed for bird nesting in spring and summer and for hunting Oct through early Jan. Hunting is prohibited on Sun. Be sure to call ahead for details.

Fees/permits: Entrance fee per vehicle; bicycles and pedestrians free. Backcountry permit required; register at the Toms Cove Visitor

Center. Backpackers must depart at least 4 hours before sunset, with enough daylight to hike 12 miles to the State Line or Pope Bay backcountry campsites in Maryland. Visit www.nps.gov/asis for camping rules and regulations. **Facilities/features:** Restrooms, educational and visitor centers, lifeguarded beach, kayak launch on the Virginia end of the island. Primitive camping is allowed across the Maryland border only (12 miles one way); there are portable toilets, but all freshwater must be carried in. **NatGeo TOPO! map:** Chincoteague East **NatGeo Trails Illustrated map:** Delmarva Peninsula **Other maps:** Refuge and Park Service maps available at visitor center and online.

FINDING THE TRAILHEAD

 From the new Chincoteague Bridge (VA 175): For the Wildlife Pond/Beach-front Loop, stay straight to go on Maddox Boulevard (VA 2113). Drive 1.2 miles to a traffic circle and follow Maddox Boulevard through the circle. In 1.4 miles, reach the refuge entrance gate, where Maddox Boulevard becomes Beach Road. Enter the refuge and in 0.3 mile, turn left into the parking area for the Herbert H. Bateman Educational Center at 8231 Beach Road. This ecofriendly building serves as the visitor center, with nature exhibits inside. For the Beachfront Backpack, after entering the refuge, continue past the educational center and enter the Assateague Island National Seashore. In 1.5 miles, reach the Toms Cove Visitor Center on the right to obtain a backcountry permit and parking tag. **Visitor center GPS:** N37 54.544' / W75 21.337'. *DeLorme: Virginia Atlas & Gazetteer*: Page 63, A5.

THE HIKE

Screams and cries rise off the oceanfront as hungry gulls and terns scavenge for food along the surf. Beyond Assateague Island's low sand and inland pine, snow geese float restlessly in a freshwater pool. Suddenly, on some silent, unseen signal, a single goose, then two, three—then the entire flock rises in flight. Their *whonk-whonk* joins with cries of shorebirds in a resounding cacophony.

An explosion of snow geese off the water draws the birder's eyes skyward. Here, a broad-winged raptor swoops high above the pond. Its brown wings tilt slightly left, then right in a jittery act of balance. The telltale white head and yellow, hooked bill soon come into focus. This bald eagle, its search for a meal frustrated, soars out of sight behind crowns of loblolly pine.

This winter struggle between prey and predator will end when snow geese fly north in spring. Closer to the ocean, a different life struggle begins in spring when piping plover descend upon Chincoteague National Wildlife Refuge on the southern tip of Assateague Island. After a brief courtship, breeding pairs build a nest in the sand. Up to four eggs will hatch within a month of being laid. For 5 critical days, the young chick's life consists of dodging predators and finding enough food to survive. Days turn to weeks, and the handful of chicks that survive face new dangers. Camouflage, the tiny, sand-colored plover's best defense, leads to unintended consequences: Humans inadvertently step on nests. Off-road vehicles run them over. Gulls harass adult plovers and carry away chicks. Other predators, raccoons and foxes among them, raid nests. Storms send tidal surges crashing over protective dunes—violent weather has destroyed entire nesting seasons at Chincoteague.

Storms routinely overwash the beach parking areas as Assateague Island experiences erosion, sea level rise, and a westward migration. Animals fend for themselves on a daily basis in a never-ending search for an advantage—and a meal. Humans represent an interference in this delicate balance. The side of the scale on which we place our weight makes all the difference. In the case of the Delmarva fox squirrel, farming and homes had, by 1900, destroyed habitat in all but a tiny spot in Maryland. The balance tipped in the squirrel's favor in 1945, however, when Maryland set aside land for its protection. In 1971 it became illegal to hunt the large fox squirrel, which can weigh up to 3 pounds and measure 30 inches in length. On reserves in Virginia, Maryland, and Delaware, squirrel populations increased. From a population of thirty squirrels in 1970, Chincoteague now keeps its numbers around 350, shipping out squirrels to other suitable habitats if their numbers exceed this level.

Hike just across the state border into Maryland for legal camping on Assateague Island.

Human intervention, often the cause of ailing animal populations, is just as often the cure. When plover chicks hatch in late May, refuge staff begin a 16- to 18-hour vigil over nesting sites. Nesting areas are signed and roped off, and occasionally beach roads are closed to vehicular traffic. Assateague Island, along with neighboring barrier islands, accounts for the majority of the piping plover's breeding population in Virginia.

The Chincoteague refuge also played an instrumental role in the recovery of breeding peregrine falcons in Virginia. By the 1960s breeding peregrines had disappeared from the state, suffering from a fate similar to the bald eagles'—contamination from the pesticide DDT. Weakened eggshells broke, and chicks hatched prematurely. DDT was banned in 1972. In the late 1970s scientists began releasing pairs of peregrines in Virginia, both in coastal and mountain regions. In 1982 they hit gold when a pair of peregrine falcons was found nesting on Assateague Island, the first documented breeding pair in the state in nearly a half a century. As of 2010 Virginia supports twenty-three known breeding pairs of peregrine falcons, nearly all within the state's portion of the Eastern Shore. A delisting of the peregrine from an endangered species to a threatened species reflects national success in reintroducing breeding populations.

KID APPEAL

With rare exceptions, everyone wants to catch a glimpse of the famous Chincoteague wild ponies, which reside in the refuge and national seashore. The 1.6-mile Woodland Trail leads through a pine forest to an overlook where pony sightings are common. The new Bivalve Trail is a 0.2-mile spur off the Woodland Trail that leads to the shores of Toms Cove with a view of the old Assateague lifesaving station.

A mother and baby pony at Chincoteague Wildlife Refuge

And yet even in a managed environment, disaster strikes. When several storms inundated the maritime forest of lower Assateague Island—which encompasses the whole of the Chincoteague refuge—volumes of saltwater weakened the resident loblolly pines. The stress caused by a lack of freshwater made the pines susceptible to the southern pine beetle. Recovery from this trauma can be seen today along the Wildlife Loop Trail—where amid low shrubs and grass, pine saplings have made a vigorous comeback.

For years, protection of Assateague Island extended to correcting nature itself. After every major storm, the Park Service rebuilt dunes with the goal of keeping an ocean ecology from slipping away. Littoral drift, the term for a shift in barrier islands westward, moves Assateague, on average, 30 feet every decade. But not everything needs protecting. Park managers have decided against rebuilding dunes and there is a perennial debate over the wisdom of building (and rebuilding) parking lots near the beach. Whatever conditions a storm leaves the barrier island in, staff are now inclined not to tamper with it. Humans, and not the environment, will adapt to conditions. Briefly, balance tips back to Mother Nature.

MILES AND DIRECTIONS

Wildlife Pond/Beachfront Loop

0.0 Start from the parking lot for the Herbert H. Bateman Educational Center. Opposite the visitor center, a boardwalk trail leads away through a pine forest.

0.3 Merge onto the paved Wildlife Loop Road, which is open to vehicles from 3 p.m. to dusk, and continue straight. Views of Snow Goose Pool, a freshwater impoundment, open up on the left.

0.7 Continue straight on the Wildlife Loop Road past the Black Duck Trail, which exits to the right and leads 0.5 mile to paved Beach Road.

1.4 Continue straight, past Swan Cove Trail, which exits to the right and is part of the return leg of this loop.

2.5 Cross Snow Goose Pool on a dike and turn right onto a gated dirt road, which is closed to public vehicle traffic except between Memorial Day and Labor Day, when sightseeing trams operate. **Option:** To return to the educational center, turn left at this T junction and follow the paved Wildlife Loop Road.

3.1 Continue straight on the gravel road past C-Dike. **Note:** This earthen embankment is closed and may not be used to access the beach.

3.6 Turn right onto D-Dike and hike 0.3 mile to the oceanfront.

3.9 Emerge from the dunes onto the beach. Turn right and head south along the beachfront.

5.5 Turn right and walk through the beach dunes onto Swan Cove Trail. **Note:** This trail may be closed during periods of high rainfall.

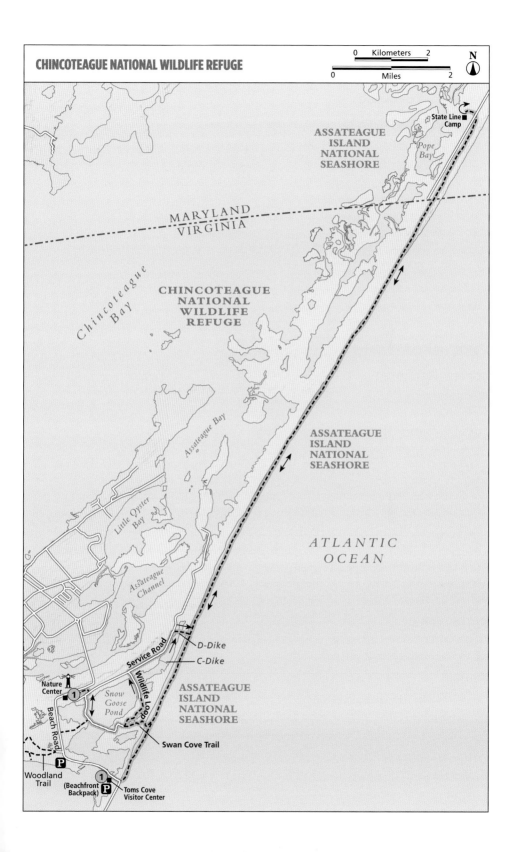

CHINCOTEAGUE NATIONAL WILDLIFE REFUGE

0   Kilometers   2

0   Miles   2

N

ASSATEAGUE
ISLAND
NATIONAL
SEASHORE

State Line
Camp

Pope
Bay

MARYLAND
VIRGINIA

Chincoteague
Bay

CHINCOTEAGUE
NATIONAL
WILDLIFE
REFUGE

Assateague Bay

ASSATEAGUE
ISLAND
NATIONAL
SEASHORE

ATLANTIC
OCEAN

Little Oyster
Bay

Assateague
Channel

Service Road

D-Dike

C-Dike

Wildlife Loop

Nature
Center

Snow
Goose
Pond

ASSATEAGUE
ISLAND
NATIONAL
SEASHORE

Beach Road

Swan Cove Trail

Woodland
Trail

(Beachfront
Backpack)

Toms Cove
Visitor Center

| 6.0 | Swan Cove Trail ends at Wildlife Loop. Bear left to return to the educational center. |
| 7.5 | Arrive back at the Herbert H. Bateman Educational Center parking area. |

Beachfront Backpack

0.0	Start from the Toms Cove Visitor Center, where you must obtain a backcountry permit and inquire where to park overnight. Head to the beachfront, turn left, and walk north. **Note:** To eliminate a couple of miles walking in the sand, ask about parking across from the lighthouse and hiking on the Service Road to the beach.
2.9	Pass a dune crossover to D-Dike on the left. Continue straight.
9.4	Pass Old Fields crossover, a route leading left through the dunes to an interior service road. Continue straight.
11.0	Cross the Maryland state line and enter Assateague Island National Seashore. Continue straight.
12.5	A tent sign in the dunes to the left indicates State Line campsites, primitive sites with no running water, and chemical toilets. Camping is permitted amid dunes only. Turn around and return to the Toms Cove Visitors Center. **Note:** If State Line camp is booked, Pope Bay on the bayside of Maryland's Assateague Island is 0.5 mile north.
25.0	Hike ends at Toms Cove Visitor Center.

HIKE INFORMATION

Local Information

Chincoteague Chamber of Commerce, (757) 336-6161, www.chincoteaguechamber .com

Local Events/Attractions

Annual Pony Swim and Penning, last week in July, Chincoteague, (757) 336-6161. An event of national renown running for 100 years, Chincoteague ponies are herded off the refuge to swim across a small water passage to Chincoteague Island for an auction to benefit the Chincoteague Volunteer Fire Company. There are also spring and fall round-ups, which are less crowded to attend.

Lodging

The resort town of Chincoteague has a wide array of lodgings, from motels and B&Bs to rental homes. Visit www.chincoteaguechamber.com for listings.

There are several commercial campgrounds in Chincoteague, but backcountry camping is allowed only at Assateague National Seashore in Maryland.

Restaurants

Nearly thirty Chincoteague restaurants serve up fare ranging from seafood to homemade ice cream to the standard burger and fries.

Tours

Refuge staff lead interpretive programs. Call (757) 336-6122 for information.

Organizations

Assateague Island Alliance, www.assateagueislandalliance.org

Other Resources

Eastern Shore of Virginia Tourism, (757) 331-1660, www.visitesva.com

2 FALSE CAPE STATE PARK/ BACK BAY WILDLIFE REFUGE

Barrier islands serve as an ecological first line of defense for our shores. Storms batter them, waves wear them down, wind strips them clean. Tucked out of harm's way behind the islands lie sheltered bays and marshes teeming with grasses, shellfish, birds, and small animals. False Cape State Park and Back Bay National Wildlife Refuge showcase just one of Virginia's many barrier island and lagoon ecosystems, albeit a critical one. The preserves stand within striking distance of Hampton Roads' 2 million residents and all the incumbent pressures (pollution, development, overcrowding). Sprawl stops at the park boundaries, and hikers and bird watchers are assured a quiet afternoon with space to walk and think, or watch and listen.

Start: Little Island Park for overnight. Back Bay NWR for day hikes (no overnight parking).
Distance: 14.7-mile lollipop
Hiking time: About 7 hours
Difficulty: Moderate due to length
Trail surface: All aspects of seashore ecology are present, from the beach to dunes to maritime pine and oak forests.
Land status: National wildlife refuge and state park
Nearest town: Virginia Beach, VA
Other trail users: Cyclists, anglers, hunters (in season), and bird watchers
Accessibility: Back Bay NWR has an ADA-compliant visitor center, restrooms, and some boardwalks to wildlife-viewing stations and the beach. The visitor center at False Cape is ADA compliant. The park operates a tram from Back Bay with advance notice. The park's visitor center has a beach-accessible wheelchair.
Canine compatibility: Leashed dogs are permitted in False Cape State Park, but there's no access allowed through the Back Bay NWR, so they can only arrive by boat. Pets are not permitted in Back Bay NWR at any time.
Trail contacts: False Cape State Park, Virginia Beach, (757) 426-7128 (camping reservations: 800-933-PARK), www.dcr.virginia.gov/state-parks/false-cape. Back Bay National Wildlife Refuge, Virginia Beach, (757) 301-7329, www.fws.gov/refuge/back_bay
Schedule: False Cape SP and Back Bay NWR are open daily dawn to dusk; East and West Dike Trails may be closed Nov through Mar for wintering waterfowl.
Fees/permits: Parking fee charged at Little Island Park Memorial Day to Labor Day. Entrance fee charged at Back Bay NWR Apr through Oct. Camping fee charged at False Cape State Park. All campers *must* receive their confirmation letter and information packet via email before camping at this park. You must bring two copies of the confirmation letter, one to display on your vehicle dashboard and the other to clip to your site marker.
Facilities/features: False Cape State Park has primitive camping, pit toilets, flush toilets at Environmental Center, and drinking water in the Barbour Hill area. Back Bay NWR has a visitor center, kayak/canoe launch, restrooms, and day-use parking only.
NatGeo TOPO! maps: North Bay, Knott Island
NatGeo Trails Illustrated map: Delmarva Peninsula
Other maps: A Trail Guide/Map is available at the park and downloadable on its website.

FINDING THE TRAILHEAD

From Virginia Beach, take the Indian River Road exit 286B off I-64. Proceed east on Indian River Road for 13.4 miles, then turn left onto New Bridge Road. In 1.3 miles, turn right onto Sandbridge Road. After 3.1 miles, turn right onto Sandpiper Road. Drive south on Sandpiper for 3.8 miles to Little Island Park on the left, where overnight parking is permitted. **GPS:** N36 41.588' / W75 55.473'. *DeLorme: Virginia Atlas & Gazetteer*: Page 35, C7.

THE HIKE

Barrier islands are a habitat of extremes. The same beach where sunbathers flock for relaxation also harbors some of the earth's harshest living conditions. Waves beat upon it unceasingly, but those same waves bring ashore food that nourishes microorganisms, shellfish, birds, and small animals. Unfettered wind reduces shrubs and trees to bonsai proportions; wind also spreads beach grass and sea oat seeds, two species that help prevent sand-dune erosion. Then there is sand itself, barren of most nutrients, yet it creates the very reefs and dunes that preserve our coast.

A hiker must adapt to False Cape State Park and Back Bay National Wildlife Refuge (the park and refuge form a 20-mile contiguous stretch of protected coastal habitat between Virginia Beach and the North Carolina border). Forget mountain grandeur. Forget tall hemlocks or yellow poplar trees. Here, wind-lashed holly, oak, and pine eke out a precarious living. Deer, raccoons, opossums, and foxes rustle the shrubby thickets. Migratory birds capture the imagination—shorebirds in the spring, songbirds in spring and fall, and nesting birds in summer; in winter, it's the ducks and geese. Plant and animal life here have had more time to adapt than humans. Wax myrtle has a coating on its leaves that protects it against the relentless sun and moisture loss from high winds and salt exposure. Salt marsh cordgrass is able to overcome both the presence of saltwater—which would kill less hardy plants—and a severe lack of oxygen in the dense, mushy marsh soil. It solves the problem of saltwater through reverse osmosis, whereby it balances saltwater intrusion with freshwater within its vascular cells. Oxygen, meanwhile, is pulled from the air and transported down the stem to the roots. Look closely at the muddy fringe of a salt marsh at low tide and look for red stains in the otherwise black mud. This is a botanical version of rust, a by-product of oxygen mixing with iron sulfide.

Every dune, especially on the lagoon or wash side, features plants whose progression reveals their place in the ecology of the island. On the fringe grows sea rocket, a member of the mustard family. Higher on the dune, beach grass, native to northern barrier islands, and sea oats, commonly found on dunes from Virginia southward, coexist. In areas flooded daily by the tide, salt marsh cordgrass grows nearest to water, while salt marsh hay and black needlerush occupy higher areas of marsh. In the afternoon, at low tide on a clear day, the sun will glint off oxidized salt particles clinging to tall stems of these grasses, giving the impression of light bouncing off thousands of tiny mirrors. Beneath the grasses and puddles of brackish water, juvenile blue crabs reach maturity and fish spawn.

Plants that seem withered and dead during dry spells spring to life after rain. False heather jumps to life under moist conditions. Looking something like a small cedar, the heather's yellow flowers coat the ocean side of dunes. Because it grows low to the ground and spreads, heather helps stabilize the sand.

Down on the beach, sanderlings dart hither-and-thither, first chased by a crashing wave, only to turn and pursue it back into the ocean. This small bird pecks at the spongy

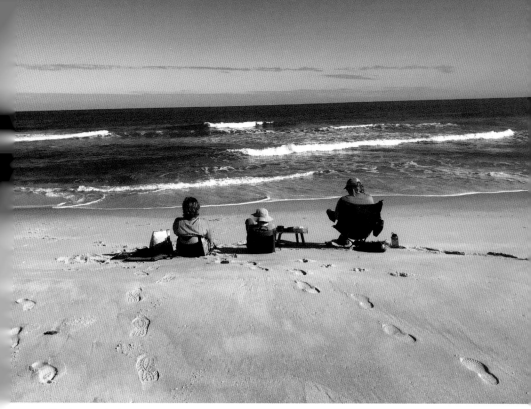

Resting on the beach

sand, digging deep for shellfish. During the summer as many as 30 million clam larvae will occupy 1 square meter of surf. There are snails beneath the sand, too, and small crabs and worms. At nighttime, sandhoppers (small crabs) emerge from holes by the thousands to pick food from shells and seaweed coughed up by waves. Luminescent and quick, the sandhopper has startled more than a few nighttime beach strollers. Rest assured, by the time you've figured out it's an animal and not a ghost, the critter is out of harm's way. It digs a hole in the sand at a speed of 6 feet in 10 minutes, putting it well out of reach of prying eyes and bird beaks.

Given this diversity and complexity, it's worth considering how the wilds of False Cape and Back Bay might have developed were it not for the park and refuge. A few miles up the beach, Virginia Beach's boardwalk teems with humans on hot summer days. Sunbathers, surfers, and beach strollers crowd miles of white Atlantic beach. The city spends millions to preserve this, fighting nature with "beach replenishment projects," a process of pumping sand from offshore back onto shore.

The process they're fighting is the gradual drift of barrier islands (and our eastern coast, generally) to the south and west. Left to its own devices, the white sands of Virginia Beach would, in a couple hundred years, move, shifting south along the coast in the fashion of all barrier islands. Scientists call this *littoral drift*. Each wave picks up sand and transports it down the shoreline. A calm day or two will see tons of sand displaced. A hurricane or nor'easter will move those same tons in a few hours. The inlet below Ocean City, Maryland, which separates that resort town from Assateague Island, was carved by a single hurricane in 1933.

There was no dramatic event responsible for Back Bay and False Cape. In the 1800s some 300 people lived in the Wash Woods, a section of False Cape State Park. They fished for a living, and a few raised livestock and farmed. (Interestingly, Wash Woods settlers were survivors of a shipwreck off the coast; their first homes and church were built from what they could salvage from the ship.) Like the island itself, they lived at the mercy of the ocean. Over hundreds of years, farmland turned to marsh. Sand replaced fertile soil. Soon, sportsmen outnumbered inhabitants, and hotels and sporting clubs sprang up. Four-legged game was slim pickings. The waterfowl, on the other hand, were plentiful.

It can be taken as a sign of progress, then, that over time Virginia has moved from hunting wildfowl on this small barrier island to protecting them. Like other barrier islands up and down the East Coast, this island hosts neotropical birds migrating to Central and South America. Waterfowl nest here. In September, vireos, yellowthroats, and warblers arrive. By October, yellow-rumped warblers have alighted to spend winter. In all, bird spotters have recorded 288 bird species in the Back Bay refuge. (This is typical of barrier islands lining the East Coast; Chincoteague National Wildlife Refuge on Virginia's Eastern Shore lists 300 bird species spotted.)

On these slivers of sand, the equivalent of an interstate highway rest stop, birds find the amenities they need: nesting spots, food, and, quite frankly, a spot to rest weary wings. And they seem to be more than willing to share it with hikers.

MILES AND DIRECTIONS

0.0 Start at Little Island Park. Walk to the south end of the parking lot. At a picnic pavilion, turn toward the beach and surf.

1.5 Hike straight along the beach, past a boardwalk that leads up into the dunes on the right. **Note:** The boardwalk leads to a Back Bay NWR ranger station and visitor center.

4.7 Reach the boundary of False Cape State Park. Continue straight on the beach.

5.0 A beach path leads right up into the dunes toward Barbour Hill primitive campsites and the state park's contact station, a turnoff marked by a small metal post with a yellow tent. From this junction, it is 0.7 mile across the island to the contact station. **Note:** If you are continuing farther down the beach, Barbour Hill is your last chance to supply drinking water; it is near the contact station and near the two camping areas there.

6.7 Turn right onto False Cape Landing Trail. **Note:** If you're walking in the surf far below the dune line, keep an eye peeled for a sign reading "False Cape Landing Trail." There are primitive campsites in dunes after you turn onto the trail.

FALSE CAPE STATE PARK/BACK BAY WILDLIFE REFUGE

Kilometers
0 2

Miles
0 2

N

Shipps Bay

To Virginia Beach

LITTLE ISLAND PARK

Overnight Parking

Sandpiper Rd.

Tram (Apr–Oct)

2

Seaside Trail

Contact Station

Dune Trail

Bay Trail

Beach Trail

ATLANTIC OCEAN

Long Island

East and West Dike Trails closed November-March

BACK BAY NATIONAL WILDLIFE REFUGE

West Dike Trail

Pool C

East Dike Trail

Redhead Bay

Pool B

Sand Bay

Pool A

Ragged Island

Barbour Hill Beach Trail

Barbour Hill

FALSE CAPE STATE PARK

South Inlet Trail

Main Trail

Beach Trail

Cedar Island

False Cape Landing

False Cape Landing Trail

Back Bay

Wash Woods Beach Trail

Wash Woods Interpretive Trail

WASH WOODS EEC

Wash Woods Cemetery & Church Site

Wash Woods Cemetery Trail

Big Ball Island

Horse Island

Dudley Island Trail

VIRGINIA
NORTH CAROLINA

Crossing the dune boardwalk at False Cape State Park

7.1 Turn right onto Sand Ridge Trail, a wide dirt road. The ocean is now on your right, out of sight over the dunes. Back Bay is on your left. *Note:* Straight on False Cape Landing Trail, there is a boat landing in 0.3 mile, as well as bay-side campsites.

8.4 Sand Ridge Trail arcs right at a junction with South Inlet Trail. Follow the road right. *Note:* South Inlet Trail leads left for 0.4 mile to a sheltered reach of water with scenic views.

9.0 Turn left onto Barbour Hill Beach Trail. There is a ranger station on the right side of the road. Past the ranger station, turn right onto Barbour Hill Interpretive Trail.

9.6 Pass an observation deck on the right side of the trail.

9.8 Leave False Cape State Park and enter Back Bay National Wildlife Refuge. Turn left onto the Dike Trail, which is a gravel and dirt road that runs alongside wildlife impoundments, large pools of water that attract waterfowl and migrating birds. This hike follows the western leg of the Dike Trail.

10.1 Where the trail forks, bear right onto the Dike Trail. *Note:* The left-bearing trail is a short spur to the bay.

10.9 Hike straight past a road that turns right and leads between two impoundments.

11.4 Follow the trail as it jogs left then right and continues its northward route. A road branches right, leading between impoundments. Within 0.2 mile, hike past a third road that branches right.

13.2 The Dike Trail merges with its eastern leg. Continue on past a pool on the right side of the trail.

13.4 Reach the Back Bay visitor center and ranger station. At the station, turn right onto the Seaside Trail boardwalk.

13.5 Descend off the boardwalk and dune and turn left. Head north along the beach.

14.7 Arrive back at Little Island Park.

HIKE INFORMATION

Local Information

Virginia Beach Convention & Visitors Bureau, (800) VA-BEACH (822-3224), www.visit virginiabeach.com

Local Events/Attractions

The Winter Wildlife Festival takes place late Jan through early Feb in Back Bay NWR, False Cape State Park, and other locations throughout Virginia Beach, (757) 385-2990.

The Friends of False Cape State Park holds beach cleanups throughout the year. (757) 426-7128, www.falsecapefriends.org

The Virginia Aquarium & Marine Science Center, Virginia Beach, (757) 385-3474, www.virginiaaquarium.com. More than 800,000 gallons of aquariums with sharks, sea turtles, and dolphins.

Lodging

There are four primitive campgrounds in False Cape State Park. Sites hold between four and six people. The closest is a 6.9-mile walk from Little Island Park, where campers must park. Campsites have pit toilets; there are flush toilets at the kayak shed and Environmental Education Center. Drinking water is available at three locations in the Barbour Hill area (one by the contact station and two in the camping areas). False Cape Landing campers must bring their own containers to transport water from the water source. Open fires are not permitted. Reservations by phone are required at least 1 day in advance: (800) 933-PARK.

The Wash Woods Lodge can accommodate day visitors or 16 people overnight. The center offers a kitchen, restrooms, and a shower. Call the park for details.

Restaurants

Virginia Beach has literally hundreds of restaurants. For a unique locals spot on Back Bay, check out Blue Petes, 1400 N. Muddy Creek Rd., Pungo; (757) 426-2278; www .bluepetespungo.com.

Tours

False Cape State Park conducts tram, canoe, hiking, birding, and astronomy tours; call (757) 426-7128.

Organizations

Friends of False Cape State Park, www.falsecapefriends.org

Tidewater Appalachian Trail Club maintains some trails in False Cape, www.tidewater atc.com.

3 FIRST LANDING STATE PARK

The ultimate surf-and-turf park, First Landing State Park is Virginia's most-visited state park, yet it feels like a quiet oasis in Virginia's largest city. The "surf" is the mouth of the Chesapeake Bay, where it flows into the Atlantic Ocean; the "turf" is a landward trail network through an ecosystem that mixes southern plants with northern, temperate species. Spend an afternoon here among bald cypress swamps decked with Spanish moss, towering loblolly pines, and salt marsh. High, forested dunes offer great views of the water. Boardwalks take you safely through blackwater swamps, but at high tide be prepared to get your feet wet and muddy on more remote trails.

Start: Visitor center off Shore Drive

Distance: 6.5-mile loop

Hiking time: 2–3 hours

Difficulty: Easy due to flat terrain and a well-marked trail, with some difficult stretches along eroded trails and wet riverside routes

Trail surface: Dune trails, gravel roads, and boardwalks lead through marsh, beach, cypress swamp, and forested dunes with views of the bay

Land status: State park

Nearest town: Virginia Beach, VA

Other trail users: Cyclists, bird watchers, and joggers

Accessibility: The Chesapeake Bay Center and Trail Center are accessible, with accessible restrooms. The first loop of the Bald Cypress Trail has accessible boardwalks and bridges. There are paved walkways to the beach, and a beach wheelchair is available.

Canine compatibility: Leashed dogs permitted (leashes no longer than 6 feet)

Trail contact: First Landing State Park, 2500 Shore Dr., Virginia Beach; (757) 412-2300; www.dcr .virginia.gov/state-parks/first-landing. For camping reservations, call (800) 933-PARK or visit www .reservevaparks.com.

Schedule: Open year-round, 7 a.m. to dusk. The campground is open 24 hours a day. Note that on summer weekends the parking lot may fill and guests will be turned away. The office/visitor center is open 7 days a week, Mon–Thurs 8 a.m. to 4 p.m., Fri and Sat 8 a.m. to midnight, and Sun 8 a.m. to 8 p.m. The Trail Center is open 7 days a week, 8 a.m. to 4 p.m.

Fees/permits: Parking fee, higher on weekends Apr–Oct

Facilities/features: Environmental educational and trail centers, full-service campground and cabins, laundry, concessions at the Bay Store, beach (no lifeguards), picnic shelters, and boat launch

NatGeo TOPO! map: Cape Henry

NatGeo Trails Illustrated map: Delmarva Peninsula

Other maps: A Trail Guide/Map is available at the park and downloadable on its website.

FINDING THE TRAILHEAD

From Norfolk, take exit 282 (Northampton Boulevard/US 13) off I-64 and drive 4.5 miles north on US 13. Follow signs for US 60 East (Shore Drive) and drive 4.5 miles on US 60 to the park entrance. At the traffic light at the park entrance, turn right into the park and follow the main park road straight into the parking lot for the Trail Center, where you can get information on park trails and what you can expect to see. Turn left at the light to reach the park office, camping, cabins, and the Chesapeake Bay Visitor Center. **GPS:** N36 54.916' / W75 02.485'. *DeLorme: Virginia Atlas & Gazetteer*: Page 35, A6.

THE HIKE

The 6th and 20th of April, about four o'clock in the morning, we described the land of Virginia . . . There we landed and discovered a little way, but we could find nothing worth the speaking of, but fair meadows and goodly tall trees, with such fresh waters running through the woods as I almost ravished at the first sight thereof.

So wrote George Percy, a Jamestown settler, recounting his first steps on North American soil in 1607. After a rough few days at sea, terra firma no doubt thrilled Percy's group, even if the landscape did not. They would name this point Cape Henry, christening forever present-day Virginia Beach's northernmost tip, where the Chesapeake Bay meets the Atlantic Ocean. Today the land inland from Cape Henry Lighthouse and Fort Story is called First Landing State Park, in their honor. Here hikers will find riches Percy and company found commonplace: maritime forest and southern swamp and beach ecology, all preserved for a walker's enjoyment.

By Percy's account, the landing at Cape Henry was rough. Native Americans attacked and two men were injured, one fatally. It was an inauspicious welcome that might have chased lesser men back to the Caribbean. There, at least, they had enjoyed hot spring baths, fish, and fowl to their satisfaction.

But these privateers, commissioned by the England-based Virginia Company, had other plans. Explorations by foot carried them inland from Cape Henry, through land entangled in vines as thick as a man's thigh. They chased Native Americans off a pile of oysters roasting in a fire, and tasted a delicacy that would someday make the Chesapeake Bay famous around the world. By boat, they continued into the lower Chesapeake Bay and traveled to Hampton, Virginia, which they dubbed Point Comfort, met up with Kecoughtan Indians, and, instead of fighting, exchanged gifts.

When it came time to leave, the explorers staked a small cross to mark Cape Henry. Left behind were the "fair meadows and goodly tall trees," and for one reason or another, this coastal area never saw permanent settlement (save the military reservation occupying land around the lighthouse). As colonial Virginia grew in the 1600s, fishermen claimed it as common ground, launched boats, built small shelters, and laid out nets. In 1936 the state created Seashore State Park here. It was renamed First Landing in 1996.

What has been preserved? An ecology that mixes subtropical and temperate-zone plants for a species diversity one would normally find farther south. Loblolly, eastern, and pitch pines tower 100 feet and higher. Broad bald cypress stand in oily blackwater swamps, their small knees poking through primordial-like ooze. White sand dunes are topped with clingy grasses—and bones. Archaeologists unearthed remains of twenty-six Chesapean Indians here, predecessors of the Kecoughtan tribe that attacked Percy's group. The Smithsonian Institute housed the artifacts until 1998, when they were returned and reburied in a ceremonial mound near the park's visitor center.

HEADS UP
In warm months be prepared for ticks, mosquitoes, and snakes. During high tide, portions of the Osprey Trail may be messy, or even impassable. Be sure to stay on the trails, and ignore the bushwhacked side trails.

You can start on an incredibly diverse hike at the Trail Center parking lot. The Bald Cypress/Long Creek/Osprey Trail loop takes you from cypress swamp through tidal marsh, bayside beach, dune forest, and back to swamp. Bring your binoculars. In one afternoon you're likely to see osprey nests, snowy egrets, and great blue herons.

On Bald Cypress Trail, Spanish moss hangs from the cypress. (This is the northernmost reach of the moss, a parasitic plant.) Larger specimens of this tree may date from 500 years ago. Around it, water lilies float on still water that reflects rainbow patterns—not from pollution, but from oils secreted by trees. It's possible, park interpreters say, that Captain John Smith and others replenished their casks of water here for a long return trip to England. The water, which colonists say tasted like strong iced tea, was so tannic, it could last 6 to 8 weeks at sea.

Long Creek Trail takes you to the edge of Broad Bay and a view of large homes on the opposite bank—reminders of development this park escaped. Virginia Beach is the state's most populated city; First Landing is the state park system's most visited, attracting more than 1 million visitors annually. Yet it can handle the load. Solid trails built by Civilian Conservation Corps crews are well maintained, a considerable feat given the constant erosion. It helps that most people hike short interpretive trails near the visitor center, or hike and bike the wide Cape Henry Trail.

Hikers will find quieter moments on the hiker-only Long Creek Trail. Where the trail skirts White Hill Lake—more of a marsh than a true lake—American egrets and great blue herons wade in relative peace. Look for an osprey's huge nest atop dead loblolly and oak trees at the junction with the Osprey Trail. You might see muskrat and mink lodges in the tidal marshes. (You can identify muskrats by their flat, naked-looking tail.) If you're hiking early in the morning, sit for a while on the shore of Long Creek, near shallow or

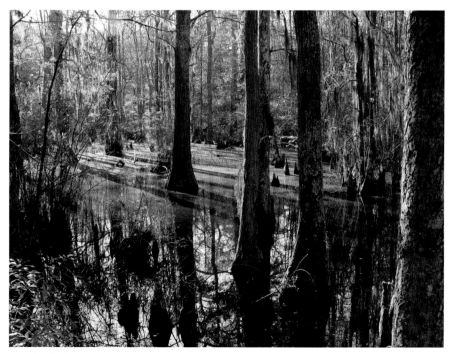

Boardwalks lead hikers through a magical bald cypress swamp. VIRGINIA STATE PARKS

This Chesapeake Bay beach was the first landing of the Jamestown settlers in 1607.
VTC/BILL CRABTREE JR.

First Landing's beach offers more than sunbathing, and summer isn't the only time to visit. Bird watchers with binoculars flock to Cape Henry in winter for views of northern gannets that winter offshore in the mid-Atlantic region. During feeding, gannets tuck their wings and narrow themselves for a plunge of 100 feet or more into ocean depths. Also here, the chicken turtle ranks as a critically endangered species in Virginia, with five or fewer known to be in existence.

marshy water. A slick head will break the water's surface, swivel left and right, then disappear beneath the water. Each time it surfaces, it emits a hasping noise, as if it's clearing its nostrils. The muskrat survives primarily on aquatic vegetation, but its morning feeding ritual may yield clams, frogs, or an occasional fish.

Back on the trail, look for the partridgeberry, a trailing evergreen common in the park. The white pairs of tubular flowers bloom in June and July; the red berries and shiny green leaves are visible all winter. Curiously, partridges don't eat them, but Native American women drank a partridgeberry tea during the last weeks of pregnancy to lessen the pain of childbirth.

You can link again with Long Creek Trail by hanging a left at the end of Osprey Trail. This section gains a little elevation as you hike giant sand dunes covered with vegetation. It's the primary landform in the park—and it's constantly shifting, if ever so slowly.

MILES AND DIRECTIONS

0.0 Start from the Trail Center parking lot. Walk down a wide gravel path that parallels the park entrance road. Walk straight past a footpath that breaks left and is a shortcut to the Cape Henry Trail.

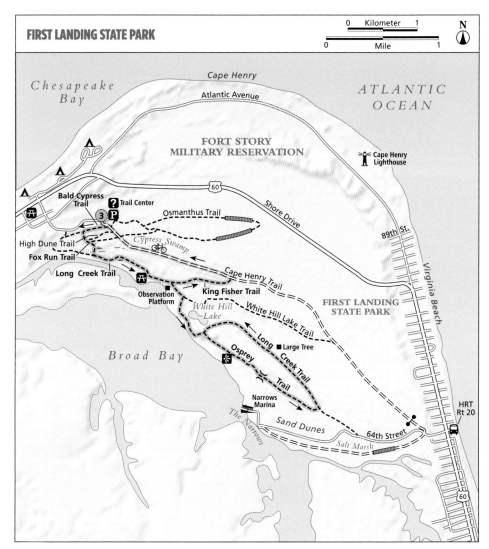

FIRST LANDING STATE PARK

0   Kilometer   1

0   Mile   1

N

Chesapeake Bay

Cape Henry

ATLANTIC OCEAN

Atlantic Avenue

FORT STORY MILITARY RESERVATION

Cape Henry Lighthouse

60

Shore Drive

Bald Cypress Trail

? Trail Center

P

3

Osmanthus Trail

Cypress Swamp

High Dune Trail

Fox Run Trail

Long Creek Trail

Cape Henry Trail

89th St.

Observation Platform

King Fisher Trail

White Hill Lake Trail

White Hill Lake

FIRST LANDING STATE PARK

Virginia Beach

Large Tree

Broad Bay

Long Creek Trail

Osprey

Trail

Narrows Marina

Sand Dunes

64th Street

HRT Rt 20

The Narrows

Salt Marsh

60

0.05 Turn left onto the Cape Henry Trail, a wide multiuse trail popular with bicyclists and joggers.

0.08 Turn right onto Bald Cypress Trail. The fence across the trailhead indicates this is a hiker-only trail.

0.1 Across the trail lies a nurse log, noteworthy for the shoots growing from the mossy, rotted lumber—shoots growing into small trees themselves. On your left is a sand dune thick with holly and pine. To your right is a cypress swamp. The chicken turtle (*Deitrochelys reticularia*), an endangered species, lives here, as do more common frogs and wading birds.

0.15 An unmarked path climbs the dune on your left. This is the first of many unmarked trails that spread like a spider web throughout the park. Hiking them might provide adventure, but it also contributes to erosion. Stay on the marked trails.

0.2 The Bald Cypress Trail makes a hard left. Climb five wooden steps, then turn left onto the Fox Run Trail. **Note:** A right turn leads to the park entrance road.

0.6 Cross a sand dune and come to a T intersection with the Long Creek Trail. Turn left onto Long Creek Trail.

0.7 Pass by a wide opening in the trees and underbrush with views onto Broad Bay.

0.8 Ignore two unmarked trails that split left off the Long Creek Trail. Long Creek Trail follows the riverside, separated from water by only marsh grass.

1.1 Top out on a sand dune with views over Broad Bay. This is a good spot for a picnic.

1.35 Stay straight on Long Creek Trail as King Fisher Trail enters on the left.

1.4 An observation deck on the right side of the trail allows for great views over the tidal wetlands that buffer Broad Bay. This structure marks the beginning of a series of boardwalks spanning sensitive habitat.

1.5 At a fork in the trail, bear right on Long Creek Trail. Cross a concrete spillway and skirt the south side of White Hill Lake.

1.8 Begin a brief steep climb to the top of the "white hill" sand dunes that lend the lake its name. Broad Bay is to the right.

2.0 Turn right and descend on the Osprey Trail. **Note:** The Osprey Trail skirts the water's edge. During high tide, it may be washed out. In all cases, prepare for wet hiking.

2.4 Cross a small wooden bridge.

2.7 Trail leaves behind its wet portions and climbs onto a low, wooded finger of land bounded by marsh.

3.1 Turn left onto Long Creek Trail.

4.3 Pass the Osprey Trail on the left.

4.5 Turn right onto King Fisher Trail. **Note:** Numerous unmarked paths lead off in different directions from this trail. Use the white blazes to keep you on track.

5.1 On the hillside to your left, notice the series of enormous loblolly pines. This species is a valuable commercial lumber. Native Americans called it the *loblolly*—meaning "mud puddle"—for the environment in which it grows well.

5.4 Turn left onto Cape Henry Trail.

6.3 A portion of the Bald Cypress Trail crosses the Cape Henry Trail. Continue straight on the Cape Henry Trail.

6.45 Reach the junction with the parking lot access trail. Turn right to return to the parking lot.

6.5 Arrive back at the parking lot.

Bikes on the trail at First Landing. VTC

HIKE INFORMATION

Local Information
Virginia Beach Convention & Visitors Bureau, (800) VA-BEACH (822-3224), www.visit virginiabeach.com

Local Events/Attractions
The Fall Festival in Oct and Party in the Park in early Nov are held by the Friends of First Landing State Park: www.friendsoffirstlandingstatepark.com.

The Chesapeake Bay Center (located on the Chesapeake Bay side of the park) houses exhibits on the First Landing in 1607, natural resource displays, and the park's visitor information.

Lodging
The park has 180 campsites and several yurts, open Mar to early Dec. There are sites with and without electric and water. The twenty full-service cabins are open year-round. For reservations and information, call (800) 933-7275 or visit www.reservevaparks.com.

Organizations
Friends of First Landing, Virginia Beach, (757) 412-2300, www.friendsoffirstlandingstate park.com

Tidewater Appalachian Trail Club maintains some trails in First Landing, www.tide wateratc.com.

4 YORK RIVER STATE PARK

The worm-eating warbler, common to Virginia's Blue Ridge province, is also found in the coastal environment of York River State Park. After walking through the park's forests, thick with mountain laurel and holly, shaded by chestnut oaks and American beech, hikers will agree with the songbird: This park feels a lot like Virginia's mountain regions. Most paths here lead through mature hardwood forests to overlooks onto the York River. Land underfoot holds evidence—pottery shards, arrowheads—of settlement dating from tens of thousands of years ago. Perhaps the park's most interesting story is still being recorded—that of the Taskinas Creek Estuary, a vital marsh and hardwood swamp monitored by scientists as a gauge of the Chesapeake Bay's health.

Start: Park contact and fee station
Distance: 7.7-mile loop
Hiking time: 1–4 hours
Difficulty: Easy due to flat terrain, well-marked trails, and options for shorter hikes
Trail surface: Wooded paths, boardwalks, and gravel and dirt roads lead through marsh, fields, hardwood swamps, and upland forests.
Land status: State park
Nearest town: Williamsburg, VA
Other trail users: Cyclists and equestrians
Accessibility: Paved paths along native plant arboretum to canoe dock, 0.5-mile path around day-use area, and 0.75-mile ADA backwoods trail
Canine compatibility: Leashed dogs permitted (leashes no longer than 6 feet)

Trail contact: York River State Park, 9801 York River Park Rd., Williamsburg; (757) 566-3036; www.dcr.virginia.gov/state-parks/york-river
Schedule: Open daily year-round, 8 a.m. to dusk. The park visitor center, office, and gift shop are open from 8 a.m. to 3:30 p.m. daily.
Fees/permits: Per-vehicle entrance fee
Facilities/features: Visitor center, concessions, gift shop, ADA restrooms, picnic shelters, boat launch, and kayak and canoe rentals on a 7-acre pond and on Taskinas Creek
NatGeo TOPO! map: Gressitt
Other maps: A Trail Guide/Map is available at the park and downloadable on its website.

FINDING THE TRAILHEAD

From I-64, take the Croaker exit 231B and go 1.2 miles north on Croaker Road/VA 607. Turn right onto VA 606—also called Riverview Road—and drive 1.7 miles to VA 696. Turn left onto VA 696 (York River Park Road). The fee station is in 2 miles. Parking lots for the visitor center, picnic area, and trails are just beyond the fee station. **GPS:** N37 24.718′ / W76 42.847′. *DeLorme: Virginia Atlas & Gazetteer*: Page 50, A1.

THE HIKE

Offshore of Taskinas Creek Trail, salt marsh cordgrass sways with a stiff breeze. On the creek's muddy flats, spotted sandpipers and black-bellied plovers dart in earnest pursuit

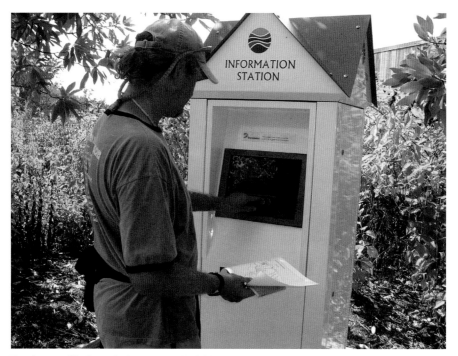
Touchscreen kiosks make it easy to print hiking maps at many state parks in Virginia.

of food. A cluster of fiddler crabs scuttle for shelter. As you climb away from the creek on a trail beneath oak and beech trees, a great blue heron, startled, lumbers toward open water, letting loose a *gaaak* as a parting shot.

How much, you might wonder, can these scenes differ from those of 300 years ago? The Native Americans of eastern Virginia were a riverine people; their lives revolved around what the rivers provided. Men hunted meadow and wood for white-tailed deer, turkey, and other prey, but the water provided all things necessary for life: food; fertile soil; shells for ornaments, tools, and trading; reeds for mats and baskets; and even transportation. At low tide, women foraged in freshwater marsh for arrow arum, whose root, tuckahoe, is edible when boiled. Thick-stemmed saltwort, pickled or preserved, made a tasty delicacy.

English settlers called it a "hand-to-mouth" existence, and yet their survival, too, depended on it. On a monthly—sometimes biweekly—basis, Native Americans sent gifts of food to the James Island fort in 1607–8, sustaining settlers during spring "starving times," when the previous fall's harvest had run out and new forest growth made hunting more difficult. When English farmers spread beyond fort walls onto the James/York River Peninsula, they found why the Native Americans could afford generosity: Chiskiack Indians planted maize, beans, and squash among burned tree stumps, remnants of field clearing. It was a high-yield, if not terribly efficient, farming system.

York River State Park's Powhatan Forks Trail crosses high peninsula meadows, then enters the shade of hardwood forest. A person who has spent time in Virginia's mountain woods may sense something familiar. The trees—chestnut oak, American beech, green ash—and a forest understory of mountain laurel, holly, and berry-producing shrubs thrive here thanks to soil conditions normally found in western Virginia. York River State Park soil contains marl, a limestone-heavy clay similar to soils of the Shenandoah Valley. Elsewhere in the park, the Yorktown rock formation sinks as deep as 150 feet or more underfoot. This is a calcium-rich soil, thick with deposits of ancient seashell and sand. Prehistoric seas washed over Virginia's coastal region several times. Erosion along the York River constantly churns up fossils pointing to past aquatic life. Unearthing 5-million-year-old shells and whalebones is not an uncommon occurrence here.

Where the north branch of Powhatan Forks Trail drops into a marshy area, an expansive view of the river opens up. This approach is much gentler than the Riverview Trail's abrupt ending on high river bluffs a half-mile downstream, yet both permit an unobstructed view of Purtan Bay on the opposite shore. Captain John Smith, hoping to save a struggling colony, took in a similar vista in the fall of 1608. (Today, homes dot that far shoreline and recreation boats bob in the water.) In Captain Smith's time, Purtan Bay was one home of Powhatan, chief of the eastern Native American empire that bore his name. His tribe, the Werowocomoco, built huts along the shallow bay and its three tributaries and used fragile bridges strung across tidal flats as links with each other.

In what must have been an embarrassing moment for the adventurous John Smith, he and a party of men crossed the York River to meet Powhatan, but landed in the wrong spot. Some men disembarked and tried crossing a stream by way of a bridge made of forked stakes and planks. It defeated the heavily clad men, and the Werowocomoco ferried them, a few at a time, across the creek. Later, after negotiating for corn, Smith and company tried returning to their ship, but his canoe ran aground on a mudflat. Powhatan's men trudged out to retrieve them; Smith asked instead for "some wood, fire, and mats to cover me." He spent the night thusly, waiting for the tide to return and float his boat off its hang-up.

Despite initial feebleness, the expanding colony soon had Powhatan's empire in retreat. Nathaniel Bacon Jr., a settler, led a group of armed, discontented landowners against the Native Americans in the summer of 1676. Miffed by the colonial governor William Berkeley's inability to keep Indian raiders in check, Bacon's men soon hounded the governor into hiding. Given virtually free rein, Bacon used outposts throughout the Tidewater to launch attacks. As a result, travelers today will see his name attached to innumerable homes, old forts, backroads, and "hideaways" throughout the region. York River State Park is no different. Near the park stands the Stonehouse site, a 17th-century military outpost during Bacon's Rebellion, now listed on the National Register of Historic Places. The Occoneechee tribe fell in May 1676, and the Pamunkey fell in August of that same year.

Bacon died of natural causes in October 1676 and Berkeley regained control of the Virginia colony. In February 1677, English settlers and Native Americans struck the Treaty of Middle Plantation. Besides war reparations—prisoners, land, weapons, tools— the treaty made remnants of a once-powerful Indian empire formal subjects to the king of England. It called for an annual tribute of three arrows and twenty beaver pelts in exchange for reservation land near West Point, Virginia. More than 300 years later, the Treaty of Middle Plantation remains in force. Each autumn, Mattaponi (matta-PO-ni) and Pamunkey Indians trek to the governor's mansion to pay their rent for reservation land—a deer strung on a pole, with tribesmen dressed in full regalia supporting either end of the stick.

0 1 2 3 4 5 6 7

200'   200'
START   Powhatan   END
150'   Forks Cut-off   150'
                                                    Backbone
100'   Trail   100'
         York River   York River
50'   50'
     Riverview
     Trail
0'   0'

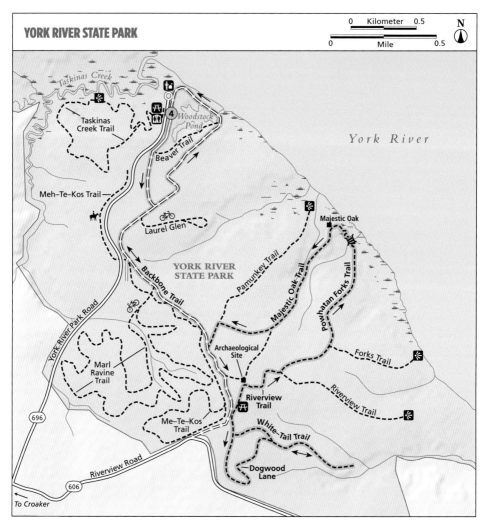

YORK RIVER STATE PARK

0   Kilometer   0.5

0   Mile   0.5

N

Taskinas Creek

Taskinas
Creek Trail

Woodstock
Pond

York River

4

Beaver Trail

Meh–Te–Kos Trail

Laurel Glen

Majestic Oak

YORK RIVER
STATE PARK

Backbone Trail

Pamunkey Trail

Majestic Oak Trail

Powhatan Forks Trail

Archaeological
Site

Forks Trail

York River Park Road

Marl
Ravine
Trail

Riverview
Trail

Riverview Trail

696

Me–Te–Kos
Trail

Riverview
Trail

White–Tail Trail

Dogwood
Lane

Riverview Road

606

To Croaker

MILES AND DIRECTIONS

0.0 Start from the park contact and fee station. Follow a paved path alongside the park entrance road. In a few hundred feet, this paved path becomes a gravel-lined two-track path as it enters woods. There is a yellow sign on the right for the Backbone Trail. **Note:** Park trail maps identify this stretch as combined Backbone Trail/Woodstock Pond Trail.

0.16 Pass the Beaver Trail on the left. **Option:** Beaver Trail is a 0.6-mile alternative for circling Woodstock Pond. It ends near the York River at a junction with Woodstock Pond Trail. Use Beaver Trail to complete a shorter loop around the pond that will return you to the park visitor center.

0.4 At the junction of Woodstock Pond Trail, turn right on Backbone Trail, a hard-packed dirt road that runs 1.4 miles to the park's south boundary. Both cyclists and hikers use this trail. The Meh-Te-Kos bridle path (for horses) intersects it at numerous points. Following Woodstock Pond Trail left leads back to the visitor center in 0.8 mile.

1.2 Walk past the Pamunkey Trail, which branches left off Backbone Trail. **Note:** At this intersection, a power line cuts across Backbone Trail. Stick to the roadway bearing right.

1.4 Continue straight on Backbone Trail past a junction on the left for Powhatan Forks Trail.

1.6 Arrive at a junction with Riverview and White-Tail Trails on the left. Veer left onto White-Tail Trail. (There's a picnic table here.)

1.65 Turn right onto Dogwood Lane Trail, a rutted narrow dirt road flanked by mountain laurel on the high-banked dirt roadsides.

2.0 Stay on Dogwood Lane Trail as a service road veers right. From here, Dogwood continues as a singletrack path through heavy woods flush with turkeys, pheasants, and deer.

2.4 Bear right onto White-Tail Trail.

2.8 White-Tail Trail ends in a large clearing that has limited winter and spring views of the York River. Turn around and retrace your steps along White-Tail Trail.

3.2 Continue straight on White-Tail Trail past a junction with Dogwood Trail on the left.

3.5 White-Tail Trail junctions with Riverview and Backbone Trails. Veer right onto Riverview Trail, which is a wide, sandy two-track woods path.

3.7 Approach an open clearing and a junction with Powhatan Forks Trail. Continue on Riverview Trail, which bears right into the woods. A trail sign here notes that it is 1.27 miles to the end of Riverview at the York River. **Note:** The clearing is a former archaeological dig site.

3.9 Bear right onto Powhatan Forks Trail at a Y-shaped junction. The trail here is a mowed path.

4.1 Powhatan Forks Trail splits left and right. Bear left on the North Branch Powhatan Forks Trail. The trail gradually descends to the York River through a forest lush with mountain laurel and American holly trees.

4.7 A wide spot on the North Branch Powhatan Forks Trail features views of the York River and a wood bench for resting. Follow the trail as it descends off the hillside to a boardwalk across a river marsh.

4.9 On the opposite side of the boardwalk, climb the stream bank to another overview of the York River and turn left onto the Majestic Oak Trail.

5.5 Bear right on Spur Trail.

5.7 Turn left on Pamunkey Trail.

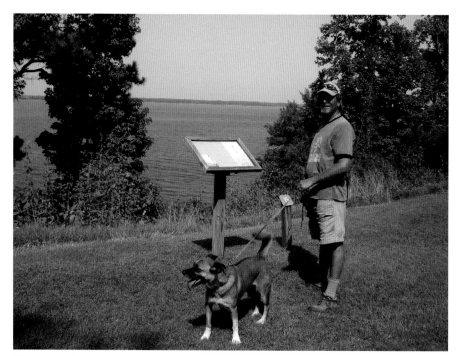
The author hikes the shoreline at York River State Park.

5.8   Turn right onto Backbone Trail.

6.7   Backbone Trail bends left to return to the park contact and fee station. Continue straight on Woodstock Pond Trail.

7.5   Ascend on Woodstock Pond Trail and follow a path as it bends left through the field and past the visitor center.

7.7   Arrive back at the state park contact and fee station.

HIKE INFORMATION

Local Information
Williamsburg Tourism Council, (757) 229-6511, www.visitwilliamsburg.com

Local Events/Attractions
Estuaries Day, late Sept. Displays, demonstrations, boat tours, and other programs centered around Taskinas Creek. Contact the park for specific dates and times.

Tours
Guided hikes and stargazing are offered in the park year-round.

Organizations
Friends of York River State Park, Williamsburg, (757) 566-3036, Facebook group

5 NEWPORT NEWS PARK

Newport News Park, a 7,700-acre preserve, is one of the largest municipal parks in America. The most heavily used parts surround Lee Hall Reservoir. Trails and dirt roads make possible a hike that at times feels remote, despite being set in the middle of a large city. The White Oak Trail Road leads away from the visitor center and transports you across long stretches of marsh and past Civil War battle fortifications. Near the turnaround of this 5-mile hike, there is a 1-mile detour into adjoining Yorktown Battlefield, where the last major battle of the Revolution secured American independence.

Start: Park Discovery Center
Distance: 5.0-mile loop
Hiking time: About 2.5 hours
Difficulty: Easy
Trail surface: Gravel road, dirt footpaths, mountain bike trails, and boardwalks
Land status: City park
Nearest town: Newport News, VA
Other trail users: Cyclists and joggers
Accessibility: There is a memorial plaza at the end of the Dam Bridge that is paved, and the bridge itself is accessible.
Canine compatibility: Pets are allowed on leash. Rabies certificate required to stay in campground.

Trail contact: Newport News Park, 13560 Jefferson Ave., Newport News; (757) 888-3333; www.nnparks.com
Schedule: Open daily year-round, sunrise to sunset
Fees/permits: None for day use
Facilities/features: Discovery Center, visitor center, bicycle rentals, picnic shelters, fishing, rentals (rowboat, paddleboat, canoe) on freshwater reservoir, full-service campground, camp store, laundry, two 18-hole golf courses, disc golf, archery range
NatGeo TOPO! map: Yorktown
NatGeo Trails Illustrated map: Delmarva Peninsula
Other maps: A trail map is downloadable from park website.

FINDING THE TRAILHEAD
From I-64 in Newport News, take exit 250B. Keep left to take the VA 143 West ramp toward VA 105. Turn left onto Jefferson Avenue/VA 143 and drive 0.4 mile to the park entrance on the right. **Trailhead GPS:** N37 10.905' / W76 32.236'. *DeLorme: Virginia Atlas & Gazetteer*: Page 50, C2.

THE HIKE
On April 16, 1862, Union forces under General George McClellan launched a military campaign from Fort Monroe in Hampton, Virginia. The goal was to push forward up The Peninsula, as the land between the James and York Rivers was called, all the way to Richmond, capital of the Confederacy.

A campaign planned as a quick thrust into the heart of the Confederacy faced its first test on the banks of the Warwick River in the vicinity of Lee's Mill, in what today is Newport News. There, Union forces met a Confederate army entrenched behind a series of earthen breastworks and trenches. Three times that day, Union forces rushed forward, only to be repelled by Confederate artillery. Soldiers from two Vermont regiments suffered the heaviest losses: twenty-six dead and more than sixty wounded. It

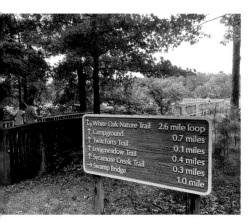

Trails in Newport News Park are well marked.

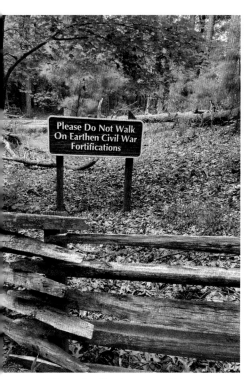

Civil War fortifications can still be seen in Newport News Park

marked the start of a 3-week siege that ultimately ended in a draw and a serious blow to McClellan's Richmond plans.

The ground that saw this long-ago action is now within Newport News Park. The Warwick River has been dammed to form Lee Hall Reservoir, a vast lake that is home to waterfowl and beloved for water sports like fishing and paddle boating. In the surrounding 8,000 acres, protected to ensure good water quality, hikers, joggers, and bike riders can access a huge outdoor playground of trails in one of Virginia's largest metro areas.

One mile into this hike, after turning onto Wynn's Mill Loop Trail, a hiker can see firsthand the remains of breastworks that protected Confederate and repelled Union soldiers. As you walk, notice a pronounced trend in the landscape that develops on each side of the trail: On the left, mounded dirt (now significantly overgrown with trees, but still visible in form) indicates breastworks, while on the right stand the swampy backwaters of a Lee Hall Reservoir tributary. Great blue herons are a common sighting here. Adult herons can stand chest-high to a person; to watch them stalk their fish and crab prey in the shallow edges of the swamp is a study in predator virtuosity as the heron spears a fish and quickly chokes it down its gullet.

Waterside vegetation in this area indicates a freshwater source, a contrast to salt-tolerant habitats along the region's tidal creeks. Rather than salt marsh grasses, these watery guts are flush with lotus lily, arrow arum, pickerel weed, and cattails. The shrubby shorelines are thick with bayberry and groundsel tree. The latter is recognized easiest in fall, when seed pods open and white bristles emerge. A dense shoreline of groundsel tree (also called *silverling*) in autumn can appear to have received a light dusting of snow.

The habitat is dynamic in that zone where water and land meet and interact. Eastern box turtles and common musk turtles slide off the mud banks as you approach, their presence marked by a *kerplunk* and ripples on the water surface. Songbirds forage for food in the bayberry and holly trees. The cardinal is the flashiest, but there are some one

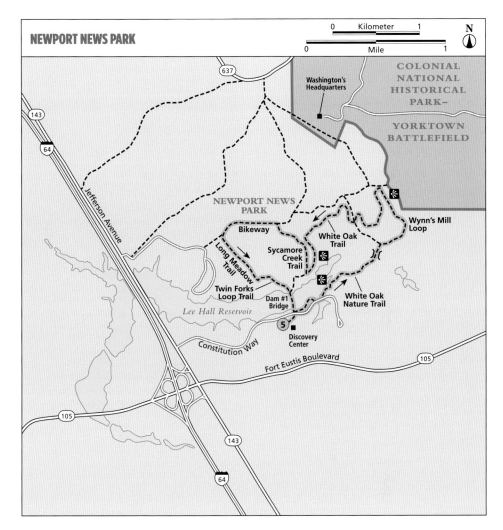

hundred other songbird species on the park's bird list. On a hot, sunny day, stay alert for a northern black racer or rat snake sunning itself on an open stretch of trail. As you cross the many boardwalks and bridges, mallard ducks slip away and Canada geese *honk honk,* as if to warn you about getting too close.

Newport News Park is beloved by residents as an oasis amid their ever-growing city— a major interstate, I-64, is within earshot of the park entrance. When you take time to delve farther into its substantial forest, you can truly appreciate its importance as both a nature refuge and a slice of American history.

MILES AND DIRECTIONS

0.0 Start at a trail board in front of the park Discovery Center. Look left for a wooden sign that reads "Nature Trail" and follow a boardwalk leading into the woods. Emerge from the woods to cross the paved park road, then turn right and follow a paved path that in about 20 feet becomes hard-packed rock and dirt.

0.3 Veer left at a fork in the trail and cross a boardwalk bridge. Trail signs indicate you are walking on the White Oak Nature Trail, not to be confused with the White Oak Trail that comprises a later portion of this route.

0.9 Cross Swamp Bridge. At the far side, turn right onto Wynn's Mill Loop. Look for Civil War–era breastworks, which are earthen berms that afforded soldiers protection during battle.

1.6 Turn left to continue on Wynn's Mill Loop. *Side trip:* Turn right for 0.8 mile to the site of George Washington's headquarters during the Yorktown battle. This side trip adds approximately 2 miles.

2.2 Continue straight through a four-way junction with Swamp Fire Trail. Within a few feet, reach a second four-way junction and turn left on White Oak Trail.

3.0 Turn right on Sycamore Creek Trail, which is a wide, hard-packed dirt road.

3.5 Turn left on the park bikeway, a gravel road.

3.9 Turn left on Long Meadow Trail, a wide, grassy doubletrack.

4.3 Continue straight on Long Meadow Trail past a left turn (this is one leg of the Twin Forks Loop). In a few feet, turn left at a second junction. *Note:* A sign at this junction points the way to the Discovery Center.

4.6 Cross the Dam #1 Bridge. At the far side, walk through a small circular plaza area with a monument to the Battle of Lee's Mill, cross the park road, and enter the woods at a sign that reads "Nature Trail."

5.0 Arrive back at the park Discovery Center.

Biking is popular in Newport News Park and neighboring Yorktown Battlefield.

HIKE INFORMATION

Local Information
Newport News Tourism, (888) 493–7386, www.newport-news.org. The Newport News Visitor Center is located at the park entrance.

Local Events/Attractions
Fall-O-Ween takes place in the park the first weekend in Oct.

Celebration in Lights transforms the park into a magical drive-through light display, Thanksgiving through New Year's Day.

Lodging
Newport News Park's full-service campground has 188 sites. Call (757) 888-3333 for reservations, or reserve at www.nnparks.com. If you bring a pet, be prepared to show proof of rabies vaccination.

HONORABLE MENTIONS: EASTERN VIRGINIA

A. BELLE ISLE STATE PARK

Bird watchers, hikers, horseback riders, and cyclists in the mood for wide-open spaces find this an ideal destination. Trails trace cornfields, cross tidal marshes, and wind through pine and hardwood filter strips—ribbons of woodland that separate fields from sensitive wetlands. Well-marked and easy to follow, trails feature interpretive boards explaining Chesapeake Bay ecology. (804) 462-5030; www.dcr.virginia.gov/state-parks/belle-isle. **GPS:** N37 46.931' / W76 36.203'. *DeLorme: Virginia Atlas & Gazetteer.* Page 60, B2.

B. SANDY BOTTOM NATURE PRESERVE

Located off the Hampton Roads Center Parkway at 1255 Big Bethel Rd. in Hampton. From exit 261A off I-64, follow the parkway west to the nature preserve entrance, just past the intersection of Big Bethel Road on the right. There are 12 miles of trails in the 456-acre park. Trillium Trail is the longest at 3.3 miles. Former borrow pits that supplied fill to build nearby I-64 are now lakes. The 10,000-square-foot Nature Center over-looks Sandy Bottom Lake. Boardwalks cross wetland habitat, while graded dirt paths pass through hardwood forest. Fishing, recreational boating, biking, and primitive camping are allowed. There are canoe and kayak rentals, eleven primitive campsites, and four tent cabins. (757) 825-4657; www.hampton.gov/sandybottom. **GPS:** N37 03.713' / W76 25.998'. *DeLorme: Virginia Atlas & Gazetteer.* Page 50, D3.

C. BEAVERDAM PARK

Located minutes from Gloucester Court House on Virginia's Middle Peninsula. From Business US 17 north, turn right onto VA 616/Roaring Springs Road. In 2.4 miles the road dead-ends at the park's main entrance at 8687 Roaring Springs Rd., Gloucester. There are 9.5 miles of multiuse trails for horses, mountain bikers, and hikers, as well as a 3-mile hiker-only trail. The main hiking trail passes along marshy fringes of the reservoir and through an upland hardwood forest. (804) 693-2107; www.gloucesterva.info. **GPS:** N37 26.906' / W76 32.040'. *DeLorme: Virginia Atlas & Gazetteer.* Page 50, A2.

D. HICKORY HOLLOW NATURAL AREA PRESERVE

Located on the Northern Neck near Lancaster Courthouse. From Kilmarnock, follow VA 3 toward Lancaster. Just before you reach Lancaster, turn right onto VA 604. The preserve is on your left. This is a special hike along the wooded bluffs overlooking Western Branch. Spur trails plunge off the hillside into the stream's marshy backwaters. Lancaster County once considered developing this 254-acre spot into an industrial park; bird watchers and nature lovers fought off the proposal with the aid of the Northern Neck Audubon Society, which now owns it. (804) 225-2303; www.dcr.virginia.gov/natural-heritage/natural-area-preserves/hickory. **GPS:** N37 46.329' / W76 26.655'. *DeLorme: Virginia Atlas & Gazetteer.* Page 60, B3.

E. CALEDON STATE PARK

Located in King George County at the top of Virginia's Northern Neck, 11617 Caledon Rd., King George. From US 301, follow VA 206 to VA 218, then head east on VA 218 for 1.2 miles to the entrance. Created to provide nesting and roosting spots for bald eagles, Caledon has more than a dozen color-coded trails totaling about 15 miles. Several lead to bird-watching spots along the Potomac River. Some trails may be temporarily closed to protect nesting birds. Sandy bluffs in the Horsehead Cliff area are embedded with fossils. Day use only. Many guided activities are scheduled spring through fall. (540) 663-3861; www.dcr.virginia.gov/state-parks/caledon. **GPS:** N38 20.032' / W77 08.594'. *DeLorme: Virginia Atlas & Gazetteer:* Page 71, B5.

NORTHERN VIRGINIA

What is northern Virginia? Is it coastal or Piedmont? Urban or suburban? Could it even be rural? Northern Virginia is, in fact, all of these. First and foremost, it is a metropolis, with all the baggage this carries: highways, pollution, sprawl. Such conditions do not, however, negate quality outdoor experiences. This area—which encompasses the pastoral hills of Fauquier County, the ragged 90-foot cliffs at Great Falls, and the calm estuaries around Pohick Bay and Mason Neck—ranks as wildly diverse as any in the state. Absent the mountains of western regions, the area features streams that, over centuries, have carved out channels through granite, schist, and metagraywacke. Healthy forests of hardwoods crown river bluffs. Microcosms of Appalachian cove forest—with its stunning array of flowers, trees, mosses, and animals—pop up along quiet, secluded streams. Virginia's fall line bisects the region, creating picturesque waterfalls and cascades that transport you hundreds of miles away.

Northern Virginians work hard for these special environments. They work hard to find them, and they work hard to protect them. Preserved tracts of land on the Potomac, below Washington, DC, are recognized as top spots in the East for nesting and roosting bald eagles. Even land that has been logged, farmed, mined, and left to waste away—as was the case with Prince William Forest Park—has rebounded to a state of natural and scenic beauty. Years of preservation work in northern Virginia have made possible just about every type of outdoor pursuit, from walking to rock climbing, bird watching to hunting.

The author with her niece, Vanessa Kubick, hiking Scotts Run Nature Preserve

Whatever natural wonders await the explorer in northern Virginia, history makes doubly rewarding. More than a few chief executives have left their mark. Roosevelt Island, a vacation spot for Theodore Roosevelt, is

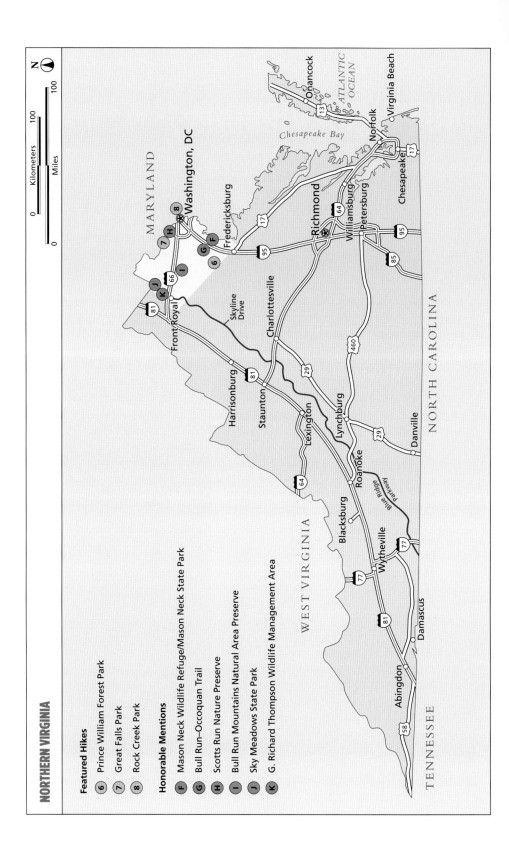

NORTHERN VIRGINIA

Featured Hikes

- (6) Prince William Forest Park
- (7) Great Falls Park
- (8) Rock Creek Park

Honorable Mentions

- (F) Mason Neck Wildlife Refuge/Mason Neck State Park
- (G) Bull Run–Occoquan Trail
- (H) Scotts Run Nature Preserve
- (I) Bull Run Mountains Natural Area Preserve
- (J) Sky Meadows State Park
- (K) G. Richard Thompson Wildlife Management Area

prominent among them. James Madison fled a burning Washington, DC, during the War of 1812, stashing the Declaration of Independence in an old gristmill now preserved as a museum. Less prominent, but just as intriguing, are Civil War raiders who prowled eastern foothills of the Blue Ridge. Archaeologists have unearthed the garbage heaps of prehistoric residents who encamped along the Potomac. And on the shores of America's river, the Potomac, Chicocoan Indians watched Captain John Smith sail as far as the waterfalls at Georgetown during his legendary explorations of 1608.

The paths of our history are today the paths of hikers, bird watchers, and nature lovers. The stories behind place-names and old buildings are as much a part of the outdoor experience in northern Virginia as the flowers, birds, and trees.

THE HIKES
6. Prince William Forest Park
7. Great Falls Park
8. Rock Creek Park

HONORABLE MENTIONS
F. Mason Neck Wildlife Refuge/Mason Neck State Park
G. Bull Run–Occoquan Trail
H. Scotts Run Nature Preserve
I. Bull Run Mountains Natural Area Preserve
J. Sky Meadows State Park
K. G. Richard Thompson Wildlife Management Area

NOVA HIKING CLUBS
The northern Virginia area (popularly known as NoVa) has several very active hiking clubs that schedule regular hikes not only in the NoVa region of Virginia/Maryland/DC, but also in nearby Shenandoah National Park. Some groups have migrated hike schedules to Meet Up, but basic information is available at the websites listed:

Capital Hiking Club, www.capitalhikingclub.org. Hikes and trips in Virginia, Maryland, and Pennsylvania.

Northern Virginia Hiking Club, www.nvhc.com. Hikes and trips in Virginia, Maryland, DC, and beyond.

Potomac Appalachian Trail Club (PATC), Vienna, (703) 242-0315, www.patc .net.

Wanderbirds Hiking Club, www.wanderbirds.org. Hikes in Virginia, West Virginia, Maryland, and Pennsylvania.

Washington Women Outdoors, Germantown, MD, www.washingtonwomen outdoors.org. Outdoor adventures for women, including hiking, kayaking, rock climbing, and biking.

Roughly 100 miles inland from Virginia's coast, a geologic boundary called the fall line marks a change in the landscape. Here the sandy soil of Virginia's coastal plain segues into the bedrock underlying the Piedmont. The effect is pronounced on rivers, where waterfalls and rapids form. Historically, these acted as barriers to ocean-faring vessels. Towns formed up and down the fall line to handle commerce between inland farmers and coastal traders. Prince William Forest Park, a small national park straddling the fall line in Prince William County, is tied to this history through the tobacco farmers and miners who used the nearby port town of Dumfries to ship their goods. Today the park still receives heavy use, but now hikers, cyclists, and nature lovers are drawn by the cascades, wildlife, rare plants, and historic ruins.

Start: Laurel Loop Trail map board behind Pine Grove picnic pavilion
Distance: 14.6-mile loop
Hiking time: About 5 hours
Difficulty: Moderate due to length, well-graded and clearly marked trails, and elevation change
Trail surface: A combination of dirt forest paths, dirt roads, and paved roads lead through hardwood forests and along streams to small cascades, rock outcrops, and waterfalls.
Land status: National park
Nearest town: Dumfries, VA
Other trail users: Joggers, cross-country skiers, and mountain bikers
Accessibility: The 0.2-mile Piedmont Forest Trail is a paved loop with footbridges, boardwalks, and benches. A section of Scenic Drive between Parking Area D and Oak Ridge Camp is one way, with one paved lane suitable for wheelchairs.
Canine compatibility: Dogs permitted

Trail contact: Prince William Forest Park, 18100 Park Headquarters Rd., Triangle; (703) 221-7181; www.nps .gov/prwi
Schedule: Park open daily, sunrise to sunset, year-round
Fees/permits: Entrance fee and camping fee; permit required for free backcountry camping, but includes a reservation fee levied by Recreation .gov
Facilities/features: Visitor center, historic cabins, and seasonal 100-site campground for tents and RVs. Campground reservations: Recreation.gov. Cabins must be reserved through the park at www .nps.gov/prwi. Chopawamsic Backcountry Area is a 1,500-acre area with 8 primitive campsites accessible from the 2-mile loop trail. There is no fee, but campers must reserve a site through Recreation .gov, which levies a reservation fee.
NatGeo TOPO! map: Quantico, Joplin

FINDING THE TRAILHEAD

From I-95, take exit 150B and turn west onto VA 619/Joplin Road. Drive 1.7 miles and turn right into Prince William Forest Park. In 0.5 mile, turn left at a sign for Pine Grove Picnic Area. Immediately turn right into the long-term parking area. Walk up the small knoll and locate the Laurel Loop Trail map board at the edge of the woods between the Pine Grove Picnic Area and the visitor center.
GPS: N38 33.644' /W77 20.943'. *DeLorme: Virginia Atlas & Gazetteer*: Page 76, D3.

THE HIKE

There is plenty of rough, broken-up terrain along the Quantico Creek and South Fork Quantico Creek stream valleys. Mountain-laurel slicks coat steep hillsides. Stream water flows over bedrock slate, which, where exposed, creates small rapids and riffles. Quantico slate is super-resistant—water simply bounces over it and flows on its merry way. Here in Prince William Forest Park, it's a last hurrah of sorts. Within a mile or so, the small streams of Prince William Forest Park empty into Quantico Creek. The descent over Virginia's fall line is complete.

The fall line—a geologic formation that defines the bedrock boundary between the Piedmont and Coastal Plain regions—is one defining natural feature of this national park. Old fields that have reverted to meadows, young forest, beaver ponds and associated wetlands, and the 37 miles of hiking trail that span all of these are others. Climbing out of the South Fork stream valley, young trees of a third- and fourth-generation forest fall away, replaced by meadow. Tobacco was the cash crop of choice throughout colonial Virginia, and the men who tilled land along Quantico Creek were no different. These farmers had the added benefit of being close to Dumfries, Virginia's oldest continually chartered municipality, established in 1749. Town fathers drew up the boundaries and voted the town into creation a mere 3 hours before Alexandria, a few miles north. Unlike Alexandria, however, Dumfries's usefulness as a port declined soon after the Revolutionary War. Relentless tilling on land surrounding the town, including Prince William Forest Park, caused massive soil runoff. Dumfries's harbor filled with silt, and ocean ships could not sail into port.

The Taylor family was the last to farm inside the park proper. High Meadows Trail passes through their old lands between the South Valley Trail and Turkey Run Ridge. An off-trail detour leads to two tombstones in the family plot, surrounded by sun-dappled woodland. There are no marked trails, only vague animal paths. Dry leaves

A waterfall in Prince William Forest Park

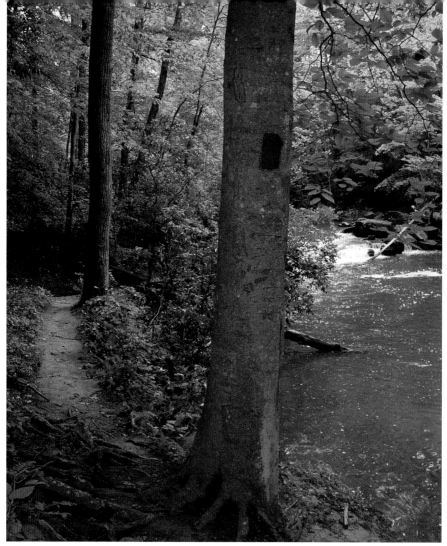

Prince William Forest Trail

crackle underfoot. Hidden amid the leaf debris are small green stems. Somewhere, behind a shrub or camouflaged by other spring flowers, might grow a small whorled pogonia, an endangered species.

Since it's the commonwealth's most urban region, northern Virginia seems the last place to look for a rare plant. Loudon, Fairfax, and Fauquier Counties, however, are among the fastest growing in the country. Development, then, is the biggest single threat to the small whorled pogonia. The US Fish & Wildlife Service lists it as threatened; Virginia ranks it as endangered.

This woodland orchid's bloom lasts a preciously short time. Within 2 weeks of the first yellow-green sepals, an entire colony will flower and lose its bloom. Following this, the flower reverts to a modest green-stemmed plant, with five or six slender leaves arranged in a whorl midway up the stem. There's a perplexing aspect to all this. The flower, when it reproduces, stores upwards of 1,000 seeds in a small capsule. Despite the potential, it's rare for a community to number more than twenty-five plants. Scientists can't say why.

Prince William Forest Park shelters not only the rare, but the common as well. A log-book at the visitor center lists sightings of deer, raccoon, turkey, and falcons, a diversity of wildlife that stands in sharp contrast from when the federal government took over the area. After the last farmer pulled up stakes here, and after a pyrite mine closed in the 1920s amid labor strife and strikes, the federal government took over as protector of the waters that flow into Quantico Creek. The area was first used as a demonstration site for land reclamation methods such as tree planting and erosion control. Gradually the emphasis shifted to recreation and protecting the Quantico Creek watershed.

The process of recovery is ongoing. The boundaries of old tobacco fields are still visible. Thistle and milkweed grow in them now. Ecologically, these weeds prove a better return for wildlife than tobacco ever did for humans. A threatened butterfly, the regal fritillary, prefers the thistle for food. Like the small whorled pogonia, this is a minor threatened species whose plight rarely receives notice. In Virginia, where it is considered critically imperiled, sightings have been recorded from Prince William Forest Park to mountainous regions of far southwest Virginia. There are, however, five or fewer confirmed population clusters of the regal fritillary in Virginia; biologists have had more success reintroducing this insect in Midwest states, where the tallgrass prairies make an ideal habitat. Pennsylvania is believed to have the only viable population of these orange and black butterflies in the East.

From a distance, the butterfly looks like a monarch. A female is distinguishable by the off-white circles on its rear, or hind, wings. A better way of identifying one is to watch mating rituals. A female regal fritillary signals her displeasure with a male suitor by flying straight up, as much as 100 feet, then entering a nosedive that scares away the unlucky male.

With such varied terrain and so much room to explore, it's easy to imagine seeing a regal fritillary, or a small whorled pogonia, as you hike about Prince William Forest Park. Finding either would be considered an accomplishment—they aren't imperiled or threatened because they're plentiful. But half the fun is knowing they're there, some-where. That, and appreciating the sanctuary that can harbor them.

MILES AND DIRECTIONS

0.0 Start from the Laurel Loop Trail map board behind the Pine Grove picnic pavilion. Do not enter the woods here, but rather turn left (north) and follow a narrow well-worn dirt path through a grassy area. You'll pass a playground and then enter a field at the far end of a paved parking lot. Walk down the right edge of the field, keeping the woods hard to your right. In the far northeast corner of the field, locate the yellow blazes for the alternate Laurel Loop trailhead, marked by a yellow blaze on a tulip poplar and a concrete trail post with a metal band that gives the trail's name and mileage to the next junction.

0.5 Turn left (west) and cross the South Fork Quantico Creek on a cable-supported bridge. On the opposite side, turn left (west) on a dirt road that is the combined South Valley Trail and North Orenda Road. *Bailout:* Don't cross the bridge; instead, bear right and follow a combination of Laurel Loop and Birch Bluff Trail to return to the Pine Grove Picnic Area for a quick 2-mile loop.

0.7 Turn left (south) on South Valley Trail as it splits off North Orenda Road.

1.4 Stay straight at a T junction with Turkey Run Ridge Trail. Ahead, South Valley Trail winds through bottomland forest formed by a bend in the stream and then turns

PRINCE WILLIAM FOREST PARK

north. **Note:** It is 1.4 miles on Turkey Run Trail to the Turkey Run Education Center, which has bathrooms and nature exhibits.

1.5 Bear left on South Valley Trail. **Note:** The trail straight becomes Turkey Run Ridge Trail where the cutoff from 1.4 miles merges on the right.

1.6 Cross over Scenic Drive.

2.1 Cross a footbridge over a small stream. Ahead, South Valley Trail climbs a hillside on switchbacks.

2.6 Cross beneath Scenic Drive via a boardwalk that hugs the concrete bridge abutment.

2.8 Stay straight on South Valley Trail at a junction with Taylor Farm Road on the right.

2.9 Cross over Scenic Drive and continue west on the South Valley Trail.

4.4 Turn left (west) and follow South Valley Trail downhill at this junction with High Meadows Trail, which continues straight uphill. **Bailout:** For a shorter 10.3-mile loop, hike uphill on High Meadows Trail and return to Pine Grove Picnic Area via High Meadows, Mary Bird Branch, Quantico Falls, North Valley, South Valley, and Laurel Loop Trails.

5.2 Pass a dam across the South Fork. Above this, the creek spreads out to form a long, narrow lake.

6.0 Cross over gravel Mawavi Road and walk north on South Valley Trail up the stream valley.

6.4 Enter wetlands where, for the next 0.7 mile, the trail skirts an area of heavy beaver activity. This wet, wide-open ecosystem attracts waterfowl, songbirds, deer, raccoons, and foxes.

7.1 Begin a climb from the stream valley into dry upland forest of chestnut oak, yellow (tulip) poplar, and white oak that is in recovery from a 2006 wildfire that consumed 316 acres.

8.0 Turn right (east) on the yellow-blazed Oak Ridge Trail.

8.5 Cross straight over Scenic Drive.

9.2 After a level stretch of hiking through a young upland forest, descend into a small stream valley with a moist forest understory of fern and skunk cabbage.

9.5 Oak Ridge Trail ends at a T junction with Old Black Top Road. Turn right (south) and walk along the gravel road.

10.4 At a four-way junction with Taylor Farm Road, continue straight on Old Black Top Road.

10.9 Turn left (north) onto Mary Bird Branch Trail. There is a concrete trail post and a triple red blaze on a tree. Ahead, descend and cross Mary Bird Branch, a stream.

11.3 Cross straight over Scenic Drive and pass through the parking and Picnic Area E. Locate a white signboard for Quantico Falls Trail. Enter the woods on a footpath, following yellow blazes. **Note:** You'll periodically see brown trail blazes and trailside signs for the Geology Trail, which shares the trail from here to Quantico Creek.

11.4 Turn left onto a dirt road. Stay alert when, in less than 0.1 mile, Quantico Falls Trail branches right off the dirt road. Turn right here and follow the yellow-blazed trail through an upland deciduous forest of oak and hickory with an understory of beech, maple, and elm.

11.8 Cross over the North Valley Trail at a four-way trail junction.

12.0 A sharp descent ends at the edge of Quantico Creek. Turn right (south) and follow the stream valley. There are a scenic set of waterfalls off to the left.

12.2 Cross a footbridge over a small tributary and merge with the blue-blazed North Valley Trail. Veer left (south) and walk downstream. In summer and fall, the trail south of this junction offers good opportunities to rest and relax on exposed rock shelves in the river.

12.9 Pass interpretive signs for the Cabin Branch pyrite mine, which operated on Quantico Creek in the early 1900s.

13.0 Cross Quantico Creek on a bridge. On the opposite side, turn right to follow a footpath through river-bottom forest. *Side trip:* Before crossing the creek, walk straight ahead to another section of the pyrite mine in less than 0.1 mile.

13.2 A long boardwalk carries the trail over a wetland. Ahead, look for an overlook on the right that gives you a vantage point of the Cabin Branch mine across the stream.

13.5 After walking a short stretch on gravel road, turn right (west) and cross Quantico Creek on a bridge. On the opposite side, turn left (west) onto South Valley Trail.

14.1 Turn left (south) and cross South Fork Quantico Creek on a cable-supported bridge. After crossing, turn right onto red-blazed Laurel Loop Trail and ascend.

14.6 Arrive back at the Pine Grove Picnic Area.

HIKE INFORMATION

Local Information
Prince William County Parks and Recreation, (703) 792-7060, www.pwcva.gov

Local Events/Attractions
The Civilian Conservation Corps (CCC) Living History Day is held the second weekend of Oct. First weekend of Nov features OSS Day, highlighting activities of the Office of Strategic Services (forerunner of today's CIA) in the park.

KID APPEAL
There are thirty orienteering courses in the park and free maps and extra compasses free at the park visitor center. You can even request a ranger-led program to learn how.

Restaurants
Occoquan, a riverside town 17 miles north of the park, has many restaurants, coffee houses, and outdoor dining options.

Hike Tours
See Hiking Clubs sidebar in Northern Virginia introductory section.

Other Resources
Potomac Appalachian Trail Club (PATC), Vienna, (703) 242-0315, www.patc.net

7 GREAT FALLS PARK

Land and history are interwoven throughout Great Falls Park—the spot where George Washington championed a canal to skirt the Potomac River's 77-foot "great falls." This may be metropolitan DC, but beyond the crowds, you can find small reminders of a time when our nation's capital was a tidal backwater and our country's survival wasn't assured. Stones in a restored canal wall bear inscriptions unique to the masons who built it. Ruins of old chimneys and homes in Matildaville mark the boomtown that lived and died on hopes that the Patowmack Canal would succeed. For a time it did succeed, ferrying farm goods from western lands to eastern seaports. Then it went bankrupt, leaving us with canal ruins, inspired views over Mather Gorge, wildflowers that bloom spring through fall, and a moment of solitude.

Start: Park visitor center
Distance: 5.1-mile loop
Hiking time: 2-3 hours
Difficulty: Easy; well-traveled trails with a few short, steep sections along the Potomac
Trail surface: Rocky cliff tops, dirt footpaths, dirt roads, riverside trails, hardwood forests, and marsh
Land status: National park
Nearest town: Great Falls, VA
Other trail users: Joggers, cross-country skiers, equestrians, mountain bikers, and rock climbers
Accessibility: Overlooks 2 and 3 are fully accessible, as is the Patowmack Canal Trail to the Holding Basin and the guard gate.
Canine compatibility: Leashed dogs permitted

Trail contact: Great Falls Park, Great Falls, (703) 757-3101, www.nps.gov/grfa
Schedule: Open daily, 7 a.m. to sunset, except Christmas. *Note:* During weekends and holidays in good weather, there can be long wait times to enter this popular park. Consider coming early or late.
Fees/permits: Entrance fee, good for 7 consecutive days from date of purchase and access to Maryland's C&O Canal National Historical Park. A state fishing license is required to fish in the park.
Facilities/features: Visitor center with museum and children's room, snack bar, restrooms, and picnic facilities
NatGeo TOPO! map: Vienna, Falls Church

FINDING THE TRAILHEAD

From I-495, take exit 44 and turn left onto Georgetown Pike/VA 193 west. Go 4.4 miles and turn right onto Old Dominion Drive. Go 0.9 mile to the park. **GPS:** N38 59.820' / W77 15.277'. *DeLorme: Virginia Atlas & Gazetteer:* Page 76, A3.

THE HIKE

On a spring afternoon, an eagle soars above craggy Potomac River rocks below Great Falls, a 77-foot vertical drop of thunder, mist, and frothing water. The raptor dips and alights on the south wall of Mather Gorge. Upended boulders show distinct layers of compressed rock that built the gorge millions of years ago. Spleenwort ferns grow thick here, where the River Trail cuts dangerously close to the cliff edge. Lined with pink spring beauties in May, this 1.5-mile route follows an up-and-down course, eventually

The powerful Great Falls of the Potomac

reaching river level at the far southern end of the park. It gets heavy use, with side trails leading to gorgeous overlooks of the waterfalls. Beyond these points, however, foot traffic dwindles and the River Trail becomes a nice conduit to the less crowded areas in the park's southern reaches.

It should be expected that a park 20 miles from the nation's capital attracts a large number of visitors. Kayakers test their mettle in the surf below the falls. Rock climbers dangle off Birds Nest, one of the many mapped climbs on the cliffs of Mather Gorge. Joggers use the wide Matildaville Trail and Old Carriage Road. Painters set up easel and palette along Falls Overlook Trail. Picnickers lounge in grassy fields under shady red oaks.

All the activity makes the Swamp Trail—in the southern section of the park—that much more attractive. It's a hiker-only path that branches off the Ridge Trail. From a slight hill, it drops through a forest of tulip poplar and beech and reaches a swampy confluence of unnamed streams. Sluggish and meandering, the streams support a lush undergrowth of wood fern and wildflowers. Concave green trillium leaves spread across a widening forest floor. It's unusual to see this wildflower in such great numbers east of the Blue Ridge, but it thrives in these wet conditions nonetheless. In fact, on this brief stretch of trail, plant life approaches the variety typical of an Appalachian cove—a forest type defined by its wet, sheltered climate and diversity of trees and plants. Eastern hemlock, white basswood, tulip poplar—with a little sleuthing, you'll find representatives of each tree along the Swamp Trail.

> **KID APPEAL**
> Ages 5 and up can earn a Junior Ranger badge. Pick up the booklet at the visitor center desk.

The priceless scenery and ecological diversity we enjoy today were viewed by James Rumsey as merely supplies. Rumsey came to Great Falls in 1785 as the overseer of construction on the Patowmack Canal, handpicked by George Washington and carrying tremendous expectations. From hophornbeam trees, Rumsey's workers fashioned tool handles. White oak trees fell to make planks for supply boats. Masons carved canal walls out of the bedrock. They inscribed finished blocks with a unique symbol to ensure they could document their work for pay.

Remains of the historic Patowmack Canal at Great Falls Park

Canal Cut, the final descent on the Great Falls skirting canal, drops 76 feet through solid rock in Mather Gorge. Considered an engineering marvel in its time, the canal—and especially this last passage—evolved painfully. Dynamite was a discovery some 80 years away, so workers on the Patowmack Canal hand-drilled boreholes, poured in black powder, and ignited the volatile mix. If dust particles exploded prematurely, few within range survived. Despite the difficulties in building the canal, George Washington believed the Potomac River, with its long reach from the coast into western farmlands, would serve as a great unifier for a young nation. He wasn't the first or the last to view the river as a means to an end. From the day Captain John Smith ventured up the Potomac to Little Falls (near present-day Georgetown), Americans have had their way with this river. Explorers, canal builders, farmers, miners, theme-park promoters—each has left a mark. Today various agencies, commissions, and nonprofits pursue watershed protection and monitor stream pollutants. Industries and farms situated in the Potomac's massive four-state, 15,000-square-mile river basin discharge pollutants into its tributaries daily. Along the southern shores of the middle Potomac, northern Virginia continues to grow every year. Housing subdivisions gobble up land on such small tributaries as Bullneck Run, Pimmit Run, and Difficult Run.

But as Washington's Patowmack Canal illustrates all too well, the river has the final say. Despite herculean efforts, seasonal fluctuations in water levels made the canal operable only a few months during the year. It declared bankruptcy in 1828.

GREAT FALLS PARK

0 Kilometer 0.5
0 Mile 0.5

N

Aqueduck Dam
Lock 20

? Great Falls Tavern
Visitor Center

Great Falls

Potomac
River

Macarthus Boulevard

Lock 19

Lock 18

Olmsted
Island

Lock 17

Entrance
Station

7

Canal Trail

River Trail

Rocky
Islands

Lock 16

MARYLAND

C&O CANAL NATIONAL
HISTORICAL PARK

738

Matildaville
(Ruins)

Patowmack
Canal Cut

Matildaville Trail

Mather Gorge

Lock 15

Old Carriage Road

River Trail

C&O Canal Trail

Swamp Trail

VIRGINIA

GREAT FALLS
PARK

Swamp Trail

Sandy Point

C&O Canal

BEAR ISLAND

Ridge Trail

Cow Hoof
Rock

Matildaville
Trail

Potomac River

738

P.I.S.S.
Shack

Old Carriage Road

193

Georgetown Pike

Ridge Trail

Difficult Run Trail

Difficult Run Trail

Difficult Run

Old Dominion Drive

193

P

To 495
Exit 13

For 26 years the Great Falls Canal moved thousands of pounds of flour, corn, livestock, and farm goods from western territories to eastern ports. Each boat that passed through finished its journey by dropping through Canal Cut. This same passage today bears little resemblance to its heyday. Trees cling to the hard-hewn cliff walls. Weeds grow everywhere. And beyond it all, the Potomac, America's river, keeps on rolling.

MILES AND DIRECTIONS

0.0 Start from the park visitor center. Walk around the building on a wide, graded path of dirt and crushed rock. Where the path splits, bear right (southeast). Once past the visitor center, turn left (east) onto Falls Overlook Trail, which leads past Overlooks 1, 2, and 3.

0.2 Bear left (southeast) onto blue-blazed River Trail. The route starts out as a wide dirt path, then narrows into a rocky footpath. *Note:* The trail straight from this junction is the Patowmack Canal Trail and marks the return portion of this hike.

0.5 Turn left (east) at a four-way trail intersection and descend a set of stairs to the edge of the Potomac. When you're finished exploring, return to this junction and turn left (east) to resume hiking the River Trail.

0.8 Turn right (west) on a dirt footpath for a detour around Canal Cut. Cross two boardwalks, and then turn left (south). Within 0.1 mile, the route returns to follow the cliffs high above Mather Gorge.

1.2 Cross straight over a paved service road and reenter woods opposite. Stay alert over the next 0.1 mile when River Trail runs close and parallel to the Matildaville Trail on the right.

1.4 Look for remains of a redbrick fireplace off the left side of the trail. A few hundred yards beyond this, look downhill to the left, where a sandy beach is visible. The trail here crosses exposed rock, and footing is tough and technical as you come to Cow Hoof Rock. This promontory is your last chance to catch stellar views of the Potomac as it flows through Mather Gorge.

1.6 A steep climb ends at a T junction with Ridge Trail. Turn left (south) onto Ridge, which is a wide dirt road.

2.1 Turn right (south) and descend to Difficult Run Trail. In 0.1 mile, reach Difficult Run Trail and turn right (north) on a wide road of hard-packed dirt and gravel. *Option:* Stay straight at this right turn on Ridge Trail. A steep footpath dives off the hillside to reach Difficult Run near its confluence with the Potomac. This short, steep descent is a bushwhack on an unmarked trail. If you chose this route, descend to Difficult Run at its confluence with the Potomac River and turn right.

2.8 Turn right (north) on an unmarked footpath that climbs steeply uphill. *Note:* This is a bushwhack on an established but unmarked trail. There are no trail signs or blazes at this junction. Prior to reaching it, look for a clearing on the right side of the trail that has the appearance of an old quarry—or a severely eroded hillside. If you reach Georgetown Pike, you've gone too far; turn and retrace your steps.

3.0 Veer left (north) onto Ridge Trail and descend in 0.1 mile to a junction with Old Carriage Road. Cross straight over the road and climb.

3.2 Turn right (north) onto the Swamp Trail Connector.

3.5 Turn left (northwest) onto Swamp Trail. *Note:* This junction may not be marked, and the trail straight ahead (leading to Old Carriage Road) seems like the more obvious route. Swamp Trail is a singletrack woodland path, while the spur is a wide, grassy path elevated above the low, wet ground on a berm.

3.9 Turn left (north) onto Old Carriage Road.

4.1 Turn right (south) onto Matildaville Trail. There is a restroom a few feet north of this junction.

4.3 Veer left and downhill where Matildaville Trail branches right and enters the woods as a narrow footpath. Descend to a T junction with Patowmack Canal Trail. Turn right and follow the old canal route to Lock 1. After exploring the ruins, return to this junction and continue straight (north) on Patowmack Canal Trail. Look for side trails on the left that lead to ruins of the canal superintendent's home and other Matildaville homes.

4.6 Turn right at a fork in Patowmack Trail and cross the canal's holding basin. Within a few feet, a footbridge spans a small creek that was dug to control water levels in the holding basin. Beyond this footbridge, continue straight past a trail on the right that descends on a set of stairs to River Trail.

4.7 Stay straight as a leg of Patowmack Canal Trail merges on the right.

5.1 Arrive back at the visitor center.

HIKE INFORMATION

Local Information
Visit Fairfax, (703) 790-0643, www.fxva.com

Local Events/Attractions
Wolf Trap National Park for the Performing Arts, Vienna, (703) 255-1800, www.nps .gov/wotr. National park dedicated to performing arts. Three different facilities offer year-round performances. The Theater in the Woods is geared especially toward children.

Restaurants
Old Brogue Irish Pub, Great Falls, (703) 759-3309, www.oldbrogue.com. Traditional Irish fare and live entertainment.

Deli Italiano, Great Falls, (703) 759-6782, www.deliitaliano.com. Grab a sandwich before heading into the park, or a slice of pizza afterward.

Hike Tours
Park staff lead nature and historical tours throughout the year. See the schedule of events at www.nps.gov/grfa or call (703) 757-3101 for information.

Also see Hiking Clubs sidebar in Northern Virginia introductory section.

Organizations
Fairfax Trails & Streams, www.fairfaxtrails.org, is a partner with the Potomac Heritage Trail Association, www.potomactrails.org. Champion of the Pimmit Run Trail and Fairfax Cross-County Trail, with links to other northern Virginia hiking and preservation efforts.

Other Resources
Chesapeake & Ohio Canal National Historical Park, Sharpsburg, MD, (301) 739-4200, www.nps.gov/choh. The C&O Canal along the Potomac River in Maryland succeeded where Washington's Patowmack Canal failed by linking farm markets west of the Appalachians to eastern seaports.

Potomac Appalachian Trail Club (PATC), Vienna, (703) 242-0315, www.patc.net. Contact for maps, book orders, cabin rentals, scheduled hikes, and membership. PATC Map D covers Great Falls and vicinity.

8 ROCK CREEK PARK

As far back as 1866, people recognized Rock Creek's natural beauty and fought to protect it. It would be another quarter-century before an actual park came into being. Long, narrow, and heavily wooded, this 10-mile-long park is a twisty green stripe through a sea of urbanism. It is also a magnet for hikers, joggers, horseback riders, and others. The spacious northern section of the park is big enough to hold them all. Here, it is hilly and wooded, with room to roam.

Start: Rock Creek Nature Center
Distance: 7.1-mile loop
Hiking time: 2–3 hours
Difficulty: Moderate due to distance and some confusing trail junctions
Trail surface: Paved paths, dirt woodland paths, and roads
Land status: National park
Nearest town: Washington, DC
Other trail users: Horseback riders, joggers, walkers, in-line skaters, and cyclists
Accessibility: The Edge of the Woods Trail at the Nature Center is paved and has a rope guide for the visually impaired.
Canine compatibility: Leashed dogs permitted
Trail contact: Rock Creek Park, 5200 Glover Rd. NW, Washington, DC; (202) 895-6000; www.nps.gov/rocr
Schedule: The park is open daily during daylight hours.
Fees/permits: None, except for groups using picnic areas
Facilities/features: There are restrooms at the Nature Center and a chemical toilet at the Boundary Bridge parking area. The Nature Center features natural history displays and a planetarium. Throughout Rock Creek Park are historic buildings, tennis courts, a golf course, and an equestrian center.
NatGeo TOPO! map: Washington West
Other maps: PATC Map N: Rock Creek Park Area
Special considerations: The park closes sections of Beach Drive between Military Road NW and Broad Branch Road NW to cars from 7 a.m. Sat through 7 p.m. Sun and on federal holidays for recreational use by hikers, bicyclists, runners, and in-line skaters.

In the south region of the park, the Rock Creek and Potomac Parkway traffic flow is altered for weekday rush-hour traffic. From Connecticut Avenue, it is one way going south from 6:45 to 9:30 a.m., and one way going north from 3:45 to 6:30 p.m. Also, access streets like Glover Road, Ross Drive, Bingham Drive, and Sherrill Drive are not maintained after heavy snowfall or in icy conditions.

FINDING THE TRAILHEAD

From northern Virginia, cross the Potomac on I-66/US 50 (Theodore Roosevelt Memorial Bridge). Take the Independence Avenue exit (right lane) and keep right to merge onto Rock Creek and Potomac Parkway. In 0.7 mile, continue straight at an intersection with Virginia Avenue. As road signs indicate Connecticut Avenue approaching, stay right and follow signs for the National Zoo and Beach Drive. (**Note:** The Rock Creek and Potomac Parkway ends at Connecticut Avenue; Beach Drive becomes the main north–south route through Rock Creek Park.) Continue straight on Beach Drive at Klingle Avenue on the left and Piney Branch Parkway on the right. There is a traffic light at Beach Drive and Park Road/Tilden Street. In 0.3 mile past this, bear left at an intersection with Blagden Avenue. At 100 yards past this, turn left off Beach Drive onto Broad Branch Road. (**Note:** Beach Drive from this point north to Military Road is closed on weekends and holidays.) Immediately turn right on Ridge Road NW, following signs for the Rock Creek Nature Center. In less than 1 mile, fork left and uphill, avoiding Ross Drive, which forks right and downhill. In 0.4 mile past this fork, bear right onto Glover Road and then turn right into the Nature Center parking area.

From downtown Washington, DC, follow directions above from the intersection of the Rock Creek and Potomac Parkway and Virginia Avenue. Or, take New Hampshire Avenue north from DuPont Circle for 0.6 mile. Turn left onto 16th Street NW and, in 3 miles, turn right onto an entrance ramp for Military Road. In 1 mile, turn left onto Glover Road. In quick succession, bear left at a fork and then turn left into the Nature Center parking area.

From Maryland and I-495/Capital Beltway, take exit 31B/Georgia Avenue, following signs for Georgia Avenue South and Silver Springs. Once on Georgia Avenue, stay in either of the two right lanes so that in 0.3 mile from I-495, you can exit right onto 16th Street. In 3.1 miles, turn right and merge onto Military Road. In 1 mile, turn left onto Glover Road. In quick succession, bear left at a fork and then turn left into the Nature Center parking area. Trailhead **GPS:** N38 57.594' / W77 03.103'. *DeLorme: Maryland/ Delaware Atlas & Gazetteer*: Page 46, B3.

THE HIKE

Rock Creek Park, at its broadest, is only a mile wide. It is a nearly 10-mile-long narrow stream valley park that passes as the long green swath of trees separating downtown Washington, DC, and Georgetown. But to look at it as a single homogenous unit is to miss the small details that make moving between the upland woods and streamside a joy.

Unmarked, but well used, are several angler's paths through floodplains along Rock Creek. If you're hiking the Valley Trail, you'll find one in a wide bend in the river north of Riley Spring Bridge; the other is between West Beach Drive and Boundary Bridge. They are the proverbial low road, alternatives to the higher, drier route of the official Valley Trail.

One advantage in following them is personal satisfaction. These unmarked paths bring you close to the creek. On a sandbar, a few tree logs that washed downstream in a high flood sit high and dry, perfect perches for a snack and relaxing. The stream is a melodious riffle, not so loud that you can't hear bird chatter. Rock Creek in calm water reflects back yellow and red leaves on overhanging trees, making a shimmering mirage of color.

In terms of plants, the floodplain just feels different from the upland. Here there is more smooth alder, but less holly, which is abundant in the understory of the drier forests that cover the stream valley's sloping hills. There is American hornbeam, a skinny tree whose ripply trunk and tight gray bark give the appearance of muscles. It's an apt comparison; this tough, heavy wood was preferred for making handles for axes and sledgehammers.

Yellow poplar and American beech are two of the main trees you'll find in an upland forest, but in the floodplain, they're replaced by eastern black walnut. Donald Culross Peattie, in his book *A Natural History of Trees,* ranks black walnut second only behind pecan in usefulness. Indians chewed the bark to ease toothaches, and processed black walnut shells are "soft grit abrasives" and as such are perfect for "cleaning jet engines, electronic circuit boards, ships, and automobile gear systems."

The northern section of Rock Creek Park is the perfect spot to "converse" with both the upland woods and streamside floodplains. A long stretch of the Western Ridge Trail, north from Bingham Drive to Beach Drive, covers hilly terrain. It is the largest chunk of

Rock Creek is a tributary of the Potomac River

unspoiled woodland in the park, with only Wise Road bisecting it. This is the territory of the great horned owl and the screech owl.

A detour from this heavy upland forest down along Pinehurst Branch leads to other discoveries. By October, hackberry trees are in fruit along the Pinehurst Branch Trail, offering songbirds like the cedar waxwing valuable fuel. There are three shallow-water fords across the branch on our route; the last is a scramble up the stream bank to dry ground. The trail uphill is a narrow path that in summer almost disappears beneath the crowded shrub understory. In no time you're standing atop a knoll amid red oaks and tulip poplars. In this spot, in a park that records 2 million recreational visits annually, you can hear an acorn drop.

MILES AND DIRECTIONS

0.0 Start from the front entrance of the Rock Creek Nature Center. Follow a paved path west past the Edge of the Woods Trail on the right. Where the path Ts, turn right (north) onto the green-blazed Western Ridge Trail, which here shares the route with a paved bike path. Walk downhill to four-lane Military Road and cross straight over.

0.2 Turn right at an interpretive sign for Fort DeRussy. In the next 0.1 mile, you will veer left off the paved path as Western Ridge Trail becomes a wide dirt trail. Soon after this, make a right (north) turn at a double green blaze as Western Ridge Trail becomes a narrow woods trail. *Side trip:* The wide dirt path that continues straight from this double green blaze is a horse trail. In 200 yards or so, it passes the ruins of Fort DeRussy, a Civil War–era defense. This is also the return leg of this hike.

0.5 Turn left at a double green blaze for Western Ridge Trail. *Note:* Straight ahead is Cross Trail 5 (CT 5), which descends to Milkhouse Ford on Rock Creek.

0.6 Emerge from the woods and trace a horse pasture fence on your right. At the end of the fence line, turn right (north) and walk between the pasture and a community garden on the right. The trail meets a paved road. Turn left (west) on the road, keeping a line of stubby wooden posts on your right.

0.7 Turn right onto a paved path marked by a wooden post with a green blaze for Western Ridge Trail. *Note:* This path is immediately past a gated road that will parallel the trail for a few hundred yards.

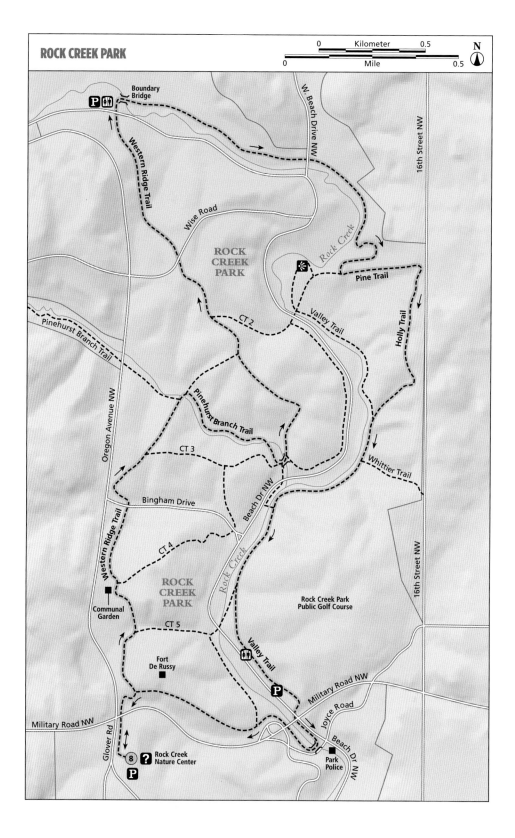

ROCK CREEK PARK

Kilometer
0   0.5
Mile
0   0.5

N

Boundary
Bridge

P

Western Ridge Trail

Wise Road

W. Beach Drive NW

16th Street NW

Rock Creek

ROCK
CREEK
PARK

Pine Trail

Pinehurst Branch Trail

CT 2

Valley Trail

Holly Trail

Oregon Avenue NW

Pinehurst Branch Trail

CT 3

Whittier Trail

Bingham Drive

Beach Dr NW

Rock Creek

16th Street NW

Western Ridge Trail

CT 4

ROCK
CREEK
PARK

Rock Creek Park
Public Golf Course

Communal
Garden

CT 5

Fort
De Russy

Valley Trail

P

Military Road NW

Military Road NW

Glover Rd

Joyce Road

Beach Dr NW

8 ? Rock Creek
Nature Center

P

Park
Police

0.9 Cross Bingham Drive diagonal left. On the far side, Western Ridge Trail is still a paved path. Within a hundred yards, follow Western Ridge Trail as it forks left. Walk another 20 feet and turn right (north) on Western Ridge, which is now a path of dirt and crushed rock.

1.1 Stay straight on the green-blazed Western Ridge Trail at a junction with Cross Trail 3 (CT 3).

1.3 Western Ridge Trail veers right at a fork in the trail. Follow it a few feet downhill to a four-way trail junction. Turn right (east) onto Pinehurst Branch Trail and descend to cross the stream at a picturesque wading pool. This trail is for foot traffic only and is one of the most scenic in the park.

1.6 Cross Pinehurst Branch again at another scenic spot. The stream, now on your left side, makes a wide bend. At low water, exposed stream rocks are a perch to sit and soak in the scenery.

1.7 Pinehurst Branch Trail reaches a four-way trail junction. Turn left (east) and descend the stream bank to cross Pinehurst Branch. On the opposite side, turn left (north) and start to climb an unnamed, unmarked footpath. The route is steep on a narrow footpath that in summer is nearly overrun by shrubs and small trees.

1.8 At a T junction with another unnamed, unmarked trail, turn left (west).

2.1 Turn right (north) onto the green-blazed Western Ridge Trail.

2.2 Stay straight (north) on Western Ridge Trail at a junction with Cross Trail 2 (CT 2), which heads downhill to the right to Riley Spring Bridge on Rock Creek.

2.5 Cross Wise Road and reenter the woods on Western Ridge Trail, which here is a dirt footpath.

2.9 Western Ridge Trail ends at Beach Drive. Walk straight across the road, and reenter the woods at a wood trail sign that marks the trailhead for the blue-blazed Valley Trail. Briefly, this dirt footpath skirts the Boundary Bridge parking area on your left. *Note:* There is a chemical toilet at the parking area.

3.0 Turn right (north) and follow Valley Trail, now a wide, graded path of dirt and crushed rock, across Rock Creek on the Boundary Bridge. A few feet past the bridge, veer right (east) off Valley Trail onto a well-trod but unmarked angler's path. *Note:* The angler's path and Valley Trail are near West Beach Road. We prefer the angler's path—the low road, if you will—because it keeps us close to the creek and is good for bird sightings like great blue heron.

3.6 Merge with Valley Trail just before a bridge on West Beach Drive. Veer right onto the blue-blazed Valley Trail and pass beneath the bridge.

4.2 Climb Valley Trail to a junction with the yellow-blazed Pine Trail. Turn left (east) onto Pine Trail and begin climbing. *Side trip:* At this junction, turn right instead and walk 0.1 mile to an overlook onto Rock Creek. After enjoying the view, return to Pine Trail and resume this route.

4.4 Pine Trail levels at a junction with Holly Trail. Turn right (south) onto Holly Trail and immediately begin to descend on a narrow dirt footpath. Climb into and out of a seasonal stream in a steep-sided gully. *Note:* Straight uphill on Pine Trail leads to 16th Street NW.

5.0 After a steep descent on Holly Trail, reach a T junction with the blue-blazed Valley Trail. Turn left (south) onto Valley Trail. Soon after, the trail passes beneath Sherrill Drive Bridge. Keep an eye out for a blue blaze on the bridge abutment.

5.1 Stay straight (south) on Valley Trail as Whittier Trail branches left (east). For the next 1.5 miles, Valley Trail is a wide, flat streamside dirt path.

5.6 Follow Valley Trail as it veers left (southeast) and uphill as a narrow, rocky footpath. *Note:* The streamside trail that continues straight from this junction is Cross Trail 5. It crosses Rock Creek at Milkhouse Ford. *Note:* The crossing at Milkhouse Ford leads to Western Ridge Trail and the Nature Center.

5.8	Pass by a Park Service bathroom on the right side of Valley Trail.
6.0	A series of switchbacks carries the Valley Trail off the hillside and down to Beach Drive. Turn left (south) and walk along the road shoulder beneath the Military Road bridge. When you see the road shoulder getting pinched into a narrow strip of grass by the looming hillside on your left, cross Beach Road and continue south on the paved bike path.
6.2	Reach the intersection of Joyce Road and Beach Drive. Turn right (west) onto Joyce Road. Cross Rock Creek and immediately, on the other side, turn right (north) onto a paved bike path. Follow it as it passes beneath Military Road. Rock Creek is through the trees off to the right.
6.4	Turn right (north) onto an unnamed horse trail that crosses the bike path. Walk a few feet to where the horse trail forks. Here, bear left and begin an uphill climb. *Note:* The right fork trail goes north alongside Rock Creek to Cross Trail 5 and eventually Milkhouse Ford.
6.8	Pass the spur trail to Fort DeRussy on the right. Within 200 yards, merge onto the green-blazed Western Ridge Trail by continuing to walk straight on the dirt trail. Avoid the green-blazed leg of Western Ridge Trail that heads right (north) at this merge. After walking a few hundred feet more, veer right onto a paved bike path, which shares the route with Western Ridge Trail.
6.9	Turn left (south) on the combined bike path/Western Ridge Trail. Walk downhill to Military Road and cross over. The path then climbs uphill alongside Glover Road.
7.0	Turn left at a sign for the Nature Center.
7.1	Arrive back at the Rock Creek Nature Center.

HIKE INFORMATION

Local Information

Destination D.C., (202) 789-7000, www.washington.org

Restaurants

Rock Creek Shopping Center on Grubb Road, Silver Spring, MD, features two local favorites: The Parkway Deli, (301) 587-1427, www.theparkwaydeli.com, and The Daily Dish Restaurant, (301) 588-6300, www.thedailydishrestaurant.com.

Local Outdoor Stores

There are five REI stores in the northern Virginia/Maryland area, including a flagship store in downtown Washington, DC. Visit www.rei.com for store locations, addresses, hours, and phone numbers.

L.L. Bean Outfitters, Tysons Corner, VA, (888) 552-9876, www.llbean.com

Tours

Ranger-led horseback tours are offered in the park. There are also a host of ranger and Junior Ranger programs led from the Nature Center.

Hike Tours

See Hiking Clubs sidebar in Northern Virginia introductory section.

Organizations

Potomac Appalachian Trail Club (PATC), Vienna, (703) 242-0315, www.patc.net. Maintains the Valley Trail, the Western Ridge Trail, and the connecting trails.

HONORABLE MENTIONS: NORTHERN VIRGINIA

F. MASON NECK WILDLIFE REFUGE/ MASON NECK STATE PARK

These two areas, nearly adjacent to each other on VA 242 (exit 163 off I-95), are known for bald eagles and trails that span freshwater marshes and shady woodland. Both the refuge and park have trails leading to marsh overlooks. Both are day use only. The state park offers picnicking and restrooms. Elizabeth Hartwell Mason Neck National Wildlife Refuge, (703) 490-4979, www.fws.gov/refuge/mason_neck. Mason Neck State Park, (703) 339-2385, www.dcr.virginia.gov/state-parks/mason-neck. **GPS:** N38 38.644' / W77 11.947'. *DeLorme: Virginia Atlas & Gazetteer.* Page 76, C4.

G. BULL RUN-OCCOQUAN TRAIL

A 17.5-mile point-to-point National Scenic Trail along the Bull Run River and Occoquan Reservoir. The southern trailhead is located in Fountainhead Regional Park off VA 123 near the town of Occoquan. The appreciable length of the trail, combined with stream crossings—some impassable after inclement weather—make this hike a real challenge. The northern trailhead is at Bull Run Regional Park off VA 28, south of I-66 near Manassas. (703) 250-9124, www.novaparks.com/parks/bull-run-occoquan-trail. **GPS:** Fountainhead Regional Park, N38 43.502' / W77 19.828'; Bull Run Regional Park, N38 48.416' / W77 28.758'. *DeLorme: Virginia Atlas & Gazetteer.* Page 76, B2, C3.

H. SCOTTS RUN NATURE PRESERVE

The most spectacular feature of this small preserve is a 30-foot multilevel waterfall that breaks just before the stream joins the Potomac River. Once known as the Burling Tract, named for one of its owners, this preserve is now linked with Riverside and Great Falls Parks farther upstream as a link in the Potomac Gorge biological system, a complex of plants and animals—some globally rare and found nowhere else on earth—that eke out a life along the turbulent Potomac River. Contact: River Bend Park, (703) 759-9018, www.fairfaxcounty.gov/parks. Trail map can be downloaded from www.fairfaxcounty.gov/parks/scotts-run. **GPS:** N38 57.591' / W77 12.328'. *DeLorme: Virginia Atlas & Gazetteer.* Page 76, A4.

I. BULL RUN MOUNTAINS NATURAL AREA PRESERVE

Located just 40 miles from Washington, DC, just a stone's throw off I-66, this reserve combines the beauty of mountainous woodlands with history dating to colonial times. Hike through coves that sheltered settler homes. (540) 422-1309; www.vofonline.org. **GPS:** N38 49.489' / W77 42.388'. *DeLorme: Virginia Atlas & Gazetteer.* Page 75, B7.

J. SKY MEADOWS STATE PARK

Located on US 17 in Fauquier County, just south of US 50. At Sky Meadows, the rolling Piedmont meets the Blue Ridge. This former farm has a historic house, hike-in primitive campsites, and wonderful views. (540) 592-3556; www.dcr.virginia.gov/state-parks/sky-meadows. **GPS:** N38 59.527' / W77 57.997'. *DeLorme: Virginia Atlas & Gazetteer:* Page 75, A5.

K. G. RICHARD THOMPSON WILDLIFE MANAGEMENT AREA

G. Richard Thompson Wildlife Management Area in Fauquier County features a network of trails including a 7-mile section of the Appalachian Trail. There is an abundance of wildflowers—the area harbors one of the largest populations of large-flowered trillium in North America. Virginia's Native Plant Society lists the Thompson Wildlife Management Area on its register of important native plant sites. (540) 899-4169; www.dgif.virginia.gov/wmas. **GPS:** Ted Lake Parking Area, N38 56.226' / W78 02.621'; Parking Area 7, N38 57.784' / W78 01.184'. *DeLorme: Virginia Atlas & Gazetteer:* Page 75, A5.

G. Richard Thompson Wildlife Management Area

CENTRAL VIRGINIA

A person traveling west from the Atlantic Coast would, after 100 miles or so, encounter a significant change in the landscape of Virginia. Around Richmond and Fredericksburg, the topography shifts from the flat lowland of the Coastal Plain to the soft hills of the Piedmont. Along rivers, impressive waterfalls mark this line of demarcation, the spot where resistant Piedmont bedrock gives way to sand and clay. A few miles downstream, the largest waterways cease acting as real rivers and instead become estuaries, filled with brackish water and ruled by the ebb and flow of the ocean's tide.

Upland from the fall line—which roughly traces I-95—Virginia's landscape begins a slow march to the Blue Ridge. The term *rolling Piedmont* borders on cliché, but remains the best description of the landscape, which dips and rises in ever-greater folds, until finally giving way to the mountains of western Virginia.

The landscape wasn't always so uniform. Piedmont bedrock shows signs of violent prehistoric mountain-building events. Large basins, some miles and miles in length and width, collected mud and silt that eroded from mountains to the west. This same material later, under intense heat and pressure, became Arvonian and Quantico slate, considered among the highest quality found worldwide. Today a thick mantle of clay and sediment covers most of the bedrock in the Piedmont. The poverty of exposed rock makes outcrops visible along Holliday Creek in Appomattox-Buckingham State Forest a rewarding experience.

Evidence of Native Americans in Virginia dates from 10,000 years ago. In central Virginia, ancestors of the Monacan Indians traveled and camped along the major rivers. The rise of the powerful Indian confederacies, the Powhatan in Tidewater and the Monacans west of the Blue Ridge, left central Virginia as a buffer between them. Both tribes hunted and traveled in this area, but archaeologists have yet to identify large permanent settlements on the scale that existed elsewhere in the state. Artifacts and stone piles near Willis Mountain point to the region possibly holding ritual or ceremonial significance for prehistoric Indians and their ancestors.

European contact in the 1600s brought the rise of the agricultural machine in the central Piedmont. Planters grew tobacco. Bateaux laden with tobacco hogsheads, livestock, and grains plied shallow streams such as the Willis and Slate Rivers. With advances in

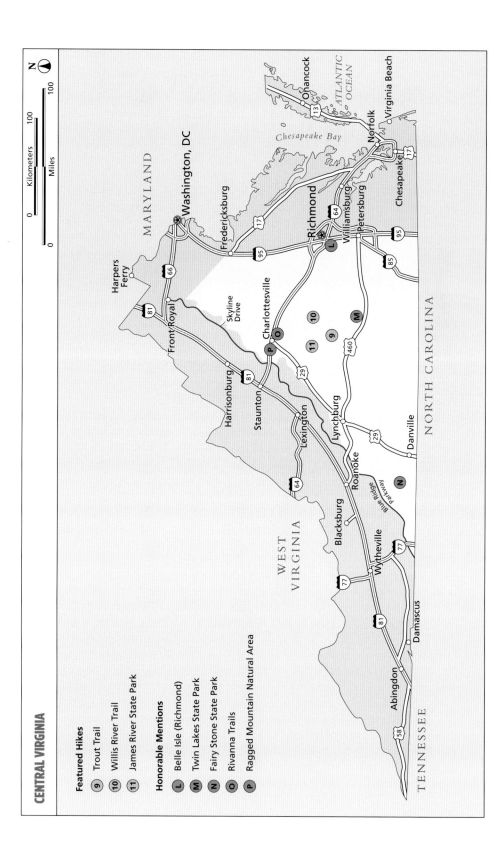

CENTRAL VIRGINIA

Featured Hikes

9 Trout Trail
10 Willis River Trail
11 James River State Park

Honorable Mentions

L Belle Isle (Richmond)
M Twin Lakes State Park
N Fairy Stone State Park
O Rivanna Trails
P Ragged Mountain Natural Area

technology came the large-scale mining of gold, iron ore, coal, slate, and other minerals.

Today those rivers that were the lifeblood of central Virginia commerce serve as natural hiking corridors. Grass- and weed-choked floodplains give way to hillsides covered with mountain laurel. And where the landscape levels into fields, Virginia pine and black oak dominate. Yet, due to this history of heavy farming, the overarching feature of central Virginia remains its wide-open landscape, a holdover from days when farmers planted acre after acre of tobacco until the soil failed, only to move west in search of fresh land. State forests created in the 1920s and 1930s have slowly rehabilitated depleted land by managing the growth of timber for commercial use. For people who enjoy the out-

Steps lead down to Holliday Lake

doors, this commercial-driven enterprise has a fortunate by-product: pockets of forest that offer quality recreation opportunities.

THE HIKES
9. Trout Trail
10. Willis River Trail
11. James River State Park

HONORABLE MENTIONS
L. Belle Isle (Richmond)
M. Twin Lakes State Park
N. Fairy Stone State Park
O. Rivanna Trails
P. Ragged Mountain Natural Area

9 **TROUT TRAIL**

Hikers are the latest folks to enjoy Holliday Creek in a line stretching back 8,000 years: Native Americans, gold miners, homesteaders, Confederate soldiers, scientists, foresters, and anglers—each found this beautiful stream suited their needs. Today, one of its greatest attributes—the scenery—enjoys protection within the largest of Virginia's state forests, the Appomattox-Buckingham. This prime Piedmont spot has mountain laurel blooms in spring, and the hills and a gorge near Holliday Lake dam defy anyone who equates Piedmont with pastoral. Throw in three unaided stream crossings and you've got an adventure that rivals any found in Virginia's mountains.

Author's note: Trout Trail is an unmarked streamside route that may be overgrown and hard to follow in summertime. For a more family-friendly experience, start at Holliday Lake State Park and pick up the Lakeshore Trail (MM 3.1) for a circle of the 150-acre lake.

Start: Woolridge Wayside off VA 640

Distance: 7.4 miles point to point, with an option for an 11.5-mile loop

Hiking time: About 4 hours

Difficulty: Moderate due to 3 difficult stream crossings and occasional bushwhacks

Trail surface: Dirt forest roads and woodland paths lead hikers along grassy stream banks, a pristine river, and steep slopes, as well as through marshes and a gorge.

Land status: State forest and state park

Nearest town: Appomattox, VA

Other trail users: Anglers; open to foot traffic only

Accessibility: Trout Trail is not accessible; however, there are accessible facilities at Holliday Lake State Park.

Canine compatibility: Dogs permitted

Trail contacts: Appomattox-Buckingham State Forest, Dillwyn, (434) 983-2175, https://dof.virginia.gov/education-and-recreation/state-forests/virginia-state-forests/appomattox-buckingham-state-forest/; Holliday Lake State Park, Appomattox, (434) 248-6308, www.dcr.virginia.gov/state-parks/holliday-lake

Schedule: Park and forest open daily year-round, dawn to dusk. Hunting is permitted in the state forest (mid-Nov through the first weekend of Jan is the busiest season). Holliday Creek is stocked in the fall, winter, and early spring. Catch-and-release rules are in effect Oct through May (artificial lures only). Open harvest extends from June 1 to Sept 30.

Fees/permits: No state forest entrance fee (a State Forest Use Permit and associated fee is required for fishing). State park parking fee and camping fee. You'll need a statewide fishing license and a trout stamp if you plan on fishing. For fees and to purchase online, visit www.dgif.virginia.gov/fishing.

Facilities/features: The state park has camping, picnicking, swimming, and boating on a 150-acre lake.

NatGeo TOPO! map: Holliday Lake.

Other maps: A Trail Guide/Map is available at the park and downloadable on its website. A free map of the state forest and Trout Trail is available at the state forest headquarters located 1.1 miles north of the Woolridge Wayside on VA 636.

FINDING THE TRAILHEAD

From Appomattox Court House, drive 8.5 miles east on VA 24 from the intersection of US 460 and VA 24. Turn right onto VA 626 and in 3.4 miles turn left on VA 640 (Woolridge Road). In 0.3 mile after this intersection, pass the state park entrance road on the right. Continue straight another 1 mile on VA 640 to the Woolridge Wayside on the left side of the road. **GPS:** N37 25.585' / W78 39.447'. *DeLorme: Virginia Atlas & Gazetteer*: Page 45, A7.

Shuttle point: From Woolridge Wayside, turn right and drive south on VA 640 for 1 mile. Turn left on VA 692/State Park Road and continue straight at an intersection with VA 614. In 3.8 miles, reach the ranger contact and fee station. Once inside the park, follow signs for the beach and picnic areas. The southern trailhead for the Lakeshore Trail is adjacent to picnic area #1. **GPS:** N37 23.712' / W78 38.336'. *DeLorme: Virginia Atlas & Gazetteer*: Page 45, A7.

THE HIKE

Virginia's Piedmont isn't exactly a hot spot for rocky gorges and deep stream valleys. Yet here you stand on the stream bank of Holliday Creek in Appomattox-Buckingham State Forest, watching water froth, twist, and turn through a narrow cleft between two steep hills. Stream boulders stir up rapids. Off one hillside, a small stream feeds the frenzy with spring runoff.

Watching the water tumble over a small cascade, you might consider how a prospector would view this scenery. The base of a waterfall, it turns out, is a great place to find gold.

Virginia settlers were first in the nation to mine gold. A lode deposit in Spotsylvania County triggered a rush that faltered only when California gold lured miners west in 1848–50. Around Buckingham County, gold ushered in some high times. Twenty or so mines operated, a few even into the 1900s. One near Dillwyn in Buckingham produced nuggets 3 pounds in weight, the largest found anywhere in the state. Up the road from Dillwyn, the name of the town Gold Hill speaks for itself—the precious metal was prospected here for a number of years.

Bridge across Holliday Lake

Early miners focused on streams such as Holliday Creek, using a technique called placer (plas-ser) mining, whereby they panned up sandy streams for gold dust until the trail ran cold. Then they scouted surrounding hillsides, looking for the vein that produced the stream residue. If they found one, they sank a shaft. Mine sizes varied. The Buckingham Mine in Dillwyn dug 183 feet. The Burnett Mine, also near Dillwyn, needed only 58 feet before hitting gold. After striking a vein, the difficult work of extracting gold began. Workers at the Buckingham Mine crushed 20 tons of ore a day to produce 130 hundred-weight (or 208,000 ounces) of gold per year.

Gold is just one mineral among many Virginia's Piedmont has yielded over the course of European settlement. Upstream from the confluence of the Appomattox River and Holliday Creek, the lake dam marks one end of a long, low ridge. Contained in the bed-rock is another rock worth mining—Buckingham slate, considered in the slate industry to be among the highest quality produced in the United States today. Much of the activity centers around Arvonia, a village settled by immigrants of a Welsh town of the same name. Slate carving in Arvonia, Virginia, is an art. Eaves of some homes are trimmed in decorative slate. Tombstones in the cemetery, carved out of slate, are in the shape of household furniture, like beds, couches, and baby cribs.

Also in the vicinity of Holliday Lake stands the privately owned Willis Mountain, which is mined for kyanite, a mineral used in heat-absorbing products—like the white ceramic on a motor spark plug. Some people believe wearing a piece of this bluish-white mineral on a necklace or holding it in your hands induces a calm feeling during times of distress and aids meditation. (Kyanite also flakes and crumbles into tiny, sharp points and shards that may cause splinters. This, in turn, will produce a sensation quite opposite that of calm. So be careful if you handle it.)

If crystals aren't your thing, the clear waters of Holliday Lake produce a calming sensation as well. Works Progress Administration (WPA) workers dammed Holliday Creek and formed the 150-acre lake in 1938. Similar public works projects at Bear Creek Lake State Park in Cumberland County and Twin Lakes State Park in Prince Edward County served as a source of work for unemployed men during the Great Depression and a means of reclaiming overfarmed, barren land for recreational uses. Conspiracy buffs will enjoy the rumor circulating in Buckingham County about the size and location of Holliday Lake. Some will have you believe this long lake was built as a practice landing strip for amphibious aircraft pilots-in-training. This is undocumented, but still interesting. What's certain is that pike, pickerel, largemouth bass, and bluegill thrive in its water, and anglers are welcome to cast their lines here.

An archaeological dig at the mouth of Holliday Creek has unearthed Native American arrowheads and pottery shards dating from 8,000 years ago. Signs of permanent settlement—domestication of plants and animals—date back 500 years. Anthropologists believe that prior to European colonization, the state was split between the Powhatans of eastern Virginia and the Monacans, who laid claim to land west of the James River headwaters. The region we call central Virginia lay between them and acted as a kind of buffer zone between these sometimes-warring empires. Native Americans traveled regularly through the area, but did not settle the land. Instead, they treated it as a prehistoric preserve (or, in modern terms, a demilitarized zone) available to both for hunting and fishing. After 8,000 years and so many different uses, Holliday Creek has come full circle, enjoying status today as a preserve of the state.

MILES AND DIRECTIONS

0.0 Start at the Woolridge Wayside on VA 640. Exit the wayside by turning right (south) on VA 640 and walking downhill.

0.3 Cross Holliday Creek on VA 640 and immediately turn left (east) onto the Trout Trail, which is a faint road trace overgrown with grass. A wood gate blocks vehicle traffic. Follow this road trace downstream. Trout Trail is not blazed, but follows old roadbeds for all but a short stretch. *Note:* Late spring through summer, the trail is overgrown with thorny greenbrier and tall grass.

0.5 The trail ends at Holliday Creek. A steep-sided hill on the right forces a stream crossing. Passage during periods of low water may be aided by a sandbar that divides the stream into two shallow channels.

0.8 A road enters the trail from the left. Continue straight on the Trout Trail.

1.2 The trail reverts to a narrow path as the hillside on your left steepens.

1.4 Cross a small tributary of Holliday Creek. There is a great swimming hole amid the shallow pools formed by the rocks and stream. *Note:* This is a rugged section of trail. Use caution.

1.7 Look closely at the exposed rock on your left. It's shot through with small dikes of a white, crystal-like rock. The gray mass is felsic volcanic rock that oozed through crevices in the Piedmont landscape 800 million years ago. During ensuing periods of metamorphism, the white rock, called pegmatite, shot through the volcanic rock under incredible heat and pressure. Geologists consider this outcrop one of the finer examples of this region's underlying rock strata.

1.9 Climb up a short hill to a junction with the Carter Taylor Multi-Use Trail. Turn right (east) and walk a few feet to paved VA 614/Walker Road. Turn right (south) again, walk down the road and cross the stream on the road bridge, then turn left down a gravel road. Near the stream bottom, avoid a short right-arching spur trail, which leads to a metal shed and a USGS water-quality testing facility.

2.0 The gravel road dead-ends at Holliday Creek, forcing another stream crossing. The water is deeper here and there are no sandbars to aid hikers. After crossing, walk up the stream bank and turn right on the combined Trout Trail/Carter Taylor Multi-Use Trail.

2.1 At a fork in the trail, veer right (south) and downhill toward the stream's edge. *Note:* The Carter Taylor Multi-Use Trail veers left at this junction.

2.4 Cross Holliday Creek and continue hiking the Trout Trail downstream.

2.9 Turn right (north) at a T junction with the Carter Taylor Multi-Use Trail, following red blazes. *Note:* To the left at this junction is a stream crossing for horseback riders.

3.0 Veer left (west) on a footpath at a Y junction. *Note:* The red-blazed Carter Taylor Multi-Use Trail veers right and uphill.

3.1 The Trout Trail ends at the Lakeshore Trail at a clearing with a picnic table. Turn left (east) onto Lakeshore Trail and cross Holliday Creek on a wooden footbridge, then turn right. *Note:* This junction requires some alert hiking, given that the Carter Taylor Multi-Use Trail passes close by. There are also trails to a fording spot for horses.

3.5 Pass by a nature observation deck on Holliday Lake.

4.1 Bear left and uphill at a wooden sign for an overlook. It is a 0.1-mile climb to the view. The overlook trail descends the opposite side of the hill and rejoins the Lakeshore Trail.

4.8 Come around the steep side of a hill and drop to the lake dam on a set of very, very steep stairs. *Note:* Look closely on exposed rock for fish-scale patterns. The dam is built on a fault where Holliday Creek, over millions of years, cut a path through Arvonian slate. This mica rock is softer than the volcanic rock known to exist in the hillsides around it. The effect is something like bookends. When the soft middle shifts, it creates the scale patterns.

5.3 Reach the southern tip of Holliday Lake. A fence marks the junction with a private trail leading to a 4-H Camp. Turn left and continue on the Lakeshore Trail and climb alongside Cemetery Creek into upland woods.

6.0 Reach VA 723 near the 4-H Camp gate. Walk straight across the road and reenter the woods. The trail parallels VA 723, which is on your left.

6.2 Turn right (north) onto a wide dirt and grass road.

6.6 Turn left (north) off the dirt and grass road at a blazed junction. Enter the woods on Lakeshore Trail, which is a narrow dirt woodland path.

7.1 Cross Sanders Creek on a footbridge and turn left (downstream). There are picnic areas on the hillside slope on the left side of the trail.

7.3 Enter the beach area of Holliday Lake State Park. Cut across the grass parking area to reach picnic area #1.

7.4 Hike ends at picnic area #1 and the trailhead for Northridge Trail. *Option:* To extend this hike to 11.5 miles and make it a loop, continue north on the Northridge Trail to its junction with Lakeshore Trail, and continue thereon to Trout Trail and the trailhead at the Woolridge Wayside on VA 640.

HIKE INFORMATION

Local Information
Appomattox Visitor Information Center, 214 Main St., Appomattox; (434) 352-8999; www.historicappomattox.com. Located in a historic train depot.

Local Events/Attractions
Historic Appomattox Railroad Festival, second weekend in Oct, Appomattox, (434) 363-8003, www.appomattoxrrfest.org. Food, music, crafts, a parade, and fireworks commemorate the donation of the Appomattox train depot to the town by Norfolk Southern Railroad.

Appomattox Court House National Historical Park, Appomattox, (434) 352-8987, www.nps.gov/apco. Park preserves the site where Confederate general Robert E. Lee surrendered to Union general Ulysses S. Grant, an act that formally ended the Civil War. Walking tours, interpreters, and special events commemorate this small village's big role in the war.

Hike Tours
Nature and history walks take place at Holliday Lake State Park. Call (434) 248-6308 or visit www.dcr.virginia.gov/state-parks/holliday-lake for dates and times.

Other Resources
Virginia Department of Wildlife Resources, Farmville, (804) 367-1000, www.dwr.virginia.gov. Information on fishing Holliday Creek and places to buy fishing stamps and licenses.

10 WILLIS RIVER TRAIL

Cumberland State Forest is the second largest in the state forest system, and the Willis River Trail is the longest hiker-only trail in any of Virginia's state forests. From the flat land along the Willis River, the trail passes through oak and yellow poplar forest, under plantations of Virginia and loblolly pines, and past old farm sites. Beaver keep active in the swamps. There are also signs of turkey and fox in the sand along the river.

Start: Parking area at the dead end of Warner Fire Road, 0.5 mile off VA 608

Distance: 14.7 miles point to point

Hiking time: About 8 hours

Difficulty: Moderate due to length, frequent road crossings, eroded stream banks, frequent blowdowns that block the trail, and hard-to-follow stretches of trail along the Willis River. This trail does not receive regular maintenance and may be difficult to follow in summertime when overgrown by grasses and shrubs. Hike at your own risk.

Trail surface: This route follows woodland paths, dirt forest roads, paved roads, small streams, and hilly terrain with little in the way of high peaks or deep valleys. The river flats are overgrown with grass and shrubs; the hillsides are shaded by hardwoods. Most hillcrests host plantations of loblolly and Virginia pines.

Land status: State forest

Nearest town: Cumberland Courthouse, VA

Other trail users: Hikers only

Accessibility: Facilities at Bear Creek Lake State Park, including the 0.16-mile Otter Trail

Canine compatibility: Dogs permitted

Trail contacts: Cumberland State Forest, Cumberland, (804) 492-4121, https://dof.virginia.gov/education-and-recreation/state-forests/virginia-state-forests/cumberland-state-forest/. Forest headquarters provides maps of the Willis River Trail, plus information on other forest uses. It's recommended you at least inform forest staff of your itinerary, if merely to alert them to the presence of cars at either end of the trail. Bear Creek Lake State Park, (804) 492-4410, www.dcr.virginia.gov/state-parks/bear-creek-lake.

Schedule: Open daily year-round, dawn to dusk. Hunting is permitted within the forest, and foresters report heaviest use from mid-Nov through the first weekend in Jan. Wear orange blaze during hunting seasons.

Fees/permits: No fees or permits required for hiking in the state forest. Bear Creek Lake State Park charges a parking fee and camping fees. There is also a pet fee at the park.

Facilities/features: None at the state forest; camping, restrooms, swimming, and boating at Bear Creek Lake State Park

NatGeo TOPO! map: Whiteville, Gold Hill

FINDING THE TRAILHEAD

From Cumberland Courthouse, drive east on US 60 for 1.2 miles and turn left onto VA 622 (Trents Mill Road). Reach Bear Creek Market in 3.3 miles. Drive past the market and turn right onto VA 623, which turns from pavement to gravel. After 1.7 miles, turn left onto VA 624, a paved road, and drive 2.1 miles to the intersection of VA 608. Here you turn left onto VA 608 and look on the right for Warner Fire Road in 2.2 miles. Turn right onto the fire road, which is dirt, and drive

0.5 mile to a dead end. You'll recognize the trailhead by the swinging bridge over the Willis River. **GPS:** N37 37.191' / W78 12.803'. *DeLorme: Virginia Atlas & Gazetteer:* Page 56, D3.

Shuttle point: From Cumberland Courthouse, drive east on US 60 for 1.2 miles and turn left onto VA 622 (Trents Mill Road). Reach Bear Creek Market in 3.3 miles and turn left onto VA 629. The southern trailhead is located at Winston Lake on VA 629, 1.2 miles past Cumberland State Forest headquarters. (Bear Creek Market, on VA 622, or Bear Creek Lake State Park, on VA 629, offer convenient mid-trail parking.) **GPS:** N37 30.957' / W78 18.064'. *DeLorme: Virginia Atlas & Gazetteer:* Page 56, D3.

Bailout: Bear Creek State Park makes a convenient bailout for hikers who want to trim this hike to a 10-mile point-to-point. Easiest access is from the junction of VA 622 and VA 629 (mileage cue 9.1 in Miles and Directions) or from the junction of the blue-blazed Cumberland Multi-Use Trail with the Willis River Trail (mileage cue 9.9). **GPS:** N37 31.915' / W78 16.028'. *DeLorme: Virginia Atlas & Gazetteer:* Page 56, D3.

THE HIKE

Sycamores, easily identified by their thick, white-splotched trunks, tower in open, grassy fields along the Willis River. On wooded slopes, oaks, yellow poplar, and beech lend old farmland a shady, deep forest feel. Along old dirt roads, pink-petal mallows peek out of roadside ditches. Taken together, it's land changing from farm to forest, a process that's been under way for 80 years and counting in Cumberland State Forest.

Abusive best describes how farmers once treated the soil here and elsewhere in central Virginia. By the Great Depression, the farm economy of Cumberland and neighboring counties bottomed out. A condition called *plow pan* typified the problem: White clay was compacted into a cement-like state that prevented plow blades from penetrating its surface. Rain couldn't nourish plant roots. Deprived of water, crops and trees shriveled, choked, and died.

When the US government paid pennies on the dollar for this land in 1939, it resembled the dust-bowl conditions of the nation's heartland. After Works Progress Administration (WPA) and Civilian Conservation Corps (CCC) workers built roads and dams, Virginia created state forests on the land. On the sides of roads, foresters planted farm and tree demonstration plots. Sleuthing by present-day rangers has revealed square, 1-acre stands of oak, poplar, and pines. The plots were used to show landowners not only what trees they could plant, but also how to manage forestland for a sustainable timber harvest. Restoration had begun.

The full benefits of 80-plus years of restoration are best appreciated on the Willis River Trail. Beavers have laid claim to land along the first 2 miles of the trail. Notice the small channels that crisscross the landscape as it slopes toward

Trail sign in Cumberland State Forest

A DICKENS MYSTERY

THIS IS THE GRAVE of a little Child whom God in his goodness called to a Bright Eternity when he was very young. Hard as it is For Human Affection To reconcile itself To Death, In any shape (and most of all, perhaps at First In This) HIS PARENTS can even now believe That it will be a Consolation to them Throughout their lives, and when they shall have grown old and grey always to think of him as a Child IN HEAVEN "and Jesus Called a little Child unto him, and set him in the midst of them." He was the son of ANTHONY AND M.I. THORNTON Called CHARLES IRVING. He was born on the 20th day of January 1841, and he died on the 12th day of March 1842. Having lived only 13 months and 19 days.

Charles Dickens wrote *Oliver Twist, David Copperfield*, and *A Tale of Two Cities*—all literary classics. But did you know he also wrote the tombstone epitaph above? It is located in the Thornton Family Cemetery within Cumberland State Forest.

The deceased was 13-month-old Charles Irving Thornton. Dickens was traveling in America at the time of the child's death. Why Dickens wrote the memorial is a mystery. Was he inspired by the death of such a young child? Or was he smitten with the child's mother, as Randolph W. Church speculated in a 1971 article in the *Virginia Cavalcade*? A less romantic and probably more likely theory suggests that Dickens's friend Washington Irving (of "Rip Van Winkle" fame) was close to the mother, and, perhaps, Dickens wrote the epitaph in consideration of this mutual friendship.

All that's known for certain is that the physician who attended the dying child requested that Dickens write the epitaph. Dickens mailed it back from Cincinnati, Ohio, where he was visiting. The marble headstone etched with Dickens's words is located in the state forest on the grounds of Oak Hill, the Thornton family's former homestead.

the beaver swamp on the left side of the trail. As beavers range farther afield in search of their favorite food—hardwood saplings—they build canals for safe passage. That's one theory to explain the presence of these small drainages. A more likely explanation would be field furrows, planted and replanted so many times they've made indelible marks on the landscape.

Human handiwork is evident farther along the trail, where plantations of Virginia pine are visible through the forest understory of sassafras and holly. Foresters currently manage pine plots for about 35 years and then harvest. Hardwood stands, by contrast, can take 70 to 100 years to reach maturity. In the case of both types, the lumber is used in state building projects.

Less evident along the Willis River Trail are signs of the river's busy past. At one time, flat-bottom riverboats (or bateaux) loaded with livestock and hogsheads of tobacco and/or flour congregated on this stream. The Willis River canal system, designed specifically for this shallow stream, worked most efficiently when four or five boats used a lock at once. Considered a pioneering form of navigation, the Willis River locks employed a wooden flash gate, which linked two stone jetties that stuck out into the river from either bank. Hinged at the bottom, this flash lock fell flat when opened. Boats coasted through the sluice and proceeded downstream. (Upriver navigation was a tad more difficult, relying on the brawn of bateau polers rather than gravity.) The locks made the Willis River navigable for up to 50 miles from its confluence with the James River. Gristmills and

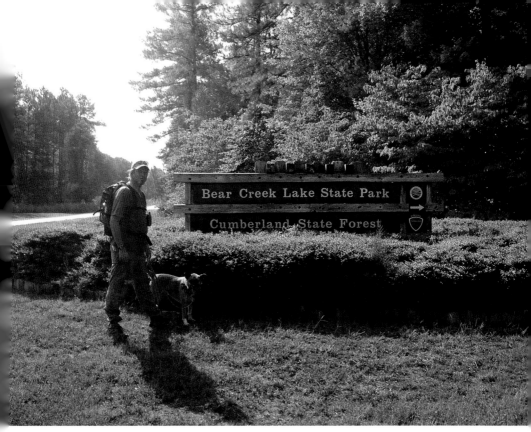

The author with trail dog Coco

inspection warehouses occupied strategic points on the water route, often near locks. Names of local roads, such as Trents Mill, a few miles past Bear Creek Market on VA 622, reference these long-ago points of commerce.

For all the innovation, commercial use of the river was cyclical. When the channel filled with sediment or wooden flash locks rotted, traffic declined. It revived when local businessmen saw fit to pay for improvements—or petition the state to fund repairs. Yet even when the James River and Kanawha Canal—the main east–west commercial route in central Virginia to which the Willis River linked—was abandoned for railroads in 1880, Cumberland County farmers continued using parts of the Willis River to ship goods to railroad depots. Use declined only when the land could not sustain enough crops to make farming profitable.

Which brings us full circle, to land once misused, now protected and plentiful with trees and wildlife. Your footsteps can roust a turkey, partridge, or deer from protected feeding areas managed by another state agency, the Department of Game & Inland Fisheries. You can walk through forests used by scientists and researchers as laboratories for cultivating genetically improved versions of loblolly pine, white pine, and Virginia pine. Or you can engage in amateur research: Rock Quarry Natural Area, midway along the trail, is one of four natural areas in Cumberland left untouched by forest personnel. Here, nature manages growth. To a forester, it represents chaos, where less valuable hardwoods crowd valuable red and white oak and yellow poplar. For this hiker, it holds some of the wildest, most scenic portions of the Willis River Trail. You be the judge.

MILES AND DIRECTIONS

0.0 Start from a parking area at the dead end of Warner Fire Road. The white-blazed Willis River Trail heads south away from the river, entering the woods at the back of the parking area. The next 0.5 mile of trail runs up and down gentle bumps in the landscape and alongside a beaver swamp. **Note:** There is a scenic swing bridge that crosses the Willis River a few feet east of the parking area trailhead. It was closed at the time of publication.

0.5 The trail begins a run on level ground amid loblolly pines. (Cumberland State Forest marks the farthest west this pine will grow in Virginia.) On this level stretch, you'll cross four drainages in succession, which makes for some wet walking in spring.

0.7 Reach VA 615 and turn left, following white blazes on the right side of the road. After crossing Reynolds Creek, turn right to reenter the woods. For the next 0.3 mile, the trail alternates between wet sections in the stream bottomland and short climbs over streamside hills. Sections of trail are often very narrow and eroded. Logs may block the path.

1.7 Cross Reynolds Creek. **Note:** Steep, eroded stream banks make this a difficult passage during periods of high water.

1.8 Crest a small hill amid a plantation of Virginia pine. The climb from the river is an ideal stretch to watch the forest transition from hardwoods (hornbeam, oak, and alder) at lower elevations to pines at the top. The trail then drops to the river.

2.5 After climbing over a small hill, descend to cross a small tributary of Reynolds Creek. The trail climbs again, entering a pine plantation.

2.8 Reach a gate and turn right onto Toll Gate Forest Road. You'll pass a clear-cut on the right, moments before reaching VA 624.

3.5 Walk straight across VA 624 and reenter the woods. The forest boundary is somewhere between the blue house on the right and the trail, so don't stray too far. As you descend on a singletrack path, a small stream forms on the right, as the terrain on the left changes from field to wooded slope.

3.6 Cross a wet ditch and climb a small hill to avoid getting your feet wet where the stream cuts close to the base of the hill.

3.9 The trail turns sharply left, away from the stream. (Through the understory of sassafras and witch hazel, you'll make out the border of a pine plantation.) The trail almost reaches the pines, then turns to run parallel to the plantation in a narrow ditch.

4.2 Cross Bonbrook Creek. Look right for white blazes and follow the trail around the base of a hill as it climbs away from the creek.

4.5 Stay alert as the trail passes closely to the state forest boundary. Barbed wire and yellow blazes on trees right of the trail mark this boundary. Through the woods on the right is a long white barn.

4.6 Walk straight across VA 624, turn left, and walk up the right side of the road. At a gated forest road with a stone apron, turn right onto a dirt road. In 0.1 mile, turn left and enter the shelter of the woods. Avoid following the forest road straight into a field.

5.0 The trail reaches the Willis River amid a field of tall grass and wildflowers. Here, the stream runs a wide, flat course. Its arrow-straight banks suggest it may have been straightened for commercial navigation. Cutting the bends out of the river allowed easier passage for bateaux, which measured 60 feet long and 8 feet wide.

5.2 Walk on the muddy bottomland along the Willis River. Keep a sharp eye out for the trail as it crosses wet ditches and passes through heavy vegetation. If you lose the trail, tend to the riverbank. You're on the mark if you see a large tree leaning out over the river.

5.4 A blue stripe on a tree marks the boundary of the Rock Quarry Natural Area, one of four in Cumberland State Forest. Natural areas are left wild and untouched. The trees here are larger, more mature species than you'll see elsewhere along the trail. The forest subcanopy is also overgrown, an appearance that results if the forest is not thinned.

6.0 Enter a clearing and turn left. This old road climbs through plantations of Virginia and loblolly pines.

6.2 Turn right onto Rock Quarry Fire Road. After a few paces, an old road goes left. Continue straight on Rock Quarry to where it dead-ends in a clearing. Here the trail bears left into the woods and takes a steep drop to the Willis River.

6.4 Reach the Willis River. The trail rides a ledge with a steep drop off the right side down to the river flats.

6.8 Descend onto the river floodplain.

7.0 Without the convenience of a double blaze, the trail takes a hard left and widens. This is confusing because a wide path also continues straight ahead. If you miss the left turn, you'll know soon enough—the riverside path peters out in a blaze of vegetation.

7.3 Reach Horn Quarter Creek and turn left to follow it upstream along the left bank. This is a good spot for lunch or photos or just a quick swim.

7.5 Cross the stream and climb the opposite bank. The trail will soon convert to a wide dirt forest road and enter a pine plantation. *Note:* Where the land levels, look for signs of an old farm. There's a crater on the left side of the trail that's likely a collapsed well. In an overgrown field on the right side of the trail are piles of concrete blocks, indicating that a house or outbuilding once stood here. The stones are covered in vinca violets.

7.7 Stay straight on the forest road trail past a clearing on the right.

8.0 At a junction with a forest road, turn right (southwest). Within 0.1 mile, this road curves right. Instead, continue straight on the white-blazed trail.

8.3 Cross a small stream and turn left (south) into the woods. The trail starts climbing a short easy incline.

8.7 Emerge from the woods at a T intersection of VA 622 and VA 623. Walk straight across dirt VA 623 and continue walking up the left side of VA 622 in the corridor cut for the power lines.

9.1 At the intersection of VA 622 and VA 629, cross the road and enter the woods opposite Bear Creek Market. A wood post with a hiker icon and trail signs marks this trailhead for the southern leg of the Willis River Trail, which is marked by white squares. *Bailout:* Walk 1.2 miles down paved VA 629 to the Cumberland Multi-Use Trailhead (CMT) parking lot in Bear Creek State Park.

9.9 Cross the blue-blazed Cumberland Multi-Use Trail (CMT), which is a dirt forest road, and reenter the woods opposite on a singletrack footpath. *Bailout:* Turn right on the CMT and in 0.2 mile reach the CMT trailhead in Bear Creek State Park.

10.3 After descending through a young hardwood forest, turn left on an old road now overgrown with grass and weeds. In less than 0.1 mile, turn left again at a junction marked by a wood trail post and hike uphill on a singletrack woods path.

10.5 Begin a very scenic section of trail along Little Bear Creek where you ascend small hills that take you from stream level to lookouts some 50 feet above the stream. You'll see pawpaw (aka the "false banana" tree) on this stretch of trail. Its peanut-shaped fruit is a food staple for squirrels, raccoons, and birds.

10.9 Cross Little Bear Creek and climb the embankment. In 0.1 mile, cross the creek again. Begin a steep ascent.

11.2 A bend in the creek carves a steep-sided natural amphitheater in the hillside and the trail traces the edge high above stream level.

11.8 Cross Bear Creek Road at a parking area for the blue-blazed Cumberland Multi-Use Trail. Reenter the woods on the white-blazed Willis River Trail.

12.0 Cross Bear Creek. (WPA work crews dammed the stream to create popular Bear Creek Lake, one of seven lakes built in central Virginia between 1935 and 1937 for recreational use.) The trail on the opposite side climbs a hill and becomes an old road.

12.7 Turn left onto dirt Booker Forest Road.

12.9 As you approach VA 628, stay alert for a double blaze on the left side of the trail that marks a left turn. Follow a power-line easement paralleling the road. In less than 0.1 mile, turn right and cut through a strip of woods that separates the easement and the road. Cross VA 628 and reenter the woods on the opposite side.

13.3 The trail passes through a wet section with many springs and seeps that mark the headwaters of Winston Lake. From here the trail climbs to higher and drier hillsides and parallels the stream, which is downhill on the right.

13.9 Descend and cross the stream. Follow the trail along the stream's edge and cross it again in 0.1 mile. After the second crossing, begin your climb out of the lowlands of Winston Lake's backwater to walk along a hillside overlooking the south side of the lake. ***Note:*** Both stream crossings are scenic stops and a great place to sit and soak in the nature around the lake's headwaters.

14.7 Hike ends as you descend a set of stone stairs and cross a wood footbridge to reach a picnic shelter and parking area for Winston Lake.

HIKE INFORMATION

Local Information

Visit Farmville, (434) 392-1482, www.visitfarmville.com

Local Events/Attractions

James River Bateau Festival, mid-June, James River: Lynchburg to Richmond; (434) 528-3950, www.vacanals.org. A weeklong celebration of a bygone era, with replicas of the bateaux that transported commerce up and down central Virginia rivers and canals in the 1800s traveling from Lynchburg to Richmond, powered by volunteers in period costume.

11 JAMES RIVER STATE PARK

Set in bucolic Buckingham County, the 1,500-acre James River State Park perches on 3 miles of riverside property that has cultural roots reaching back to pre-Revolution times and one of Virginia's most influential families. Trails range from flat paths along the James to pitchy routes through the young pine and hardwood forests on the valley hillsides. Equestrians are some of the park's heaviest users, but 15 miles of trails that span both river and forest habitats offer hikers a lesson in how a small park can still deliver big rewards.

Start: Grass parking area on the park road between the ranger contact station and nature center
Distance: 7.5-mile loop
Hiking time: About 3.5 hours.
Difficulty: Moderate due to length and pitchy terrain along woodland paths
Trail surface: Grass and dirt paths
Land status: State park
Nearest town: Bent Creek, VA
Other trail users: Equestrians and hunters (in season)
Accessibility: The 0.25-mile Green Hill Pond Loop is a paved trail with boardwalks over a scenic fishing pond featuring a universally accessible fishing pier.

Canine compatibility: Leashed dogs permitted
Trail contact: James River State Park, 104 Green Hill Dr., Gladstone; (434) 933-4355; www.dcr.virginia.gov/state-parks/james-river
Schedule: Open daily, dawn to dusk. The park is closed for hunts for a few weeks in Nov and Dec.
Fees/permits: Day-use fee
Facilities/features: Canoe rentals, visitor center, and camping
NatGeo TOPO! map: Shipman, Gladstone
Other maps: Hand-drawn map of trail system available at park

FINDING THE TRAILHEAD

From US 60 West in Buckingham County, turn right onto VA 605 (River Road). Travel 7 miles, then turn left onto VA 606 (Park Road) and immediately enter the park. **GPS:** N37 37.410' / W78 48.512'. *DeLorme: Virginia Atlas & Gazetteer*: Page 55, C5.

THE HIKE

A beautiful confluence of summertime sounds rises up from and around the James River as it sweeps around a lazy river bend. Water rushes over river rocks with a constant *shooshing*. Cicadas buzz and clatter in the tall riverside grass. Birdsong floats down from the broad sycamore and willow trees. It is a natural orchestra.

The mighty James River lends the park its name, but it is only one feature among many that make this a special place. Fields in the bottomland and forests on riverside slopes show a vigorous rebound from centuries of farming and logging. Skinny trunks amid the oaks and hickory and pine trees mark this as a young, growing forest. But they still provide welcome shade and the occasional wildlife sighting—a fox sighting along the Branch Trail wouldn't be surprising. Fields along the river's floodplain show telltale signs of old field succession, where pine saplings indicate a natural process that, if left untouched, would result in a mature hardwood forest. Other fields are kept mowed, while the high grass that lines trails through the river bottomland explodes with the bright yellows of golden ragwort and the purple of paintbrush.

Equal to the natural beauty is the impact of humans on the landscape. Ownership dates back to colonial Virginia and the Cabell family, who owned land throughout the Piedmont region. Land that is now state park was part of a larger estate called Green Hill, given in 1726 to Colonel John Cabell as a wedding present from his father.

Farming was the subsistence of the Cabell family, but they also cast an eye out onto the James River and farther west. A farmer prospers when his goods can make it to market. For that purpose, the James served farmers well, but only seasonally. It could be too shallow to navigate in the hot summer and autumn

Hiking and fall wildflowers in James River State Park

months, and too volatile, subject to raging floods, in winter and spring. Many believed the answer was a system of canals that would skirt the troublesome sections of the river and control its flow. Generations of Cabells threw themselves into developing the James River and Kanawha Canal system with the hope of linking eastern seaports with farms in the Ohio Valley and beyond. Started in 1785, it was only half completed to the Kanawha River by 1851. It ultimately stalled near Clifton Forge, Virginia, on the eve of the Civil War. That conflict and the rise of the "Iron Horse" locomotive doomed the concept of river-and-canal systems along the James.

The war also marked the end of the Cabell family's relationship to the land. In the 1870s this property was bought by the Dickens family, who owned it until purchase by the Commonwealth of Virginia in 1992—in total, nearly 300 years of ownership by only two families. The park opened in 1999.

The deep history is only one reason to appreciate a day spent hiking trails that span the river bottomland and wooded hills of James River State Park. Like old fields that grow to forest and rivers that flow to the sea, time marches on.

MILES AND DIRECTIONS

0.0   Start at a grass parking lot and trail board on Park Road between Canoe Landing Road and the cabin loop road. Turn south, cross Park Road, and enter woods opposite on a yellow-blazed trail. Within 20 feet, veer right at a fork, staying on the wide mowed path.

0.1   Stay straight and avoid the trail that splits left into the woods. You are now on Running Creek Trail, a rocky footpath.

JAMES RIVER STATE PARK

N

Kilometer

Mile

James River

Tye River Overlook

Cabell Trail

Branch Pond

Branch Trail

605

JAMES RIVER STATE PARK

Running Creek Trail

606

605

Cabell Trail

Trail Information Board

Cabell Trail

Green Hill Pond

Cabell Connector Trail

Sandbar

River Trail

Taylor Trail

Cabins

Taylor Trail

River Trail

Canoe Rental

0.2 At a fork veer left as Running Creek climbs through a young hardwood forest of oak, hickory, maple, and beech via switchbacks. ***Note:*** The right fork at this junction is part of the Cabin Loop Trail.

0.3 Cross paved Canoe Landing Road.

0.5 Reach a T junction and turn right on River Trail. ***Note:*** The trail on the left is the return portion of this loop hike.

1.0 As you descend off a hill toward a clearing, stay alert and veer right, cross two wooden footbridges, and emerge into the clearing at a trail board. Cross a dirt and gravel road and follow a grass trail downhill. The Canoe Livery is downhill on your left.

2.0 River Trail takes a hard right (east) to follow a jog around a small tributary before returning to the river's edge.

2.1 Take a moment to enjoy the James River: A footpath leads left to water's edge and a small sandbar perfect for a snack break.

2.6 The River Trail makes a sharp right and turns away from the river.

2.8 Veer left, cross a footbridge, and pass through a gate. Reach a gravel road and turn right, uphill, to access Cabell Trail. Within 0.1 mile, bear left onto Cabell Trail, which here is a mowed grass path.

3.1 Cross over the gravel Green Hill Pond access road and continue uphill on the orange-blazed Cabell Trail. At the crest of the hill, turn left and cross the park road. Cabell Trail climbs uphill as a wide dirt and gravel service road. ***Note:*** At this junction, there is a trail board with a map and several large sycamore trees that provide good shade for a midday break, as well as a park picnic area, restrooms, and a visitor center.

3.4 Continue straight past the Dixon Landing Overlook Trail on the left.

3.8 Turn left to access the Tye River Overlook. It is 0.1 mile to the wood platform with a view of the confluence of the Tye River into the James. Retrace your steps to the Cabell Trail and turn left to continue this route uphill.

4.2 Turn right and uphill as Cabell Trail leaves the service road and enters a pine forest as a woodland footpath.

4.4 Merge onto Branch Pond Connector Trail by staying straight at a trail junction where Cabell Trail turns right (east). Within 30 feet of this junction, swing left on an unmarked dirt path, avoiding a gravel road leading right, downhill, to a primitive camping area. ***Note:*** On state park trail maps, this left turn is labeled as Branch Pond Loop Connector.

4.6 Wrap around the headwaters of Branch Pond, and at a junction soon after, turn right to follow the Branch Pond Loop Trail.

5.0 Enter the Branch Pond Picnic Area. Stay alert and turn left on Branch Trail before you reach the gravel parking lot, restrooms, and picnic area.

6.2 Turn left and descend to the park road. The ranger contact station is visible uphill on the left. Cross and follow a short connector to Running Creek Trail.

6.4 Arrive at a four-way junction. Here Running Creek Trail is a wide mowed path blazed yellow.

7.1 Turn right and continue on Running Creek Trail. ***Note:*** The trail straight from this junction is the River Trail that leads to the James River and Canoe Livery.

7.2 Cross Canoe Landing Road.

7.3 Veer right onto Running Creek Trail.

7.5 Arrive back at the parking lot.

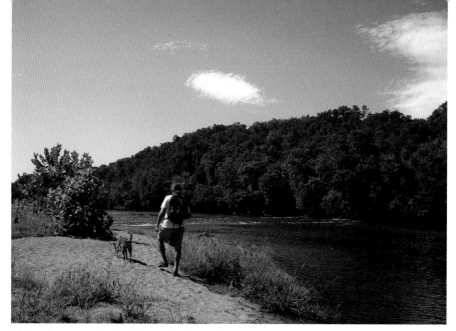
Hiking along a sandy shoreline on the James River

HIKE INFORMATION

Local Information
Appomattox Visitor Information Center, 214 Main St., Appomattox; (434) 352-8999; www.historicappomattox.com. Located in a historic train depot.

Local Events/Attractions
Rafting and tubing on the James River is a popular summertime activity. Look for seasonal outfitters based in nearby Scottsville, Lynchburg, and Amherst.

Appomattox Court House National Historical Park, Appomattox, (434) 352-8987, www.nps.gov/apco. Park preserves the site where General Robert E. Lee surrendered to General Ulysses S. Grant, an act that formally ended the Civil War. Walking tours, interpreters, and special events commemorate this small village's big role in the war.

Lodging
The park features family lodges, cabins, a large full-service campground, horse camping, and primitive camping along the river. For reservations, call (800) 933-PARK or go to www.reservevaparks.com.

Restaurants
There are grocery stores in Gladstone, but the nearest restaurants are in Appomattox (19 miles) and Amherst (22 miles).

Organizations
Friends of James River State Park, (434) 933-4355, www.virginiaparks.org/friends-jr

HONORABLE MENTIONS: CENTRAL VIRGINIA

L. BELLE ISLE (RICHMOND)

This 54-acre island is part of the James River Park System, 450 acres of city-owned parks lining the James River, in the heart of downtown Richmond. From Main Street in downtown, follow signs for Belle Isle and the Valentine Museum. There is a parking lot on Tredegar Street past the museum. A footbridge crosses onto the island from the parking lot. A wide 2-mile loop runs past ruins of ironworks and a Civil War prison. Park closes at dusk. (804) 646-8911; www.jamesriverpark.org. **GPS:** N37 32.053' / W77 27.044'. *DeLorme: Virginia Atlas & Gazetteer.* Page 58, D2.

M. TWIN LAKES STATE PARK

Located in the heart of Prince Edward–Gallion State Forest, Twin Lakes is accessed via VA 613 off US 360. You can put together a 6-mile hike around both lakes leading from high, forested hills into the marshy flow of the Sandy River at the head of the lake. There's also an 8-mile multiuse trail for hiking, biking, and horses. There are beaches, camping, and cabins. (434) 392-3435; www.dcr.virginia.gov/state-parks/twin-lakes. **GPS:** N37 10.399' / W78 16.205'. *DeLorme: Virginia Atlas & Gazetteer.* Page 46, C2.

N. FAIRY STONE STATE PARK

Located in the foothills of the Blue Ridge Mountains northwest of Martinsville on Philpott Reservoir. The park entrance is 9 miles west of Bassett on VA 57. Whiskey Run Trail offers a wide view of the parkland and reservoir. Use it to form a 4.7-mile loop with Stuart's Knob Trail and Iron Mine Trail. The name comes from the staurolite stones that crystallize into a cross-like structure. (276) 930-2424; www.dcr.virginia.gov/state-parks/fairy-stone. **GPS:** N36 47.547' / W80 07.008'. *DeLorme: Virginia Atlas & Gazetteer.* Page 26, B2.

O. RIVANNA TRAILS

This 20-mile greenbelt circles the entire city of Charlottesville, with numerous shorter loops possible. A good starting point is at Quarry Park. To get there, take exit 121 off I-64. Turn right onto Monticello Avenue, and take the first left onto Quarry Road. The park is on the left. The Rivanna Trails Foundation has interactive maps and descriptions at www.rivannatrails.org. **GPS:** N38 0.915' / W78 28.696'. *DeLorme: Virginia Atlas & Gazetteer.* Page 68, D1.

P. RAGGED MOUNTAIN NATURAL AREA

This 980-acre nature preserve is owned and managed by the City of Charlottesville, which has been adding trails. Seven miles of hiking trails circle Charlottesville Reservoir, rolling up and down the rugged and heavily forested Ragged Mountains. The parking area is at 1730 Reservoir Rd., off Fontaine Avenue, south of Charlottesville. Dogs, bikes, and joggers are not permitted. (434) 970-3260; www.charlottesville.org/raggedmountain. **GPS:** N38 01.584' / W78 33.345'. *DeLorme: Virginia Atlas & Gazetteer.* Page 67, D7.

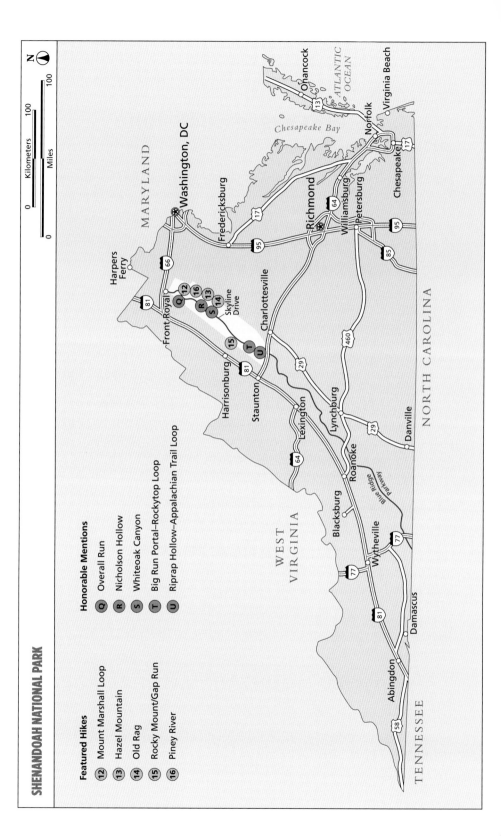

SHENANDOAH NATIONAL PARK

Featured Hikes

12 Mount Marshall Loop
13 Hazel Mountain
14 Old Rag
15 Rocky Mount/Gap Run
16 Piney River

Honorable Mentions

Q Overall Run
R Nicholson Hollow
S Whiteoak Canyon
T Big Run Portal–Rockytop Loop
U Riprap Hollow–Appalachian Trail Loop

SHENANDOAH NATIONAL PARK

In the 1920s, when the government proposed a national park along the spine of Virginia's Blue Ridge Mountains, wilderness purists scoffed. A century of farming and logging had left a legacy of barren soil and mountain slopes scarred with clear-cut. Wildlife had dwindled to near extinction. It irked some that so much time and effort would be spent on such a depleted landscape.

Oh, if the skeptics could see Shenandoah National Park today.

In a testament to nature's healing power, scars of the park's past have all but disappeared. Shenandoah is rightfully counted as one of the crown jewels in our country's national park system. Long and thin, it measures 75 miles from Front Royal in the north to Rockfish Gap in the south. Within its boundaries are some of Virginia's finest forests. From overlooks, on a clear day, views stretch east to Washington, DC, and west into West Virginia. You're as apt to see a bear or deer amble across Skyline Drive as you are another human. That's not incidental. Black bears are a park success story, having rebounded from near extirpation to several hundred in number.

On the mountaintops, a new generation of oaks and hickories has replaced the oak-chestnut forest that provided a livelihood for so many mountain dwellers. Waterfalls come in all shapes and sizes, from the reckless fury of a spring run on Big Devil Stairs to the free-form drops along popular day hikes like Whiteoak Canyon.

Above all are the mountains. Approached from the east, the Blue Ridge sweeps skyward underlaid with granite that formed more than 1 billion years ago—before recorded life on earth—making the Blue Ridge one of the oldest mountain ranges on earth. Basalt lava flows and metamorphic Catoctin greenstone indicate a violent prehistoric past when, deep in the bowels of the earth, heat and pressure formed new rocks from old, then thrust them upwards to form the mountains we see today. So large a barrier did these mountains pose to colonists in Virginia that it bred two distinct cultures: a land-owning aristocracy in the eastern Piedmont and Coastal Plains, and a Scots-Irish farm culture in the western valleys and ridges. Today, the only restriction to travel is your imagination and leg power. Hundreds of miles of trails spread through the park and its 79,500 acres of designated wilderness. Each trail invites the traveler to step from the car and explore what lies beyond what the eyes can see.

THE HIKES

HONORABLE MENTIONS

Overall Run is the highest waterfall in Shenandoah National Park.

12 MOUNT MARSHALL LOOP

The dual peaks of Mount Marshall loom large over Shenandoah's northern district. With summits above 3,000 feet and open rock cliff tops, North and South Marshall offer inspired views west over the Shenandoah Valley as you trek along the Appalachian Trail. Their counterpoint is an equally inspired view eastward from the craggy boulders that punctuate aptly named The Peak, accessed via the Bluff Trail. This steep-sided mountain, crowned with billion-year-old granite, measures just under 3,000 feet in elevation. The rugged ascent—1,000 feet in just over 0.5 mile, on a trail no longer maintained by the Park Service—makes it one of Shenandoah's lesser-known, but more-demanding, climbs. This 16-mile hike links these peaks and the breathtaking gorge carved by Big Devil Stairs, capturing what makes Shenandoah National Park so popular: great views, waterfalls, and woodland trails.

Start: Jenkins Gap parking area on Skyline Drive
Distance: 15.8-mile loop
Hiking time: 8 hours
Difficulty: Difficult due to distance and an optional side trip on a steep, unmarked path up The Peak
Trail surface: Hike mountain slopes on singletrack woodland paths, old forest roads, and a bushwhack to breathtaking views from The Peak.
Land status: National park
Nearest town: Front Royal, VA
Other trail users: Cross-country skiers
Accessibility: This trail is not accessible to people with disabilities; however, most of the facilities within the park are. Check out the accessible 1.3-mile Limberlost Trail (Mile 43).
Canine compatibility: Leashed dogs permitted (leashes no longer than 6 feet)
Trail contact: Shenandoah National Park, 3655 US 211 East, Luray; (540) 999-3500; www.nps.gov/shen
Schedule: Open year-round. Skyline Drive may close without advance warning due to inclement weather. Even when Skyline Drive is closed, hikers may still enter the park on foot. Most facilities begin opening in Mar and close by late Nov.
Fees/permits: Entrance fee required, valid for 7 days, or annual pass. Available at www.recreation.gov or at any park entrance. Free backcountry camping permits, available at www.nps.gov/shen/planyourvisit/bc-p, at ranger stations and visitor centers, are required. Campfires are prohibited in the backcountry, except in park-constructed fireplaces. Before visiting, review backcountry regulations, which cover such issues as group size, where to camp, and waste disposal. Call (540) 999-3500 for regulations. To fish in Shenandoah National Park (SNP), Virginia residents age 16 or older must have a Virginia state fishing license.
Facilities/features: The park offers a wide variety of lodging, camping, and dining.
NatGeo TOPO! map: Chester Gap
NatGeo Trails Illustrated map: Appalachian Trail, Calf Mountain to Raven Rock; Shenandoah National Park
Other maps: PATC #9: Shenandoah National Park Northern District

FINDING THE TRAILHEAD

From Front Royal, travel south on US 340 from the intersection of VA 55 and US 340 in downtown Front Royal. In 0.3 mile, turn left onto Skyline Drive. In 0.5 mile, pass the park entrance booths. Drive south on Skyline Drive to the Jenkins Gap parking area between mileposts 12 and 13, on the right (west) side of the road. There is parking for twenty cars. **GPS:** N38 48.433' / W78 10.862'. *DeLorme: Virginia Atlas & Gazetteer*: Page 74, B3.

THE HIKE

Springtime in the Blue Ridge Mountains begins not with green leaves, but with flowering trees. Lavender, white, pink, and yellow buds overflow their small calyx and coat charcoal-shaded branches with color. Tree buds appear first on warmer, southwest-facing hills and in moist creases in the mountain slopes. As April turns to May, the days lengthen and temperatures warm. The ornamental redbud—a tree preferred by George Washington over even Virginia's official tree, the flowering dogwood—strikes a note by filling its moist soil habitat with a mix of lavender, purple, and pink buds. Dogwoods, habitual to dry slopes, follow with showy white petals, cloven and red-tinged. Later in May, white and pink cups burst from the dark evergreen of mountain laurel. By June, this spring symphony will drop into anonymity. Sunlight-gobbling oaks, elms, and poplars will leaf out and overshadow all else. In these still-cold days of April and early May, though, the small trees shine as stars of the landscape.

The Bluff Trail along the east flank of Mount Marshall is hardly the only place in Shenandoah National Park to catch spring's colorful performance. The trail does, however, offer a side bonus in spring—great views down the Blue Ridge onto the small farms and crossroads of the mountain's eastern foothills. The narrow and sometimes uneven route rises to three distinct overlooks with vistas onto a wide, pastoral valley. Each view only whets the appetite for what lies ahead on top of The Peak (2,959 feet).

The Peak stands alone, separate from the main trunk of the Blue Ridge Mountains. The path to the summit fell off the park's list of maintained trails about a decade ago. USGS topographic maps still show the route, and a sharp-eyed hiker will find the trailhead at the junction of Mount Marshall and Jordan River Trails. Just minutes into your climb up The Peak and the challenges are evident: First a steep pitch, without benefit of switchbacks, then fallen trees and overgrown trail; finally, poor or nonexistent trail markers. Locals nicknamed this mountain Little Bastard. From first glimpse to final weary steps, the name fits. The exposed rock at the summit is charnockite, a billion-year-old granite found the world over. Joseph Charnock, the Englishman for whom the rock is named, founded the city of Calcutta, India. His tombstone is a charnockite rock. Legend says the explorer died from injuries when he tripped over a large chunk of this rock and struck his head. True or not, it serves as a timely reminder as you pick your way over the rough, exposed charnockite boulders descending The Peak. Watch your step!

The Peak once belonged to a family, the Millers, who owned it as part of their 6,000-acre mountain estate. For a time, they worked the tanbark trade. Workers stripped bark off chestnut trees and, using the roads we hike on today, drove mule-pulled carts across Mount Marshall to a tannery in Browntown. The process of turning animal hides into leather required the tannin found in the bark of chestnut and oak trees (also found, in smaller doses, in acorns, coffee, and tea). Tanning was a smelly, dirty job. After grinding the chestnut bark, a tanner mixed bark with water and submerged animal hides in

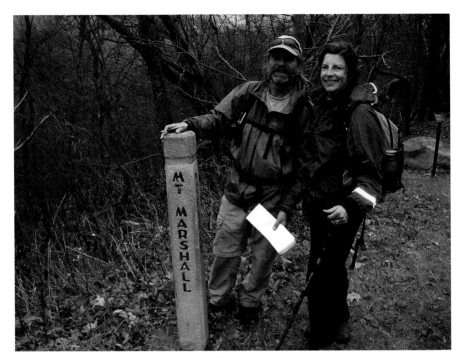

The authors on the Bluff Trail/Mount Marshall JODI URBAN

the concoction. Over a period of months, the tannic mixture cured the hide, making it leather. Until the blight of the early 1900s, the American chestnut was preferred for this process because of its high tannic content.

The road that runs along The Peak's south flank is a remnant of the tanbark trade, but today it's hard to imagine anything but foot traffic on it. Fallen trees impede progress at every turn. Thickets of mountain laurel grow off the steep-sided slopes and grass has overgrown the wheel ruts. As you climb through brush, violet pinwheeled periwinkle pokes through last fall's leaf debris, its roots spreading across the dry slope. Closer to the summit, bloodroot, great chickweed, and liverwort splotch the woods with white blossoms. The chickweed practically begs for attention, growing in large tufts that make it attractive to the butterflies that flock to its red-tipped stamens.

There are no chestnut trees left in Shenandoah National Park, or none that could produce bark in the quantity it once did. The chestnut blight stifles tree growth, and young

HEADS UP

In the Mount Marshall area, camping is closed above 3,200 feet. This means two campsites along the Appalachian Trail are closed where the trail, as described below, crosses South Marshall and North Marshall peaks. This is part of a project by SNP to protect sensitive plant communities on rocky outcrops. Educate yourself about these *rock outcrop communities* at www.nps.gov/shen, and keep in mind that while striving to leave only footprints, we always leave a trace. Mount Marshall is an extremely sensitive area, so exert caution and minimize your impacts.

chestnuts die before they can grow more than head-high. There are, however, plenty of oak trees. Hickory has replaced chestnut as a companion tree. Mountain laurel is ever-present in the understory. There are dogwoods, witch hazel, and spicebush as well. Witch hazel deserves mention, if only for how it reproduces. When the shrub's seedpods dry, they burst and release two seeds that can fly outward 30 feet. This not only explains why witch hazel seems omnipresent, but also confounds an old saying about seeds not falling far from the tree. Less reliable are claims that a forked witch hazel branch functions as a divining rod, leading a person to underground water sources. If by chance it does, credit luck, not witchcraft. The shrub takes its name from the Old English word *wych*, meaning "flexible."

The vistas off Bluff Trail spread east over the Blue Ridge foothills and Piedmont. Four mountains fill the horizon: Keyser, Jenkins, Wolf, and The Peak. Their presence illustrates just how complicated Blue Ridge geology can be. Here, within a few miles, stand mountains with marked differences in shape, not to mention rock. Mount Marshall is young—its bedrock is basalt lava, formed by a series of lava flows that oozed from the earth's crust about 550 million years ago. The Peak and its neighbors are old, weathered stubs of resistant granite that date from a billion years ago. The valley between them is more than the route of some picturesque stream. Beneath its crust lies a geologic fault. Faults, by their very nature, slip. That movement breaks rocks, and, over a period of millions of years, the land overlying them collapses. Water, seeking the easiest route downhill, finds the groove and contributes to further erosion. A crease becomes a valley. What's left? Mount Marshall and The Peak, standing like two prizefighters on either side of an imaginary line.

MILES AND DIRECTIONS

0.0   Start from the Jenkins Gap parking area on Skyline Drive. Exit the parking lot by turning right (south) on Skyline Drive and walking alongside the road shoulder. **Note:** The return leg of this loop enters Jenkins Gap parking area to the right as you exit.

0.4   Turn left (east) off Skyline Drive onto the yellow-blazed Mount Marshall Trail, which is a forest road lined with mountain laurel. The trail follows folds and contours along Mount Marshall's east slope as you descend.

1.7   Cross Waterfall Branch. There is a series of small waterfalls downstream from this crossing, and a flat area alongside the creek makes a good primitive camp.

2.6   Cross Sprucepine Branch, which is shaded by tall, straight-trunked yellow (tulip) poplars.

3.7   Cross an unnamed stream, one of several that form the headwaters of Jordan River.

3.9   Reach a T junction with the Bluff Trail on the right. Continue straight on Mount Marshall Trail. **Option:** To eliminate The Peak and shave 2.3 miles off this hike, turn right (south) on Bluff Trail and follow mileage cues below starting at mile 6.1.

4.3   Reach a T junction with Jordan River Trail on the left. From this junction, follow a distinct footpath that leads into the woods in a southeast direction. The trail is blazed intermittently with light blue paint slashes. **Note:** It is a 1,000-foot ascent in 0.7 mile to the top of The Peak.

4.6   After a steep uphill, the footpath intersects the faint trace of an overgrown road. Turn right, walk 10 to 15 feet, and look for the trail continuing uphill on the left. The trail from here to the top is a steep pitch with large boulders and outcrops. **Note:**

MOUNT MARSHALL LOOP

0 Kilometer 1

0 Mile 1

N

To Front Royal

SHENANDOAH
NATIONAL PARK

Smith Creek

Bolton Branch

12

2,882 ft.

Waterfall Branch

Sprucepine Branch

Hogwallow
Flats

B L U E R I D G E

Skyline Drive

Appalachian Trail

Mount
Marshall
Trail

Browntown Trail

South Marshall
3,212 ft.

North
Marshall
3,368 ft.

Jordan River

Jordan River Trail

Gravel
Springs
Gap

Huge
Boulders

The Peak
Trail

Bluff Trail

The Peak
2,959 ft.

Gravel
Springs
Hut

Big Devil Stairs Trail

Harris Hollow Trail

The road trace continues at a more level pace around The Peak and to a saddleback that allows a more moderate approach but adds 0.6 mile to this hike.

5.0 Reach The Peak with its open rock summit and views southeast over the Rush River valley and the town of Washington. Turn and retrace steps downhill.

5.7 Emerge from the bushwhack path and turn right (north) on Mount Marshall Trail to ascend to the junction with Bluff Trail.

6.1 Turn left (west) on Bluff Trail. The trail ascends through a boulder field on a single-track woodland path. For the next 2.5 miles, the trail follows the contours of Mount Marshall with brief inclines and several wet areas where mountain streams begin forming in the creases of the hillside.

8.4 At a junction with the trail to Big Devil Stairs, continue straight on Bluff Trail. **Side trip:** Turn left to explore Big Devil Stairs, a deep gorge carved into Mount Marshall with nice falls overlooks. There are trailside clearings for one or two primitive campsites within 0.1 mile of this side trip. The first falls overlook is in 0.4 mile, followed by a steep descent to two more overlooks. The trail to stream level near the park boundary is a 2-mile side trip.

9.3 Views open up on the left side of the trail overlooking Harris Hollow.

9.8 Turn right on Bluff Trail at a junction with Harris Hollow Trail. For the next 0.1 mile, Bluff and Harris Hollow Trails share the pathway.

9.9 After a switchback in the trail, continue straight on Bluff Trail as Harris Hollow Trail branches right and uphill.

10.0 Enter a clearing and bear left (west) toward Gravel Springs Hut. Avoid a light-duty dirt road that ascends from the clearing on the right. Near a freshwater spring adjacent to the hut, ascend a blue-blazed path that climbs the hill behind Gravel Springs. There is a spring, privy, and fireplace here.

10.3 Turn right (north) onto the white-blazed Appalachian Trail.

10.5 Pass through Gravel Springs parking area. Cross Skyline Drive and walk past a gate. Immediately past the gate, turn right on the white-blazed Appalachian Trail.

11.5 Summit the 3,212-foot peak of South Marshall, with clear views to the west and north.

12.0 Cross Skyline Drive to the east side and begin an ascent of North Marshall on a series of switchbacks.

12.6 Cross the summit of North Marshall (3,368 feet).

13.6 An unmarked trail on the right leads 30 feet to a spring. Continue a descent through Hogwallow Flats.

14.2 Cross Skyline Drive to the left (west) side of the highway and begin an easy ascent.

15.8 Hike ends by turning right on yellow-blazed Jenkins Gap Trail and walking 150 feet to the Jenkins Gap parking area.

HIKE INFORMATION

Local Information

Front Royal Visitor's Center, 414 E. Main St., Front Royal; (800) 338-2576; www.frontroyalva.com

Local Events/Attractions

Wildflower Weekend, May, Shenandoah National Park, Luray, (540) 999-3500, www.nps.gov/shen. Guided hikes and programs throughout the park.

Lodging

Park lodges at Skyland (Mile 41.7 and 42.5), Big Meadows (Mile 51.2), and cabins at Lewis Mountain (Mile 57.5) are seasonal. Call (877) 847-19195 or go to www.goshenandoah.com for reservations.

Gravel Springs Hut has a 1-night minimum stay for hikers who are out for 3 days or longer. There is a spring, privy, and fireplace here. Tenters can use the four marked primitive tent sites uphill behind the privy; these have none of the restrictions associated with the hut. However, all park backcountry camping regulations apply.

Campgrounds are located at Matthews Arm (Mile 22.2), Big Meadows (Mile 51), Lewis Mountain (Mile 57.2), and Loft Mountain (Mile 79.5). Some are first-come, first-served. For campground reservations, call (877) 444-6777 or visit www.recreation.gov.

Six backcountry cabins are operated by the PATC. For reservations, call (703) 242-0693 or visit www.patc.net.

Shelter on the Bluff Trail

Restaurants
Full-service restaurants are located at Big Meadows Lodge (Mile 51.2) and Skyland (Mile 41.7 and 42.5), and Wayside Food Stops at Elkwallow Wayside (Mile 24.1), Big Meadows Wayside (Mile 51.2), and Loft Mountain Wayside (Mile 79.5). All restaurants are seasonal. Visit www.goshenandoah.com for information.

Hike Tours
Ranger-guided programs are offered spring, summer, and fall.

For commercial tour operators that are permitted in the park, visit www.nps.gov/shen/planyourvisit/permitted-business-services.htm.

Other Resources
Potomac Appalachian Trail Club (PATC), Vienna, (703) 242-0315, www.patc.net. Publishes maps and guides and sponsors hikes in the park.

Shenandoah National Park Association, Luray, (540) 999-3582, www.snpbooks.org. A nonprofit partner that sells guidebooks, maps, brochures, and CDs on the history, flora, and fauna of Shenandoah National Park, to benefit park activities.

13 HAZEL MOUNTAIN

Hazel Mountain and Sams Ridge once offered a sizable mountain community all the tools and products for a decent living. Today it draws people for its natural beauty. At Hazel River Falls, the stream drops 30 feet into a pool ringed by tall cliffs in the shape of a natural amphitheater. From here a trail climbs to the heights of White Rocks before dropping back to the river and more scenic cascades. Throughout the area a sharp-eyed hiker will spy evidence of mountain settlers. Trails follow old roads used to transport farm products, and old fields, apple orchards, and home foundations are visible.

Start: Trailhead at the Meadow Springs parking lot
Distance: 10.8-mile lollipop
Hiking time: About 5 hours
Difficulty: Moderate due to steep climbs along White Rocks and unaided stream crossings of the Hazel River
Trail surface: Dirt footpaths and old wagon roads lead to waterfalls and rock overhangs at Hazel Falls, views off White Rocks, streamside trails along the Hazel River, and an old homesite on Sams Ridge.
Land status: National park
Nearest town: Luray, VA
Other trail users: Hikers only
Accessibility: This trail is not accessible to people with disabilities; however, most of the facilities within the park are. Check out the accessible 1.3-mile Limberlost Trail (Mile 43).
Canine compatibility: Leashed dogs permitted (leash no longer than 6 feet)
Trail contact: Shenandoah National Park, 3655 US 211 East, Luray; (540) 999-3500; www.nps.gov/shen
Schedule: Open year-round. Skyline Drive may close without advance warning due to inclement weather. Even when Skyline Drive is closed, hikers may still enter the park on foot. Most facilities begin opening in Mar and close by late Nov.
Fees/permits: Entrance fee required, valid for 7 days, or annual pass. Available at www.recreation.gov or at any park entrance. Free backcountry camping permits, available at www.nps.gov/shen/planyourvisit/bc-permit.htm, at ranger stations and visitor centers are required. Campfires prohibited except in established fireplaces. Before visiting, review backcountry regulations, which cover such issues as group size, where to camp, and waste disposal. Call (540) 999-3500 for regulations. To fish in Shenandoah National Park (SNP), Virginia residents age 16 or older must have a Virginia state fishing license.
Facilities/features: The park offers a variety of services, including camping, dining, and lodging.
NatGeo TOPO! map: Thornton Gap, Old Rag Mountain
NatGeo Trails Illustrated map: Shenandoah National Park; Appalachian Trail, Calf Mountain to Raven Rock; Massanutten and Great North Mountains
Other maps: PATC #10: Shenandoah National Park Central District

FINDING THE TRAILHEAD

From Luray, drive east on US 211 for 8.8 miles. Turn onto the Skyline Drive access road at the Thornton Gap entrance station. Proceed south on Skyline Drive. Park at the Meadow Springs parking area on the left (east) side of Skyline Drive between mileposts 33 and 34. A concrete post at the back of the parking lot marks the start of Hazel Mountain Trail. **GPS:** N38 38.298' / W78 18.820'. *DeLorme: Virginia Atlas & Gazetteer:* Page 74, C2.

A bear crossing the trail

THE HIKE

To my considerable disappointment, Mr. Bear didn't stick around to answer questions about life on Sams Ridge. He saw me before I saw him, and my view constituted his posterior ambling into the brush. A bear in the wild ranks as one of Mother Nature's more fleeting encounters (gaping at the bear from your car on Skyline Drive does not count). But what adrenaline! My imagination worked overtime. Would the bear circle back and track us to our tent? Did bear reinforcements lie in waiting nearby? Mentally, I prepared myself for a late night banging pots around a bonfire.

Then I tripped. Rocks in the trail are a definite hazard if you're daydreaming. Abandoning the trail, I followed Mary past small shrubs and creeper vines toward a patch of uneven ground. An iron stove and a blue-and-white-specked pail lay partly buried. Faint markings of an old home foundation were visible. Of all the homesites scattered around Hazel Mountain, this spot surely qualified as prime real estate. Views carried east across the Hazel River to White Rocks' four distinct peaks. A thick mat of green broad-leafed plants crowded a nearby spring. Hazel Mountain Road, a main route across the Blue Ridge in the 1800s, passed just a half-mile up the trail.

A hike around Hazel Mountain (you never actually climb this 2,880-foot mountain) runs with ghosts of mountain settlers from beginning to end. The initial descent to the Hazel River passes by hidden ruins of settler homes, and patches of apple trees indicate old orchards. As recently as 1900, the trail itself was a busy thoroughfare through

HEADS UP
The current threat to Shenandoah's trees is the emerald ash borer, an exotic beetle from Asia that is feeding on and killing millions of ash trees throughout North America. Visitors can only bring USDA-approved firewood into the park in an effort to prevent further spreading.

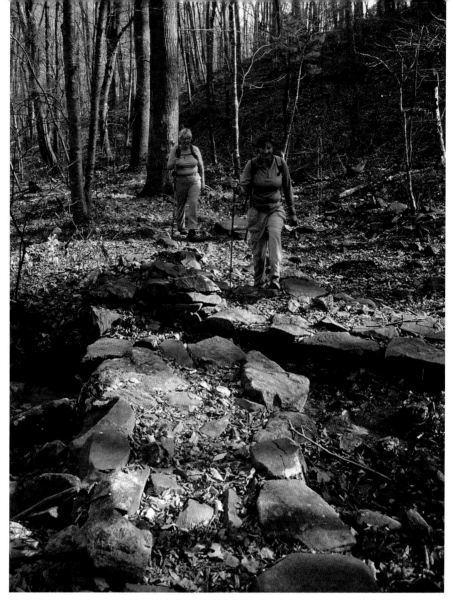
The author and friend Jodi descend the Hazel Mountain Trail.

Thornton Gap; a church and school stood at the junction of Sams Ridge and Hazel Mountain Trails. White Rocks Trail and Sams Ridge Trail were old roads as well. On White Rocks Trail—where it arcs right around a boulder field—the landscape to the right side looks suspiciously like an overgrown field. On Sams Ridge, where we found a home foundation, there also stood a fruit tree, a twisted piece of metal stove, and a pile of rocks—each a ghostly sighting of a past life in the mountains.

In the black-and-white photos of that period, mountain settlers rarely smile. But to say theirs was a hardship is misleading. Certainly by our modern standards it was hard. Fireplaces provided the only heat during cold winter months. One personal recounting of a season spent on the Blue Ridge describes how blankets froze where the sleeper's breath touched it. Otherwise, life revolved around subsistence farming. Warmer months found men and women outdoors, working fields, cutting wood, planting garden plots. Kids attended school in between chores. Small garden plots supplied most of a family's organic food; larger fields were sown with corn, rye, or oats to be sold in town. Through the 1800s Thornton Gap was a busy thoroughfare. A mill complex on the east side of the mountain ground corn and cut lumber. A blacksmith was located here, and a distillery, too. On the western flank of the Blue Ridge, leading to Luray, a tannery operated.

This was the age of the chestnut tree. Once the dominant tree of the Southern Appalachians, the American chestnut supplied wood for homes, nuts for eating, and bark for tanning. As the nuts ripened, kids would stand under the trees throwing rocks into the branches, trying to shake loose the round, burry fruit. Tea from the leaves, mixed with honey, made a natural cough syrup. In fall, dry leaves were gathered and stuffed in mattresses (they called these "talking beds" for the noise they made). The tree bark proved most profitable. Tanners chopped, ground, and mixed bark with water to form a thick, watery, acrid-smelling stew. Animal hides were layered in vats filled with this liquid. Over the course of a year or so, tannic acid—a harsh, bitter, yellowish substance plentiful in the chestnut tree bark—leached into the animal hide and cured it. As you climb through the gap between Hazel and Catlett Mountains on the Sams Ridge Trail, it's hardly a stretch to imagine a wagon loaded with sheets of chestnut tree bark en route to the tannery near Luray, driver perched atop the running board.

Coincidence is sometimes unsettling. In 1900 plants imported from Japan to a New York City zoo contained a blight that would destroy the mature American chestnut population within 40 years. In 1925 President Hoover proposed a national park along the Blue Ridge south of Front Royal. In the fall and winter of 1931–32, the two events—the chestnut blight and construction of a national park—converged on the upper slopes of Hazel Mountain, Catlett Mountain, and other peaks in the northern Blue Ridge. For months, standing dead chestnuts shimmered ghostly, their bark stripped, the wood bleached white. At a time when mountain residents were facing displacement and relocation for a new national park, the tree that had provided sustenance in so many ways was dying as well.

Seventy-plus years later, Shenandoah National Park faced another tree crisis affecting the mighty eastern hemlock, which succumbed to pollution, drought, and finally the woolly adelgid, a microscopic organism that coats the underside of the hemlock needles with millions of white sacs. Today you might see the remains of dead trees, but very few live hemlocks on this trail.

I don't believe in specters, but I had to agree with Mary as we climbed back to Skyline Drive: There was an unsettling feeling in the air on Sams Ridge, in the vicinity of old homesteads, and along the Hazel River, where we stared at the old hemlocks. The ghosts of people and trees—not the haunting kind—just silent reminders of how time marches on.

MILES AND DIRECTIONS

0.0 Start at the concrete post labeled Hazel Mountain Road. Walk downhill and bear right past the trailhead for the blue-blazed Buck Hollow Trail, which branches off left. Continue straight on the yellow-blazed Hazel Mountain Trail, which is an old dirt road.

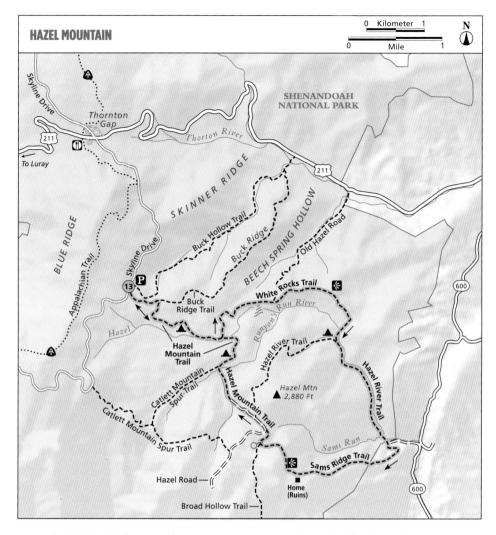

HAZEL MOUNTAIN

SHENANDOAH NATIONAL PARK

0.4 Buck Ridge Trail, marked by a concrete post, enters from the left. About 50 paces past here is an unmarked campsite on the right of Hazel Mountain Trail.

1.3 Hazel Mountain Trail begins paralleling the Hazel River, which is audible to your right. **Note:** This is not an open-harvest stream, and all fish caught must be released.

1.6 Turn left (north) onto the yellow-blazed White Rocks Trail. *Note:* Straight on Hazel Mountain Trail is the return leg of this loop.

1.7 White Rocks Trail begins a long curve right, skirting a spot that shows evidence of an old settlement or field. Trees are sparse or young growth. Shrubs and vines run riot here and dominate the understory. It was common for settlers, when clearing fields, to pile the rocks or make stone fences. Remnants of both are visible.

2.5 Enter a "four-corners" trail junction. Turn right and descend 0.15 mile down a steep, narrow footpath to the Hazel River. At the stream, turn right and hike upstream a few feet to a 30-foot waterfall. (Birds nest in the rock overhangs, and the common blue violet peeks out from thin patches of soil amid the rock boulders.) To return to White Rocks Trail, follow the route you descended.

2.8 Back at the "four corners" trail junction, turn right to continue on White Rocks Trail. The trail climbs to the four knobs whose exposed white rocks give this ridge its name. To the southeast, the lush Hazel River valley unfolds. Look left for a nice view of the remaining White Rock knobs.

Hazel Mountain trail marker

4.2 After a long descent, reach the Hazel River. Cross and bear left, walking downstream along the river. This is a good camping spot, with several established sites marked by fire rings.

4.4 Reach a T intersection with the Hazel River Trail. Turn left and follow the Hazel River Trail to the park boundary. *Bailout:* Turn right on Hazel River Trail and climb over Hazel Mountain. Reach Hazel Mountain Trail in 2 miles, turn right, and follow mileage cues below starting at 8.0 miles. This shaves 1.5 miles off the route, but avoids a steep ascent up Sams Ridge.

5.7 Turn right onto the blue-blazed Sams Ridge Trail, begin a steep ascent, and exit the park. *Option:* An alternate starting point for this hike is straight ahead on the Hazel River Trail, which empties onto VA 600.

6.2 Reenter the park. Boundaries are marked by red slashes on the trees.

7.0 The trail levels as you near the top of Sams Ridge. Around you, the vegetation changes from the hardwood-dominated ridge flanks to a lush mix of evergreens and scrub hardwoods. The woods thin and again you're entering an old settlement area. Metal stoves, pots, stone walls, and piles of rock all testify to the previous inhabitants, displaced when the federal government seized land to create this park. Spend some time and explore, but don't disturb the remains.

7.6 Broad Hollow Trail exits on the left to access trails around Catlett Mountain and Nicholson Hollow. Continue straight on the blue-blazed Sams Ridge Trail. There is a spring just around the bend from this junction.

7.8 Turn left onto Hazel Mountain Trail, marked by a concrete trail marker post.

8.0 Continue straight past a junction with Hazel River Trail on the right. *Note:* If you opted for the bailout at 4.4 miles, continue with mileage cues from this point.

8.2 Pass an established primitive campsite off the left side of the trail. The trail is now a wide, old dirt road.

8.7 Cross a small tributary stream and bear right on Hazel Mountain Trail at a junction with Catlett Spur Trail on the left. ***Note:*** Catlett Spur Trail follows Runyon's Run upstream 1.2 miles to Catlett Mountain Trail.

9.3 Pass the trailhead for White Rocks Trail and continue straight.

10.8 Arrive back at the Meadow Springs parking lot.

HIKE INFORMATION

Local Information
Luray–Page County Chamber of Commerce, Luray, (540) 743-3915, www.luraypage .com

Local Events/Attractions
Wildflower Weekend, May, Shenandoah National Park, Luray, (540) 999-3500, www.nps .gov/shen. Guided hikes and programs throughout the park.

Lodging
Park lodges at Skyland (Mile 41.7 and 42.5), Big Meadows (Mile 51.2), and cabins at Lewis Mountain (Mile 57.5) are seasonal. Call (877) 847-1919 or go to www.goshenandoah.com for reservations.

Campgrounds are located at Matthews Arm (Mile 22.2), Big Meadows (Mile 51), Lewis Mountain (Mile 57.2), and Loft Mountain (Mile 79.5). Some are first-come, first-served. For campground reservations, call (877) 444-6777 or visit www.recreation.gov.

Six backcountry cabins are operated by the PATC. For online reservations, visit www .patc.net, or call (703) 242-0315.

Restaurants
Full-service restaurants are located at Big Meadows Lodge (Mile 51.2) and Skyland (Mile 41.7 and 42.5), and Wayside Food Stops at Elkwallow Wayside (Mile 24.1), Big Meadows Wayside (Mile 51.2), and Loft Mountain Wayside (Mile 79.5). All restaurants are seasonal. Visit www.goshenandoah.com for information.

Hike Tours
Ranger-guided programs are offered spring, summer, and fall.

For commercial tour operators that are permitted in the park, visit www.nps.gov/ shen/planyourvisit/permitted-business-services.htm.

Other Resources
Potomac Appalachian Trail Club (PATC), Vienna, (703) 242-0315, www.patc.net. Publishes maps and guides and sponsors hikes in the park.

Shenandoah National Park Association, Luray, (540) 999-3582, www.snpbooks.org. A nonprofit partner that sells apparel, guidebooks, maps, brochures, and DVDs on the history, flora, and fauna of Shenandoah National Park, to benefit park activities.

14 OLD RAG

Old Rag is one of the park's most popular hikes, and also the most dangerous. What's the attraction? Old Rag is a quick drive from northern Virginia and offers day-trippers a craggy knob with eye-popping views. Beating the crowds on Old Rag means hiking in the offseason. Mountain laurel decorates the Saddle Trail with white and pink blossoms during spring. In fall, views from Old Rag across Weakley Hollow are filled with autumn colors. Whatever the season, carry a warm overshirt or jacket; wind and no tree cover can make Old Rag's summit feel positively alpine.

Start: National park parking lot on VA 600, 0.6 mile west of Nethers, VA
Distance: 9.0-mile loop
Hiking time: 7–8 hours
Difficulty: Difficult due to the route's length and strenuous climbs
Trail surface: Dirt roads and dirt trails meander through mixed hardwood forest on lower slopes and along the trout stream at the foot of the mountain; the path is mostly exposed rock face along the cliffs and through the narrow passages between house-size boulders around the peak.
Land status: National park
Nearest town: Syria, VA
Other trail users: Hikers only
Accessibility: None
Canine compatibility: Dogs not permitted on the Ridge and Saddle Trails for their own safety. On other trails they are permitted on a leash no longer than 6 feet.
Trail contact: Shenandoah National Park, 3655 US 211 East, Luray; (540) 999-3500; www.nps.gov/shen
Schedule: Open year-round. The Old Rag trailhead is outside the park boundary, so you do not have to use Skyline Drive, which may be closed during inclement weather.
Fees/permits: Mar through Nov, visitors to Old Rag Mountain, including hikers on the Saddle, Ridge, and Ridge Access Trails, need to obtain an Old Rag day-use ticket in advance through www.recreation .gov, in addition to a park entrance pass, which can be purchased at www.recreation.gov or at the Old Rag entrance station. Overnight camping is limited and prohibited above 2,800 feet. Campfires prohibited except in established fireplaces. Call (540) 999-3500 for regulations.
Facilities/features: Chemical toilets at the registration station, and 2 shelters on the trail for day use only
NatGeo TOPO! map: Old Rag
NatGeo Trails Illustrated map: Shenandoah National Park; Appalachian Trail, Calf Mountain to Raven Rock; Massanutten and Great North Mountains
Other maps: PATC #10: Shenandoah National Park Central District

FINDING THE TRAILHEAD

From Sperryville, drive south on US 522 and in 0.8 mile, turn right onto VA 231. In 8 miles, turn right onto VA 601 and follow signs to the parking area, about 3 miles; the road number changes from VA 601 to VA 707 and finally VA 600. It is a 0.8-mile walk to the trailhead. Parking at the trailhead and along the roadside is prohibited. **GPS:** N38 34.243' / W78 17.196'. *DeLorme: Virginia Atlas & Gazetteer*: Page 74, B3.

THE HIKE

The climb up Old Rag leads from mountain slopes thick with oak and tulip poplar to a rugged, exposed landscape of rock and straggly table-mountain pine. The forest floor, littered with dead leaves along Hughes Run near the trailhead, sports a thick mat of pine needles at higher elevations. Where you had once seen witch hazel growing in the forest subcanopy, now mountain laurel sinks its tenacious roots into thin, rocky soil. For the hiker, this is a noticeable change with a subtle, less noticeable effect on the mountain. Near the summit, those pine needles collect in puddles of water on open rock. Nitrates released from the needles mix with billion-year-old granite rock, and the erosion process begins. Bowl-shaped depressions form in rock boulders. And just like that, another piece of Old Rag wears away.

As sturdy a mountain as the Blue Ridge ever produced, Old Rag is nonetheless a still-evolving mountain. Still evolving is a curious description for a peak of such stature that, by park estimates, 100,000 people climb it annually. But it explains both how Old Rag's signature summit came to exist and how it continues to change. Millions of years of weathering led to the exposure of granite boulders at the summit. More recently, rain-triggered rock slides reshaped the mountain's east slope (which is well known to only the most experienced bushwhackers and rock climbers). The exposed rock in the recent slides has triggered new interest in Old Rag among geologists. Carbon dating of rocks in the last few years debunked a long-held belief that Old Rag granite is the oldest rock in America's oldest mountain range. Samples of rock taken near Mary's Rock on Skyline Drive date a few hundred million years earlier. This new information doesn't diminish or change Old Rag; it merely adds to a story that is being written in small ways every day.

> Byrds Nest No. 1 and Old Rag Shelters are day use only. If you're hiking on the weekend, arrive early to beat the crowds.

Climbing the last mile on the Ridge Trail demands strength and balance. At one point, a narrow rock ledge is all that separates you from a long fall onto a pile of loose rocks. At another point, you may need a boost from behind to climb over a boulder. The trail negotiates steps made of Catoctin greenstone, rock pillars and boulders as large as a house, and short tunnels between the first false summit (where the trail emerges from the forest) and the true summit at 3,268 feet. The difficulty of the last mile, coupled with the crowds that flock here from June to October, will cause climbing delays.

Approaching Old Rag on the Saddle Trail is less popular, but it recommends itself for exactly that reason: Few people hike it. Hiking on Weakley Hollow Road, views open in the forest canopy and stretch all the way to the mountain. If you bushwhack off Weakley Hollow Road, it's possible to find relics of Old Rag village. In the 1780s there was a post office, school, church, and homes. (The post office stood at the junction of the Saddle Trail with Old Rag Road.) Local mountain men were employed by Skyland Resort to carry packs for the visitors climbing and camping out on Old Rag. Byrds Nest Shelter No. 1, a mountaintop picnic spot just shy of the peak, was donated by another well-heeled Old Rag climber: Virginia governor and senator Henry Flood Byrd Sr. climbed the mountain every year on his birthday.

Land at the foot of Old Rag was once one of the most populated and developed areas of Shenandoah National Park. Archaeologists estimate 460 people lived in a network of hollows and coves, including Weakley Hollow. Recent surveys have identified nearly

The view from Old Rag

ninety sites that were once homes, gristmills, churches, or schools. It is from Weakley Hollow—and the communities in neighboring Nicholson and Corbin Hollows—that the image of Appalachian mountain folk as barefooted, moonshine-swilling hillbillies emerged. A 1933 sociological study called "Hollow Folk" described residents of the Blue Ridge as "unlettered folk, sheltered in tiny mud-plastered log cabins and supported by a primitive agriculture." That description went a long way in swaying public and political opinion to evict residents in favor of building Shenandoah National Park.

Seventy years later, archaeologists with the Colonial Williamsburg Foundation began revisiting these hollows and rewriting the history. Material collected, from calendars and watches to medicine bottles and music, paints a picture of inhabitants not as primitive people who lived hand to mouth. Rather, they were rural people who faced and overcame weather, soil, and social conditions that might have humbled people of lesser character—and probably did. Testament to the power of catalog marketing, the Sears Roebuck Company probably did more to bring the outside world to hollow folk as any technological advancement.

The 2004 book *In the Shadow of Ragged Mountain,* by archaeologist Dr. Audry Horning, systematically disputes "Hollow Folk."

Climbing away from the remains of Old Rag village, the Saddle Trail passes by thick patches of blackberries. A shredded log shows where a bear ripped away soft, rotted wood hunting for grubs. Unlike deer, which were reintroduced to the park in 1935, bears returned to the park on their own. They now number between 250 and 300 (deer number in the thousands).

HEADS UP

Camping is prohibited above 2,800 feet in the Old Rag area. Also, no camping is permitted in the vicinity of the Byrds Nest Shelter. This is part of a project by SNP to protect sensitive plant communities on rocky outcrops. Educate yourself about these *rock outcrop communities* at www.nps.gov/shen, and keep in mind that while striving to leave only footprints, we always leave a trace.

On a quiet day, the staccato of a woodpecker echoes through the woods. In winter, the source of sound may well be a yellow-bellied sapsucker, a bird species that extracts sap from tulip poplars. Nestled below a rock outcrop at lower elevations along Saddle Trail, dusk wraps around the mountain. Wind buffets the peak and drifts downslope. It whistles outside the tent. One gets the sense that the mountain is alive.

MILES AND DIRECTIONS

0.0 Start from the park's official parking lot/entrance station on VA 600 (Weakley Hollow Road). Walk west to the park boundary.

0.8 A chain blocks vehicle traffic from passing. Follow the road as it drops to Hughes Run, crosses on a bridge, and begins a long, steady climb.

1.9 Continue straight on Weakley Hollow Road as Corbin Hollow Trail enters on the right. **Note:** Corbin Hollow Trail leads up Brokenback Creek and intersects with Old Rag Road in just more than 2 miles.

2.0 Continue straight on Weakley Hollow Road as Robertson Mountain Trail enters on the right. **Note:** Robertson Mountain Trail leads across the top of Robertson Mountain and intersects with Old Rag Road in 2.4 miles.

2.9 Turn left onto Old Rag Road. In a few feet, turn left again onto the blue-blazed Saddle Trail, an old road overgrown with grass. The signboard has information on park fees and the "leave no trace" ethic.

3.3 Pass the Old Rag Shelter and a spring on the right side of the Saddle Trail. **Note:** The shelter is for day use only. The spring is marked by a concrete post with yellow striping. If you drink water from the spring, make sure you treat it first.

3.6 Saddle Trail narrows and crosses a boulder field.

3.9 Pass around a boulder the size of a small house. Steps lead uphill to a switchback in the trail.

4.3 Reach Byrds Nest Shelter No. 1. **Note:** An unmarked and unnamed footpath leads past the day-use-only shelter to a perch overlooking Weakley Hollow. Use caution when walking on exposed rock or near cliff edges. The views are beautiful, but they're not worth dying for. Another unmarked trail descends down the east slope of Old Rag. This trail is abandoned and ends at private property with no public access.

4.5 Saddle Trail forks. Bear right and switchback to continue ascent of Old Rag.

OLD RAG

0   Kilometer   0.5

0   Mile   0.5

N

Brokenback Creek

Weakley Hollow Road

Corbin Hollow Trail

WEAKLY HOLLOW

600   Overflow Parking

14

Robertson Mountain Trail

Weakley Hollow Road

Hughes Run

Ridge Trail

SHENANDOAH NATIONAL PARK

Old Homesite
Old Rag Road

Saddle Trail

Boulder Fields

MOUNTAIN

Old Rag
Mountain
▲ 3,268 ft

Ridge Trail

Old Rag
Shelter

Berry Hollow Road

OLD RAG

Rock Scramble

Byrds Nest Shelter #1

Ragged Run Trail
(No access from opposite end)

4.8   Reach the top of Old Rag. A concrete post marks the end of the Saddle Trail and beginning of the Ridge Trail. ***Note:*** For views, turn left at the concrete post and climb the rocks. To descend on the Ridge Trail, return to the concrete post and turn left.

5.3   Begin rock scrambling beneath boulders wedged in crevices. The next 0.5 mile brings steep dropoffs and tricky passages around and over the rocks.

5.5   Pass over the "false summit" of Old Rag. A look back up the trail nets a nice photo op of the Old Rag summit.

5.9   The Ridge Trail leaves Old Rag's exposed granite and reenters the woods under a canopy of oak and yellow poplar.

8.2   Cross a small bridge and arrive back at the Weakley Hollow trailhead, marked by a chain and post.

9.0   Arrive at the park's official parking/lot entrance station on VA 600.

HIKE INFORMATION

Local Information
Rappahannock County Tourism, Visitor Center, 3 Library Rd., Washington; (540) 675-3153; www.rappahannockcountyva.gov

Local Events/Attractions
Prince Michel Vineyard, Winery and Brewpub is one of the East Coast's oldest and largest wineries. 154 Winery Ln., Leon; (800) 800-WINE; www.princemichel.com

Lodging
Graves Mountain Farm & Lodges near the base of the mountain, offers lodging and a farm-to-table restaurant. (540) 923-4231; www.gravesmountain.com

Park lodges at Skyland (Mile 41.7 and 42.5), Big Meadows (Mile 51.2), and Lewis Mountain Cabins (Mile 57.5) are seasonal. Call (877) 847-1919 or go to www.go shenandoah.com for reservations.

Campgrounds are located at Matthews Arm (Mile 22.2), Big Meadows (Mile 51), Lewis Mountain (Mile 57.2), and Loft Mountain (Mile 79.5). For campground reservations, call (877) 444-6777 or visit www .recreation.gov.

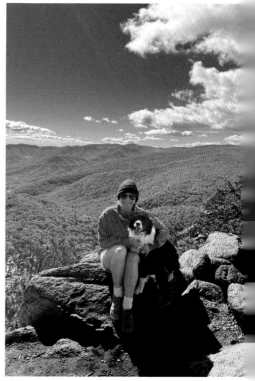

Robertson MountainTrail is a good pet-friendly alternative to Old Rag. SARAH SCARUTO

Backcountry camping at Old Rag is prohibited above 2,800 feet. Campfires are prohibited. You must obtain a free backcountry camping permit at www.nps.gov/shen/planyourvisit/bc-permit.htm.

Restaurants
Full-service restaurants are located at Big Meadows Lodge (Mile 51.2) and Skyland (Mile 41.7 and 42.5), and Wayside Food Stops at Elkwallow Wayside (Mile 24.1), Big Meadows Wayside (Mile 51.2), and Loft Mountain Wayside (Mile 79.5). All restaurants are seasonal. Visit www.goshenandoah.com for information.

The town of Madison, about 14 miles away, has several good restaurants, as does Sperryville, about 19 miles.

Hike Tours
For commercial tour operators that are permitted in the park, visit www.nps.gov/shen/planyourvisit/permitted-business-services.htm.

Other Resources
Potomac Appalachian Trail Club (PATC), Vienna, (703) 242-0315, www.patc.net
Old Rag Master Naturalists, www.oldragmasternaturalists.org

15 ROCKY MOUNT/GAP RUN

Rocky Mount's western flank is a demanding climb of 850 feet in just over 1 mile. If you're not breathless at the top, the view will steal what breath is left. A series of ridges and peaks intersect and rise in succession to the limitless horizon. A return hike on Gap Run Trail takes you from soaring heights into shaded forest. It's said trails in the south district of Shenandoah National Park get less use than other areas of the park. The Rocky Mount/Gap Run loop is proof of this. As a day hike, it is a strenuous full-day trip. Overnighters will find that a quiet tent site along Gap Run allows time to tarry and enjoy the deep-woods scenery.

Start: Concrete post on the west, or southbound, side of Skyline Drive, 0.1 mile north of Twomile Run Overlook
Distance: 10.1-mile lollipop
Hiking time: About 7 hours
Difficulty: Moderate due to a steep climb up Rocky Mount
Trail surface: Make your way along dirt and grass footpaths, rock slides, high-water washes, old streambeds, and rock outcrops on Rocky Mount to the old-growth chestnut oak forests and the dark, sheltered stream valley.
Land status: National park
Nearest town: Elkton, VA
Other trail users: Hikers only
Accessibility: This trail is not accessible to people with disabilities; however, most of the facilities within the park are. Check out the accessible 1.3-mile Limberlost Trail (Mile 43).
Canine compatibility: Leashed dogs permitted (leash no longer than 6 feet)
Trail contact: Shenandoah National Park, 3655 US 211 East, Luray; (540) 999-3500; www.nps.gov/shen
Schedule: Open year-round. Skyline Drive may close without advance warning due to inclement weather.

Even when Skyline Drive is closed, hikers may still enter the park on foot. Most facilities begin opening in Mar and close by late Nov.
Fees/permits: Entrance fee required, valid for 7 days, or annual pass, both available at www.recreation.gov or at park entrances. Backcountry camping permits, available at www .nps.gov/shen/planyourvisit/bc-permit.htm and at ranger stations and visitor centers, are required. Campfires prohibited except in park-constructed fireplaces. Before visiting, review backcountry regulations, which cover such issues as group size, where to camp, and waste disposal. Call (540) 999-3500 for regulations. To fish in Shenandoah National Park (SNP), Virginia residents age 16 or older must have a Virginia state fishing license.
Facilities/features: The park offers visitor centers, wayside pull-offs, dining, and lodging.
NatGeo TOPO! map: McGaheysville
NatGeo Trails Illustrated map: Shenandoah National Park; Appalachian Trail, Calf Mountain to Raven Rock
Other maps: PATC #11: Shenandoah National Park South District

FINDING THE TRAILHEAD

From the south, take exit 99 off I-64 and proceed north on Skyline Drive for 28 miles. Twomile Run Overlook is at Mile 76.2, on the west side of Skyline Drive. From the north, access Skyline Drive from US 33 in Swift Gap. Drive south on Skyline Drive for 11 miles to reach Twomile Run Overlook on the west side of the highway. From the overlook, walk 0.1 mile north along the west shoulder of

Skyline Drive to reach the Rocky Mount trailhead, marked by a concrete post. **GPS:** N38 17.944' / W78 38.826'. *DeLorme: Virginia Atlas & Gazetteer:* Page 67, B6.

THE HIKE

Gap Run can be a monster. That much was clear from tree limbs and other forest debris scattered across its floodplain. Rocks larger than a human head lay piled around the base of larger trees, some 20 feet removed from the actual stream bank. Thinking of the torrent that moved them made me reconsider the small, puddling, barely moving flow that trickled past my campsite. You see, in late July, Gap Run is anything but a monster: a puddle here and a puddle there, and not much else.

A few feet upstream, my nephew, Matthias, took advantage of summer's low-water conditions to scramble over streambed rocks in search of a crayfish or salamander. I had gone over with him proper streambed hunting techniques: Squat or hunch down on a rock, I said, and just stare at one spot in the stream. Then slowly, with two fingers, lift one stone at a time. Give the silt time to settle, then, if you don't see what you're looking for, replace the stone where you found it. A lot of critters call this stream their home, I said. And no one likes to come home and find his house rearranged.

These are the good times, I thought as I watched him explore. A few hours earlier, it was all about adjusting packs, lightening loads, tending to blisters and hot spots, and helping a struggling 7-year-old come to terms with carrying his food, water, and clothing for miles on end, all so we could sit in the woods, eat prepackaged food, and sleep on hard ground.

Leadership training, whether for business or wilderness adventure, preaches the importance of monitoring your group's morale. A happy camper interacts better with others

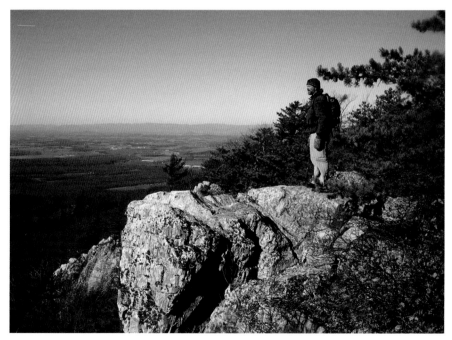

The author stands on a rock outcrop on Rocky Mount.

and is more willing to help the group. With children, this is especially true. There usually comes a time, a critical moment—almost always after a difficult stretch of trail—when an uncomfortable thought settles in: This, they state plainly, is too much like work.

Our group—Mary, myself, and our niece and nephew, Sarah and Matthias—began the hike off Skyline Drive on Rocky Mount Trail. It started nicely on a dirt footpath that posed little risk of injury, on a gentle slope with sporadic views southwest to Twomile Ridge. When the trail steepened and curved around the east side of a small knob, legs weakened. Complaints started drifting back my way and I heard someone say they were dizzy. All indicators pointed to a much-needed rest. The opportunity presented itself once the trail reentered the shade of forest.

Every leader needs a bag of tricks and the next 2 miles exhausted my personal stash. We played "Trail-Wheel of Fortune." We set group challenges to hike a certain distance in a certain period of time. We sang songs. Every time a view opened on the trail, I used it as a topographic lesson by pointing out where we stood. We juggled loads, adjusted shoulder straps, medicated sore feet, and, before long, we hit a nice campsite on the Gap Run Trail. Three miles in 6 hours—the pace left a little to be desired, but a successful first day by all other measures.

Sigurd Olson, author of *Campfires*, wrote "anyone who has traveled in the wilds knows how much he looks forward to the time of day when he can lay down his burden and make camp." I'm not sure Olson ever hiked with children, because for them, camp means one thing: Work. Unpack your backpack. Help set up tents. Prep dinner. Get firewood. Get water. Then a chorus of don'ts: Don't go in the tent with shoes. Don't throw dirt at your sister. Don't touch that plant. Don't eat that bug . . .

At this delicate point, when commands are flying fast, it pays to remember: The poor kids have already completed a herculean task just getting here. More importantly, if their needs aren't met, they can hardly be expected to meet someone else's.

With imagination, jobs can be fun. Matthias and I drew water duty, which led us to search Gap Run for some running water, which in turn led to not getting water at all. Instead, we moved up and down the dry wash, checking out small pools for aqua-critters. A *snap-crackle* brought us to the shoreline where, in dry oak leaves, a turtle the size of a half-dollar pumped tiny legs in a vain attempt to escape detection. We tracked it for 10 minutes or so, until I remembered that without water, we wouldn't eat. We filtered and headed back to camp.

Anticipation motivates. Over breakfast the next morning, Mary and I announced the day hike would be without packs. That prospect sent Matthias and Sarah up the trail like shots. When we caught up, their flushed faces and panting told the story: It's hard to keep an excited kid down, but it's also difficult to run up Rocky Mount. As we approached the white outcrops of the summit, I told the kids to be on the watch. The Erwinian quartzite is pocked with small fossil wormholes that date from a period when this incredibly hard rock was the beach of a prehistoric ocean. As amazing as that sounds, I witnessed something even more mind-boggling: two kids running uphill the last tenth of a mile, each trying to be the first to the summit.

Atop Rocky Mount, we stared across to Rocky Mountain and Twomile Ridge, each of us alone in our thoughts. Turkey vultures rode air currents, wings shifting to-and-fro as they held a tricky balance of speed and direction. "This," said 11-year-old Sarah, "is the most awesome thing I've ever seen in my entire life."

MILES AND DIRECTIONS

Rocky Mount Trail marker

0.0 Start at the Rocky Mount trailhead 0.1 mile north of Twomile Run Overlook on Skyline Drive.

0.6 The trail climbs briefly, then drops to an easy stretch along a footpath. **Note:** The trail shows signs of once being a road. In fact, this route once served as a fire road up from Berrytown, a town at the foot of the Blue Ridge west of Rocky Mount. Occasional views open west to Twomile Ridge and east into the Hawksbill Creek valley and Weaver Mountain.

1.0 Hike along an exposed stretch of trail as you make a brief, 200-foot climb up over a small knob. The trail reenters the woods as it descends the northwest side of this hill.

2.2 Come to the intersection of Gap Run Trail and Rocky Mount Trail. Continue straight to climb Rocky Mount. **Note:** Gap Run Trail heads off to the right and descends past the headwaters of Gap Run. It junctions with the opposite end of Rocky Mount Trail in 2.2 miles.

2.5 Begin a steep climb up Rocky Mount. Views of Twomile Ridge open up when the trail switches back to the right.

2.9 Exposed chunks of chalky rock become more frequent. Close examination reveals fossilized wormholes in this Erwin quartzite.

3.2 About 40 yards shy of the wooded peak on Rocky Mount are cliffs with views of Twomile Ridge, and six ridges rising in succession beyond. **Note:** There is rocktripe lichen on the rocks at this summit. It appears brown, with folded-up edges, and is brittle to the touch. *The Audubon* field guide describes this lichen as "rarely seen," so take a minute to enjoy.

3.8 A large slab of rock becomes increasingly visible on the left side of the trail as you descend. Old-growth chestnut oaks line the trail on your right, and the forest understory is a mix of blueberries, sassafras, and scrub oak. (The sassafras has quite a history. Explorers and colonists treated it as a cure-all. It shrinks less than any southern hardwood, thus was favored in building fences and boats, but its odor supposedly drove away bedbugs, which made it a favored wood for building a bed frame. It was once used widely as a flavor agent. Lately, scientists have found that safrole, a clear oil found in the roots of sassafras, is a cancer-causing agent. Its use in food and drinks is forbidden in the United States.)

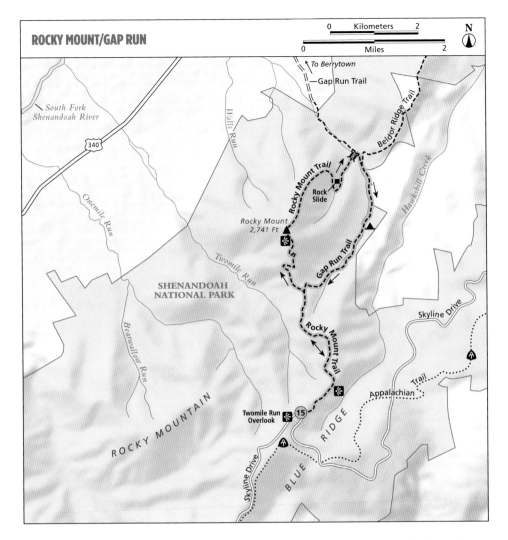

4.7 Cross the first of several rock slides that have covered the mountain below and above the trail with boulders. (Be careful when crossing the rock slides. There is no danger of further slippage, but footing is tricky.) After this the trail descends via switchbacks to a small tributary of Gap Run.

5.1 Cross a small stream and follow the right bank downhill. Within several hundred yards, you'll hop back across the stream and follow the left bank. The trail is clear; stream crossings are well marked.

5.5 Cross Gap Run and reach a T intersection where Rocky Mount Trail meets Gap Run Trail. Turn right onto Gap Run Trail. **Note:** To the left, Gap Run departs the park in 0.8 mile and reaches VA 630 near Berrytown in 1.7 miles.

5.7 An open area to the right of the trail marks an established primitive campsite.

6.2 Gap Run Trail, which has followed the footprint of an old dirt road, becomes a footpath as it crosses a washed-out section of Gap Run. The stream forks into many small rivulets and the trail crosses them as it winds up the wide stream valley. In 0.1 mile, the trail reverts back to a wide, graded path.

6.4	Veer right and continue walking upstream on a woodsy footpath. **Note:** The old road veers left and uphill. Red paint slashes on the trees mark the national park boundary.
6.6	Cross Gap Run. As you climb up the stream valley for the next mile, you will cross the stream two more times.
7.6	Cross Gap Run for the final time and begin a steep ascent to a saddle and the junction with Rocky Mount Trail.
7.9	Gap Run Trail ends at Rocky Mount Trail. Turn left to return to Skyline Drive.
10.1	Hike ends at Skyline Drive. Turn right and head downhill 0.1 mile to parking at Two-mile Run Overlook.

HIKE INFORMATION

Local Information
Town of Elkton, (540) 298-1951, www.elktonva.gov

Local Events/Attractions
The town of Stanardsville has specialty shops, lodging, and dining: www.stanardsville.org.

Lodging
Park lodges at Skyland (Mile 41.7 and 42.5), Big Meadows (Mile 51.2), and cabins at Lewis Mountain (Mile 57.5) are seasonal. Call (877) 847-1919 or go to www.goshenandoah.com for reservations.

Campgrounds are located at Matthews Arm (Mile 22.2), Big Meadows (Mile 51), Lewis Mountain (Mile 57.2), and Loft Mountain (Mile 79.5). For campground reservations, call (877) 444-6777 or visit www.recreation.gov.

Six backcountry cabins are operated by the PATC. For reservations, call (703) 242-0693 or visit www.patc.net.

Restaurants
Full-service restaurants are located at Big Meadows Lodge (Mile 51.2) and Skyland (Mile 41.7 and 42.5), and Wayside Food Stops at Elkwallow Wayside (Mile 24.1), Big Meadows Wayside (Mile 51.2), and Loft Mountain Wayside (Mile 79.5). All restaurants are seasonal. Visit www.goshenandoah.com for information.

Hike Tours
Ranger-guided programs are offered spring, summer, and fall.

For commercial tour operators that are permitted in the park, visit www.nps.gov/shen/planyourvisit/permitted-business-services.htm.

Other Resources
Potomac Appalachian Trail Club (PATC), Vienna, (703) 242-0315, www.patc.net. Publishes maps and guides and sponsors hikes in the park.

Shenandoah National Park Association, Luray, (540) 999-3582, www.snpbooks.org. A nonprofit partner that sells apparel, guidebooks, maps, brochures, and DVDs on the history, flora, and fauna of Shenandoah National Park, to benefit park activities.

16 PINEY RIVER

Heavily settled prior to Shenandoah National Park's formation, the woods tucked between Piney River and Keyser Run today hold clues both obvious and obscure, from family cemeteries to low stone field walls long overgrown by a resurgent forest. Above all, it is a sanctuary of rushing water and steep cliffs. Those who like to save the best for last will appreciate our twist on conventional wisdom: Most people like to climb *up* Little Devil Stairs, but we save this knee-knocking route along Keyser Run for a finishing act.

Start: Parking area and park registration booth on VA 614/Keyser Run Road
Distance: 7.4-mile loop
Hiking time: About 5 hours
Difficulty: Moderate due to several unaided stream crossings and a moderate elevation, with one strenuous segment through Little Devil Stairs due to steep, rough terrain and numerous unaided stream crossings
Trail surface: A gravel forest fire road gives way to centuries-old roads that have reverted to singletrack paths. A majority of this hike is along streams, and in sections exposed rocks and roots make for uneven terrain. The last segment of this route is over exposed rocks, some as big as cars, and steep drop-downs. In spring, sections of trail may be washed out.
Land status: National park
Nearest town: Sperryville, VA
Other trail users: Equestrians permitted on Hull School Trail between the Bowers Family Cemetery and Piney Branch Trail

Accessibility: This trail is not accessible to people with disabilities; however, most of the facilities within the park are. Check out the accessible 1.3-mile Limberlost Trail (Mile 43).
Canine compatibility: Leashed dogs permitted
Trail contact: Shenandoah National Park, 3655 US 211 East, Luray; (540) 999-3500; www.nps.gov/shen
Schedule: Open year-round.
Fees/permits: Entrance fee or annual pass required, available at www.recreation.gov, or park entrances. If camping, obtain a free backcountry permit at www.nps.gov/shen/planyourvisit/bc-permit.htm, or at ranger stations or visitor centers. A Virginia fishing license is required.
Facilities/features: None
NatGeo TOPO! map: Thornton Gap
NatGeo Trails Illustrated map: Appalachian Trail, Calf Mountain to Raven Rock; Shenandoah National Park; Massanutten and Great North Mountains
Other maps: PATC #9: Shenandoah National Park Northern District

FINDING THE TRAILHEAD

From Sperryville, follow the combined US 211/522 east. In 2.1 miles, turn left (north) on VA 622/Gid Brown Hollow Road. Drive 2 miles and turn left onto VA 614/Keyser Run Road. Stay straight on Keyser Run Road as first VA 672 and then VA 623 branch off left and right, respectively. In 5 miles from the highway, enter a trailhead parking area with room for ten or more cars. **GPS:** N38 43.831' / W78 15.517'. *DeLorme: Virginia Atlas & Gazetteer*: Page 74 C2.

Piney River

THE HIKE

The woods that descend to Piney River are a beautiful place on a sunny morning, especially so after a strong spring rainstorm. Birdsong floats down from the tree canopy, and sunlight dapples the leaves and ground. Dry streambeds are flush with runoff. Deer poke about the forest understory, chewing on twigs. On the trailside, lush green plants grow in a seep from the rocks. Lettuce saxifrage and Solomon's seal are telltale plants that mark the spot of many natural springs.

Ephemeral streams emerge after a heavy rain. As you descend Hull School Trail toward Piney River, a run of small plate-size rocks may be visible off the left side of the trail. Your first instinct is to call it a boulder-strewn spring or streambed. Further exploration shows it's more likely a stone stream; while water runs down it after heavy rain, it is dry other times. Skinny-trunked maples grow from the rock bed, indicating soil stability not found in a consistently running stream. Crusty lichen, another indication of stability, appears on rocks near the edges of the stone stream.

Piney River, reached at the junction of Hull School and Piney Branch Trails, gushes downstream with force. Stream crossings without the aid of a footbridge force a search upstream and downstream for a fallen log or rocks suitable for hopping. In the forest near the stream's edge, small rivulets form on both sides of the Piney Branch Trail, marking points of minor flooding.

Where the Piney River passes through a steep gorge, the trail steepens as well, climbing the hillside on switchbacks. Where it briefly levels, the river can be heard, but not seen. A small window through the forest canopy does

"Why the Mountains Are Blue" by Wayne Baldwin recounts the sadder history of the creation of Shenandoah National Park.

offer a glimpse to the solid cliff wall on the opposite side. Just the spot, perhaps, a denning bear or mountain lion might prefer.

The presence of mountain lions—also referred to as cougars, pumas, panthers, and catamounts—is subject to debate. Officially, the last eastern subspecies of mountain lion, *Puma concolor cougar*, was documented in Virginia in 1882. But anecdotal sightings, if not actual documentation, continue to occur. Whether the population is a resurgence of the native eastern cougar, a wanderer from another region (Florida currently has the only population of cougars in the East, the highly endangered Florida panther, *Puma concolor coryi*), or an escaped or released pet is unknown.

Any thought of a lurking predator is dispelled as you climb away from the Piney River gorge along Pole Bridge Link Trail. In spring, the grassy fringes of the trail here are a spectacle of wildflowers, whether the ephemeral spring beauties, the white petals of giant chickweed, delicate purple wild geraniums, or common violets and buttercups. Dry, grassy spots host a profusion of common lousewort, a red-and-yellow blossom that seems more at home in a cow pasture than these woodlands.

The descent through Little Devil Stairs offers what Piney Branch Trail only hinted at: up-close interaction with rugged nature. There are at least eight stream crossings, and after a heavy rain, probably more. At one point the cliffs on either side close in so tightly, you're forced to walk down a small island that conveniently emerges from the stream.

A rock talus marking the halfway point of the descent through Little Devil Stairs highlights the geologic dynamism of the park. A "river" of its own sort, the talus covers the hillside with rocks and boulders, most of them tire-size or smaller. *Talus creep* describes the slow downslope movement of this rock slope toward the valley bottom. In a geologic time frame, this slope is considered dynamic and moving. The slope and the quartzite rock itself show no signs of the stability (lichen or vegetation) that was evident on the stone stream alongside the Hull School Trail.

Kilometer

0   1

Mile

0   1

N

Skyline Drive

Piney River

Keyser Run

Pole Bridge Link Trail

Little Devil Stairs

Little Devil Stairs Trail

Little Devil Stairs

SHENANDOAH
NATIONAL PARK

Keyser Run Fire Road

Piney Branch Trail

16   614

Keyser Run Fire Road

Cemetery

Pignut Mountain
2,531 ft.

Piney Ridge Trail

Piney River

Hull School Trail

Fork Mountain Trail

Hull School Road

MILES AND DIRECTIONS

0.0 Start from the Little Devil Stairs parking lot. Follow a gravel road uphill from the west end of the lot.

0.2 Swing right (north) on the fire road and walk past signs marking the boundary of Shenandoah National Park.

1.1 After a steady climb, enter a clearing that is the junction of Keyser Run Fire Road and Hull School Trail. The Bolan family cemetery is off to the right. After exploring, depart the clearing on the left, following yellow-blazed Hull School Trail, which descends as a narrow woodland footpath.

1.7 A small stream cuts across the trail. Ahead, in 0.2 mile, cross another stream and then swing left as the trail continues a gradual descent to Piney River.

1.8 Turn right on Piney Branch Trail at a T junction and hike upstream on the blue-blazed trail. Just before reaching this junction, study the woods off the trail on the right. Rock piles amid a young forest indicate possible field-clearing activity dating from when this park was settled. Careful exploration of the rock piles yields the presence of a freshwater spring at the base of one.

1.9 Pass a primitive campsite off the trail on the left. Soon after, cross Piney River. **Note:** After a heavy rain, you may have to explore up- or downstream for a suitable place to cross.

2.3 Continue straight (north) on Piney Branch Trail past a junction with Piney Ridge Trail on the left.

2.5 After a short stretch of trail that runs close to the stream, begin a climb from river-bottom forest up the side of a river gorge.

3.0 A vigorous climb levels briefly and the forest canopy opens to views of the imposing cliff face on the opposite stream bank. In the next 0.1 mile of trail, look for unmarked paths leading off trail right to the river's edge.

3.3 Cross Piney River on stream rocks and start a steady uphill climb on Piney Branch Trail. The stream is now on your left side.

3.5 The trail levels briefly, and off the trail to the left is a primitive campsite.

4.2 Detour off the trail to the left to explore the cliff line that gives visual proof to the elevation you've gained in the last 1.2 miles.

4.6 Turn right (east) on Pole Bridge Link Trail. Level terrain off both sides indicates you are traversing across the flat top of a ridge.

4.7 Pass a primitive campsite off the trail to the right.

4.9 Stay straight on Pole Bridge Link Trail at a junction with Sugarloaf Trail on the left.

5.4 Reach Fourway, a junction with Keyser Run Fire Road and Little Devil Stairs. Cross the fire road diagonal left and reenter woods on Little Devil Stairs Trail. The trailhead is marked by a concrete trail marker.

5.7 Begin a series of five switchbacks that carry you down a steep slope into Little Devil Stairs Canyon.

5.8 Cross Keyser Run, the first of four unaided stream crossings over the next 0.3 mile. **Note:** The next 1.1 miles descend *extremely* technical terrain as you scurry across, squeeze through, drop down off, and hop across rocks and boulders that litter this stream gorge.

6.0 Cross Keyser Run for the fourth time and pass beneath a 20-story-high cliff line that forms the right stream bank of the canyon. A talus in this area is littered with tire-size rocks, and the trail footbed is loose rubble.

6.1 Two quick stream crossings put you back on the right stream bank. Ahead, Keyser Run is squeezed by cliffs and the trail takes a middle course down an island formed by a split in the stream. Watch for blue blazes on trees for guidance. *Note:* In spring or after heavy rainfalls, this section may be washed out, requiring you ford downstream as you follow the blue trail blazes.

6.3 Cross Keyser Run from the right to left stream bank. This is the first of four stream crossings as the trail emerges from the gorge into a wider stream valley.

6.7 Cross from the left to right stream bank, the last in this dizzying descent. Ahead, the trail separates from the streamside and crosses a small knoll.

7.2 Begin a long stretch of hiking across flat bottomland forest. Just before reaching the trailhead parking lot, cross a stream.

7.4 Arrive back at the parking lot.

HIKE INFORMATION

Local Information
Rappahannock County Visitor Center, 3 Library Rd., Washington, VA 22747, (540) 675-3153, www.rappahannockcountyva.gov

Local Events/Attractions
Wilderness Weekend is held each Sept at the park's Byrd Visitor Center, milepost 51 on Skyline Drive, near Big Meadows.

Quievremont Winery, Gid Brown Hollow Road, (540) 987-3192, www.quievremont .com

Restaurants
The Inn at Little Washington is a world-renowned restaurant and inn in a small-town country setting. Middle and Main Streets, Washington, (540) 675-3800, www.theinnat littlewashington.com

Hike Tours
Park rangers lead a variety of nature, wildflower, and geology hikes. www.nps.gov/shen.

For commercial tour operators that are permitted in the park, visit www.nps.gov/ shen/planyourvisit/permitted-business-services.htm.

Organizations
Potomac Appalachian Trail Club (PATC), Vienna, (703) 242-0315, www.patc.net

HONORABLE MENTIONS: SHENANDOAH NATIONAL PARK

Q. OVERALL RUN FALLS

Start at Matthews Arm Campground for a 5-mile loop hike to view the tallest waterfall in Shenandoah National Park, 93 feet to be exact, on the western slope of the Blue Ridge at Overall Run. From the staggering falls, the mountainous panorama unfolds westward over Massanutten's double ridges, and farther off on the hazy horizon looms Great North Mountain. In dry conditions, water flow may be minimal. The falls are best viewed when there has been plentiful rain. **GPS:** N38 45.613' / W78 17.860' *DeLorme: Virginia Atlas & Gazetteer: Page 74, B2.*

R. NICHOLSON HOLLOW

Park at Stony Man Overlook at milepost 38.6 on Skyline Drive in the park's central district. Nicholson Hollow was once a populated area of 400 families. Old home foundations and other evidence of past lives are visible along this 5.8-mile one-way trail. Use Corbin Hollow Trail and Indian Run Trail to make an extended backcountry loop, with primitive campsites and swimming holes. (540) 999-3500; www.nps.gov/shen. **GPS:** N38 36.769' / W78 21.632'. *DeLorme: Virginia Atlas & Gazetteer: Page 74, D2.*

S. WHITEOAK CANYON

Parking for the Whiteoak Canyon Trail is at milepost 42.6 on Skyline Drive in the park's central district. The steep gorge features waterfalls, giant boulders, and quiet pools that make this one of the most popular and beautiful places in the park. The connecting Limberlost Trail is accessible for people with disabilities. There is no backcountry camping. (540) 999-3500; www.nps.gov/shen. **GPS:** N38 35.174' / W78 22.972'. *DeLorme: Virginia Atlas & Gazetteer: Page 74, D2.*

T. BIG RUN PORTAL-ROCKYTOP LOOP

Begin this hike at Big Run Overlook at milepost 81.2 on Skyline Drive in the park's southern district. A classic Shenandoah hike: all downhill to the park boundary, followed by a steep climb back to Skyline Drive. In total, a strenuous 14.6-mile loop. (540) 999-3500; www.nps.gov/shen. **GPS:** N38 15.229' / W78 41.046'. *DeLorme: Virginia Atlas & Gazetteer: Page 67, C6.*

U. RIPRAP HOLLOW-
APPALACHIAN TRAIL LOOP

The parking area for this 10-mile hike is at milepost 90 on Skyline Drive in the park's southern district. Chimney Rock, Calvary Rock, and a swimming hole are highlights on this trip. So are the springtime mountain laurel blooms along Riprap Trail as it descends through Cold Spring Hollow. (540) 999-3500; www.nps.gov/shen. **GPS:** N38 10.649' / W78 45.896'. *DeLorme: Virginia Atlas & Gazetteer: Page 67, C5.*

VALLEY & RIDGE

Featured Hikes
- (17) Big Schloss
- (18) Stephens Trail
- (19) Laurel Fork Area
- (20) Roaring Run/Hoop Hole

Honorable Mentions
- (V) Fridley Gap
- (W) Massanutten Mountain West/Signal Knob
- (X) Massanutten Mountain East/Duncan Hollow
- (Y) Wild Oak National Recreation Trail
- (Z) Shenandoah Mountain Trail/South

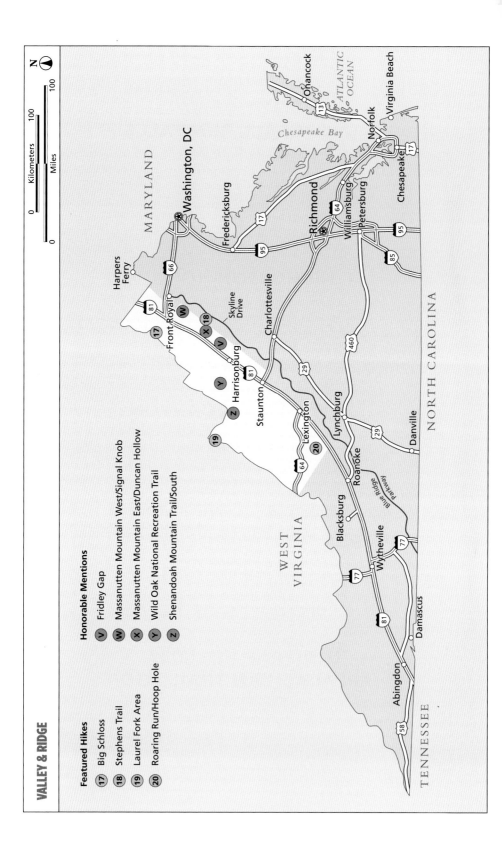

VALLEY & RIDGE

I am now in the very midst of that great congregation of hills, comprising all the spurs, branches, knobs and peaks of the great chain which has been called, with a happy attitude, the backbone of America.

James Kirke Paulding wrote this during his Virginia travels in 1816. Any person might think as much when venturing into the Allegheny Mountains today. Bringing order to this landscape is hopeless. The hills are long, straight ridges tending northeast–southwest, divided by deep, narrow valleys, like waves and troughs of the earth's crust folded and faulted by gigantic continental collisions millions of centuries ago.

Little is consistent about the Valley & Ridge region. Shoulder spurs shoot off in all sorts of directions, appearing as broad buttresses for the many rocky balds and tree-covered knobs. An otherwise straight ridge will warp with S turns, alluding to the powerful, earth-shaping forces that create mountains. Streams cut deep grooves in the

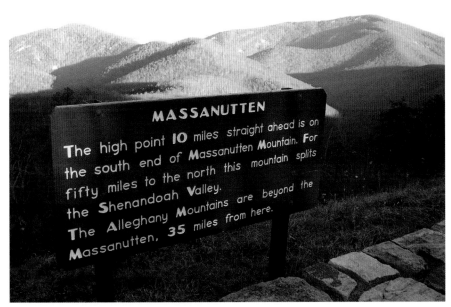

Roadside view of Massanutten Mountain

mountain slopes, and a trove of plants and trees soak up life from these veins of moisture, giving rise to the Appalachian cove forest, one of Earth's most diverse ecosystems. Rock slides inhibit forward progress in one direction, while in the other, a sharp-rising ridge presents a seemingly insurmountable obstacle.

The Appalachian Mountains, which include the Allegheny chain of Virginia and West Virginia, are among the oldest mountains on the planet. The Southern Appalachians as a whole are considered a biological wonderland. Virginia's Valley & Ridge region supports that claim with vigor. In Laurel Fork, elements of northern boreal forest inhabit the high-altitude knobs and stream valleys, while miles away, dry forests on lower ridges display the classic oak-hickory forest type. So it is that the hiker passes from dank, moist streambeds to high, exposed cliff-lines to laurel-shrouded mountain slopes in a single day.

Anyone who travels the mountains of Virginia with any regularity is bound, sooner or later, to come upon a spot so special, so utterly beautiful at that moment in time, it brings them to pause. It could be a soaring view, a mist-shrouded wilderness pond or a mountain stream, a swath of pink and white–blooming mountain laurel, or a sun-dappled cove cooled by the shade of old-growth hemlock. Wherever, whenever, this spot remains an abiding image long after the hike ends. That is the gift of Virginia's mountains.

THE HIKES
17. Big Schloss
18. Stephens Trail
19. Laurel Fork Area
20. Roaring Run/Hoop Hole

HONORABLE MENTIONS
V. Fridley Gap
W. Massanutten Mountain West/Signal Knob
X. Massanutten Mountain East/Duncan Hollow
Y. Wild Oak National Recreation Trail
Z. Shenandoah Mountain Trail/South

17 BIG SCHLOSS

In German, *schloss* means "castle." In Virginia, schloss can only refer to one geologic wonder, a towering outcrop of sandstone on Mill Mountain. Big Schloss is a popular day trip from Wolf Gap Recreation Area, a primitive camping site 2 miles south. A more strenuous trip begins far to the north, in a quiet river valley better known by hunters than hikers. The hike begins at Wilson Cove Wildlife Management Area, a 5,200-acre piece of the national forest designated for muzzle-loader buck hunting only, in late November and early December. Along Pond Run, old-growth hemlocks stand out from the smaller trees growing thick along this stream. Rock slides, steep inclines, overlooks, and quiet views off Mill Mountain follow in succession.

Start: Bridge over Waites Run on Waites Run Road (WV 5/WV 1).
Distance: 19.5-mile lollipop
Hiking time: About 12 hours
Difficulty: Moderate due to length, sections of rocky and uneven trail, and steep climbs
Trail surface: Dirt forest paths and old logging roads lead through rock formations and cove forests along Pond Run and Little Stony Creek.
Land status: National forest
Nearest town: Wardensville, WV
Other trail users: Mountain bikers, cross-country skiers, and hunters (in season)
Accessibility: None
Canine compatibility: Dogs permitted

Trail contact: Lee Ranger District, Edinburg, (540) 984-4101, www.fs .usda.gov/gwj
Schedule: Open year-round. Hunting is permitted in national forests. Wilson Cove Wildlife Management Area hosts a special muzzle-loading season in late Nov to early Dec. Deer season lasts from Nov to early Jan.
Fees/permits: None
Facilities/features: No facilities. There are primitive campsites along the trail and camping facilities at nearby Wolf Gap Recreation Area.
NatGeo TOPO! map: Wardensville, Woodstock, Wolf Gap
NatGeo Trails Illustrated map: Massanutten and Great North Mountains

FINDING THE TRAILHEAD

From Strasburg, follow VA 55 (also called Wardensville Pike) west for 20 miles, crossing into West Virginia en route. In Wardensville, bear left at the WV 55/WV 259 junction. In 0.5 mile, turn left onto Carpenters Avenue, at the 7-Eleven store. In 0.8 mile, turn right onto Waites Run Road (WV 5/WV 1). Pass a community park on the left. Enter George Washington National Forest in 1.3 miles. In 5.3 miles, reach a concrete bridge spanning Waites Run. Across the bridge a sign indicates the boundary of Wilson Cove Wildlife Management Area (WMA). There are pull-offs for cars on either side of the stream and campsites for late-day arrivals. **GPS:** N39 00.951' / W78 36.324'. *DeLorme: Virginia Atlas & Gazetteer*: Page 73, A6.

THE HIKE

The Native American phrase for *Appalachia* translates roughly as "endless mountain." That seems an apt description standing atop one of Mill Mountain's many outcrops. The view west is of one mountain rippling onto another and another, each one dissected by a

Big Schloss's dramatic rock formations resemble "castles."

narrow, wooded valley. Trees drape the entire landscape—a rare scene in these otherwise well-developed hills.

Mill Mountain attracts hikers just for these kinds of panoramas. The trail is well marked and the views easy to find. It's hard to imagine that this same trip, if undertaken 300 years ago, would be considered folly. On the whole, early settlers avoided steep uphill routes across mountains. Huge oaks and chestnut trees made passage difficult; a frustrating undergrowth of laurel, creeper, and shrubs reduced their pace to a crawl. Instead, settlers stuck to roads through the valleys, routes first blazed by Native Americans. The most famous, the Great Warriors Path, became the Great Wagon Road as settlers replaced indigenous populations. So numerous were the Scots-Irish, German, and English migrants moving south on the Great Wagon Road from Pennsylvania, it has been said travelers numbered in the tens of thousands up to the Revolutionary War.

Before settlers, Iroquois Indians had used the north–south route for hundreds of years. Virginia governor Alexander Spotswood and his companion explorers found the route when they reached the shores of the Shenandoah River. Marked by hatchet notches in trees, the Great Warriors Path aided Iroquois travel from Canada into southern regions for war and trade. It was on one such trip that a band of Iroquois stayed south and settled in villages on the Neuse and Pamlico Rivers in northeastern North Carolina, which is where European traders and explorers encountered these "mild" and "gentle" people. Their name, from the Iroquoian word for "hemp gatherers," was Tuscarora.

Whatever the English's first impression, relations between the Tuscaroras and settlers turned ugly. Broken treaties and a rash of kidnappings of Indian children contributed to a Tuscarora-led massacre in 1711, at New Bern in North Carolina. (English settlers had built New Bern on the site of a Native American town, Chattoka.) The killings were unusually brutal. Women were pinned to the floor and staked through, children killed, and homes burned. A 2-year war ensued. By 1713 the Tuscaroras were defeated. Chieftains sent word north along the Great Warriors Path to the League of Five Nations, in upstate New York, asking for help. In 1714 the Tuscaroras began migrating up the Appalachians into Virginia, Maryland, Pennsylvania, and, finally, New York. A Virginian settler in the 1750s and 1760s might see groups of these Indians, their worldly possessions piled on horseback, traveling in small bands, sometimes settling in an area for years, then moving north again. Officially, the Tuscaroras were accepted into the League of Five Nations (now Six Nations) in 1722. Their migration lasted at least another half-century beyond this date. Today their tribe numbers 600 people on reservation land near Niagara Falls.

In name and spirit, the Tuscaroras remain in Virginia to this day. At Waites Run, a hiker who steps onto Tuscarora Trail enters a forest world of mountain streams and hemlock groves. The wide-trunked evergreens show black, gnarled roots, some reaching into Pond Run, soaking in the water. Along this stream, Tuscarora Trail shares the path with Pond Run Trail. In a gap between Half Moon and Mill Mountains, Tuscarora Trail branches east. Uphill from a good spring at the headwaters of Half Moon Run, the blue-blazed route plunges left into heavy woods. The grade steepens. Boulders and small rocks make walking difficult. The fractured gray rock underfoot shows a quartz-pebble conglomerate. In these stones, the Tuscarora name crops up again as Tuscarora sandstone, a type found at the core of mountains from Virginia to Pennsylvania. (Admittedly, the term *sandstone* gives reason to pause. This is, after all, one of the most erosion-resistant rocks in the Appalachians, a fact at odds with the idea of sand, which is easily eroded. The key here is metamor-

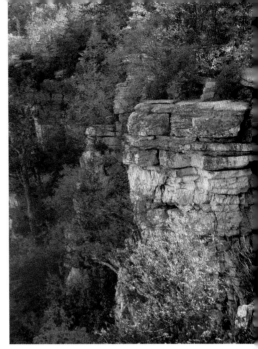

Big Schloss's fall colors

phism—a change in which a rock, subjected to intense, volcano-like heat and pressure, changes and becomes a new rock. So the chief ingredient of sandstone is recrystallized sand—sand subjected to so much heat and pressure it turned to quartzite, which is one of the most resistant rocks around.)

The hiker and Tuscarora Trail part on Mill Mountain, where the latter turns east and heads for the Shenandoah National Park while the Mill Mountain Trail follows the ridge-line south. From Waites Run, the trail has climbed 1,500 feet; the next 4 miles undulate more gently on a slope leading south to Big Schloss. It's a dry hike. Except for water at Sandstone Spring, there are no reliable sources on the ridge. There are, however, views. Short branch trails end at rough-textured rocks that will skin knees and elbows if you scramble up for a view. Finally, there is Big Schloss visible above tree line, accessible by boardwalks over crevices and steep rock faces. Free-fall views surround the high point on this rock formation—there's nothing but blue sky east-west-north-south and straight up.

From the high-and-dry altitude of Mill Mountain, Big Schloss Cut-off Trail descends through a sea of mountain laurel (peak blooms in June) to reach Little Stony Creek. Where the trail on Mill Mountain is bedded with sand and stone flints, the route up Little Stony Creek Trail is muddy, lined with ferns, and full of chirping birds. There are red-eyed vireos, Acadian flycatchers, and ovenbirds rustling about the brush. Scarlet tanagers roost on treetops, then swoop in a flash of red to feed on insects in the brush. Also present are warblers, although hardly in numbers they once were. This songbird's decline in the Southern Appalachians is an alarm for naturalists. The decline rate varies by species, but as a whole, nearly three-quarters of the fifty warbler species known to inhabit the southern forests are in decline. For an explanation, look no further than the burned and clear-cut forest along Little Stony Creek below FR 92. Habitat loss and fragmentation, whether caused by logging, development, or natural events, has impacted warblers to a degree that has made it an issue of study by the Forest Service.

Past Sugar Knob Cabin, Stony Creek Trail intersects the Tuscarora Trail and the return to Waites Run begins. Just when it feels the hike won't end, reach the gap between Half Moon and Mill Mountains. The route downhill along Pond Run leads to the trailhead, but consider shedding the pack here for one final viewpoint. Follow white blazes out of the campground to a rock outcrop on the edge of the mountain. The view from here is endless. The Indians had an apt description for this kind of view: Appalachian.

MILES AND DIRECTIONS

0.0 Start from a signboard for the Pond Run Trail (also known as the Tuscarora Trail). Standing on the concrete bridge spanning Waites Run, looking upstream, the signboard is on the right stream bank. From it, a blue-blazed dirt footpath climbs over a small hill and drops back to the water and follows Waites Run upstream.

0.4 Veer right to follow the trail up Pond Run. Prior to this, there are campsites on your left. **Note:** Green paint slashes on trees alongside the trail designate the wildlife management area, not the trail.

0.5 Make the first of eight stream crossings on Pond Run.

1.4 After crossing Pond Run once again, the trail climbs a rocky route up the right hillside. Berry bushes crop up in the understory, signaling passage from the moist environment of the stream to drier slope environs.

2.4 Reach a grassy junction. Turn left and immediately pass a campsite on the right. An unmarked footpath descends from this campsite to a rock outcrop with a beautiful view of unspoiled forestland. **Note:** One-tenth of a mile past the campsite is a spring, the last reliable water source for 3 miles.

2.7 Bear left onto a narrow, rocky, blue-blazed footpath. Avoid the old road that climbs the hill to the right. The footpath is a leg of the Tuscarora Trail and covers some rugged ground as it bends around Mill Mountain to a bluff overlooking Wilson Cove and Paddy Mountain, before cutting southeast to meet Mill Mountain Trail.

3.9 Tuscarora Trail empties into a grassy clearing. Walk straight through the clearing and onto Mill Mountain Trail, a dirt road overgrown with grass. **Note:** A left turn is the return trail from Sugar Knob Cabin.

4.3 A trail branches off to the right to a now-destroyed airway beacon site. (The trail to the old airway beacon is crowded with huckleberry, which bloom in early June.) Past this junction, the trail threads a set of concrete posts and reverts to a single-track woods path.

5.4 After a steep, rocky decline, reach Sandstone Spring. This is a good water source and campsite.

6.0 An unmarked trail to the right reaches an overlook west to Long Mountain. From here, you also get a nice view south along the spine of Great North Mountain, a range once called Devil's Backbone.

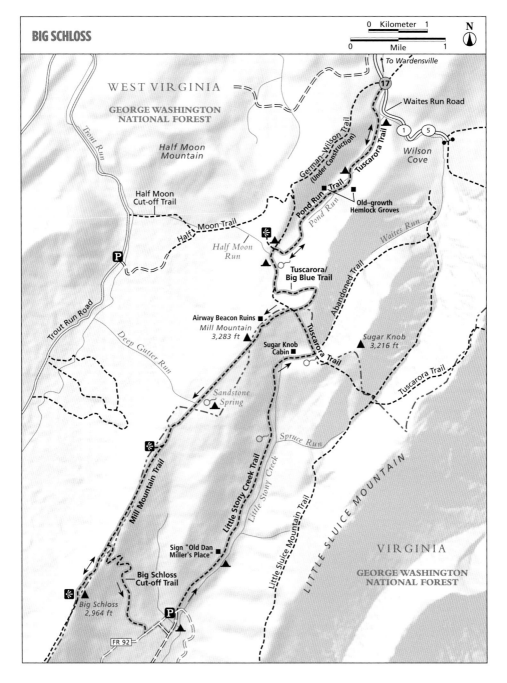

BIG SCHLOSS

0   Kilometer   1

0   Mile   1

N

WEST VIRGINIA

**GEORGE WASHINGTON
NATIONAL FOREST**

Trout Run

*Half Moon
Mountain*

Half Moon
Cut-off Trail

Half Moon Trail

P

Trout Run Road

Deep Gutter Run

*Half Moon
Run*

Tuscarora/
Big Blue Trail

Airway Beacon Ruins
*Mill Mountain
3,283 ft*

Sugar Knob
Cabin

*Sandstone
Spring*

German-Wilson Trail
(Under Construction)

Pond Run Trail

Pond Run

Old-growth
Hemlock Groves

Tuscarora Trail

To Wardensville

17

Waites Run Road

1   5

*Wilson
Cove*

Waites Run

Abandoned Trail

Tuscarora Trail

*Sugar Knob
3,216 ft*

Tuscarora Trail

Spruce Run

Mill Mountain Trail

Little Stony Creek Trail

Little Stony Creek

Sign "Old Dan
Miller's Place"

Big Schloss
Cut-off Trail

Big Schloss
2,964 ft

P

FR 92

Little Sluice Mountain Trail

LITTLE SLUICE MOUNTAIN

VIRGINIA

**GEORGE WASHINGTON
NATIONAL FOREST**

6.7 Reach the Big Schloss Cut-off Trail branching left off Mill Mountain Trail. From here, the Big Schloss rock formation is 1.2 miles straight ahead on Mill Mountain Trail. Continue straight.

7.9 Reach Big Schloss. Views span 360 degrees east across the Great Valley and west into West Virginia. To continue this loop hike, return to Mill Mountain Trail and the Big Schloss Cut-off.

9.1 Back at the junction of Mill Mountain Trail and Big Schloss Cut-off Trail, descend the east slope of Mill Mountain on the Cut-off Trail on steep switchbacks amid slicks of mountain laurel.

10.8 The trail drops to FR 92. Turn left and follow the gravel road downhill.

11.1 An unmarked logging road drops off the right side of FR 92. This marks a bush-whack to Little Stony Creek that takes you through landscape scarred by clear-cutting and fire. After descending on the logging road and passing through a clearing, find any one of a number of animal paths through the entanglement of vines and briars. Past this thick undergrowth is a dirt logging road. At this point, Little Stony Creek is audible, but obscured by a fringe of woods. Turn left and follow the logging road. This logging road remains the main trail to FR 92.

11.5 Pass a dirt road leading to campsites on Little Stony Creek. Two more roads leading to Little Stony and good campsites follow in quick succession.

11.7 Reach FR 92. Cross the gravel road and reenter the woods. Little Stony Creek Trail is a narrow yellow-blazed path that follows the stream, crosses several times, then climbs with alternating steep pitches and level stretches.

15.2 Reach Sugar Knob Cabin, a PATC-sponsored hut. There is a spring in the vicinity and several fire rings. ***Note:*** The PATC cabin is locked and for use through reservation only. Call (703) 242-0693.

15.3 Turn left onto the Tuscarora Trail, a wide road overgrown with grass.

15.9 Turn right at the junction with Mill Mountain Trail. This spot completes the Mill Mountain/Little Stony Creek loop.

17.1 Turn right onto Pond Run Trail and head down the mountain stream valley. Take time as you descend to notice how different the trees and terrain seem. You climbed this trail at the start of the hike, but it seems a different trail altogether as you descend.

19.5 Arrive back at Waites Run Road.

HIKE INFORMATION

Local Information
Hardy County (WV) Convention & Visitors Bureau, (304) 897-8700, www.visithardywv.com

LOCAL ATTRACTIONS
Lost River Trading Post, a gallery featuring local art, crafts and woodworking, plus baked goods and coffee, (304) 897-8700, www.lostrivertradingcompany.com

Lodging
For a comprehensive list of lodging, visit www.visithardywv.com.

Hawk National Recreation Area, a no-fee national forest campground near Wardensville, WV. Lee Ranger District, (540) 984-4101. Open mid-Apr through mid-Dec. No water or electric.

Restaurants
Kac-Ka-Pon Restaurant, Wardensville, WV, (304) 874-3232. Country home cooking. Open Wed–Sat 7 a.m. to 8 p.m., Sun 11 a.m. to 4 p.m..

Organizations
Potomac Appalachian Trail Club (PATC), Vienna, (703) 242-0315, www.patc.net. The PATC's North Mountain Brigade oversees trail maintenance along Great North Mountain.

18 STEPHENS TRAIL

Camp Roosevelt opened in 1933 as America's first Civilian Conservation Corps camp. Living in tents and earning $30 a week, unemployed men built the roads, campgrounds, picnic shelters, and fire towers we still use today. Their handiwork included a limestone block tower and shelter on Kennedy Peak. Its squat, low-rising design often surprises hikers expecting a tall lookout, but it's still high enough to give commanding views off the 2,600-foot Kennedy Peak. Eastward lies Page Valley and to the west Shenandoah Valley, both outlined with patchwork farms, towns, and forests.

Start: Camp Roosevelt Recreation Area in a trailhead parking lot just east of the campground
Distance: 8.3-mile loop
Hiking time: About 5 hours
Difficulty: Moderate, with a few steep climbs, loose rocks, and most of the trail following old logging roads
Trail surface: Dirt footpaths and dirt forest roads lead to ridgetops, forest coves, and the craggy Kennedy Peak, with views of the Blue Ridge and Allegheny Mountains
Land status: National forest
Nearest town: Edinburg, VA
Other trail users: Mountain bikers, equestrians, cross-country skiers, and hunters (in season)
Accessibility: The 0.5-mile Lions Tale Accessible Trail is just a few miles south of Camp Roosevelt on FR 274 (Crisman Hollow Road).

Canine compatibility: Dogs permitted
Trail contact: Lee Ranger District, Edinburg, (540) 984-4101, www.fs .usda.gov/gwj
Schedule: Trail parking open year-round. Camp Roosevelt is open May through Oct for primitive camping. Hunting is permitted in national forests, with the busiest season Nov to early Jan.
Fees/permits: Camping fee, cash or check only
Facilities/features: Camp Roosevelt has campsites with vault toilets, but no water, so you must bring your own.
NatGeo TOPO! map: Hamburg, Luray, Rileyville, Edinburg
NatGeo Trails Illustrated map: Massanutten and Great North Mountains; Shenandoah National Park

FINDING THE TRAILHEAD

From I-81 in Edinburg, take exit 279. Turn east on VA 675. At the intersection of US 11 and VA 675 in the center of Edinburg, turn left onto US 11. Make another right to turn back onto VA 675 at the north end of Edinburg. Follow VA 675 for 5.9 miles over Massanutten Mountain to a stop sign at Kings Crossing. Turn right and continue on VA 675 for 3.4 miles to intersection of VA 675, FR 274, and VA 730. Turn left, still on VA 675. Camp entrance is 0.3 mile up, on the left side of the road. Trailhead parking lot is just past the camp on the left. **GPS:** N38 43.883' / W78 31.024'. *DeLorme: Virginia Atlas & Gazetteer*: Page 73, C7; Page 74, B1.

THE HIKE

Spotted wintergreen's tolerance of poor soil makes this exotic-looking plant stand out amid the otherwise drab mountain slope leading to Kennedy Peak. From the flower's telltale green-and-white leaves rises a single, top-heavy stem crowned by five white petals that arc backward. To see the green plug-like pistil and pale yellow stamens, gently lift the flower and peek beneath.

Dry forest conditions breed more than curious-looking wildflowers. They breed forest fires, the threat of which prompted Jack Stephens to walk from his home in Fort Valley to Kennedy Peak on a regular basis. Stephens's route up Kennedy Peak varied little. From Fort Valley, he climbed on switchbacks to a small saddleback between what is now called Stephens Pass. Turning right, he walked atop the narrow Massanutten Ridge, then made his way up the steep, rocky hill to the fire tower.

Stephens's route is now engraved into the slope of Massanutten Mountain by a generation of hikers and horseback riders. Blueberries and scrub oak crowd the forest understory, a monotone landscape highlighted in places by very colorful spotted wintergreen. Grouse and turkeys and deer inhabit this woodland, too. In the saddlebacks between small knobs, grass grows waist-high. Trees are spaced and signs of old orchards and stone walls are visible.

The advantages of a tower on Kennedy Peak are clear from the moment you ascend. Massanutten Mountain stretches 55 miles from Front Royal to Harrisonburg, and along its entire length there are few if any steep or dramatic interruptions. Kennedy Peak is the exception, sticking up 200 feet from the main trunk just before the ridge descends to a small gap. The knob, barren of trees, affords unblocked views in all directions. If you could peer back in time from here as well, you would witness a time when local wardens received $5 a year to monitor fire activity in a newly created national forest. The period was World War I, and two forest units existed in northern Virginia, the Massanutten and Potomac Districts. To build pride and win over suspicious locals, the forest supervisor fostered a rivalry between them. From 1913 to 1916 wardens from each side met for a tug-of-war at the Shenandoah County Fair. The winner took home bragging rights and a wooden Forest Service shield. The rivalry ended in 1917 when the two districts merged. (For the record, Massanutten District won the tug-of-war twice, Potomac once. Both regions fall within the present-day Lee Ranger District.)

Where Stephens Trail retraces the footsteps of one man, a different route to Kennedy Peak, on the Massanutten East Trail out of Camp Roosevelt, follows the steps of hundreds of men. The first Civilian Conservation Corps camp opened at Camp Roosevelt in 1933, and for nearly a decade following, unemployed men and World War I veterans spread across what was then Shenandoah National Forest (the name was later changed to George Washington National Forest to avoid confusion with Shenandoah National Park). Nicknamed Roosevelt's Tree Army, these men planted trees to replace the acres clear-cut for charcoal and timber. To build the Kennedy Peak fire tower, they carried limestone blocks quarried from the mountains.

Limestone proved a valuable commodity for others, too: Early American blast furnaces required limestone to make pig iron. Along Stephens Trail, hikers can see clearly the red cake-like rocks, some the size of bricks, that iron ore producers craved. These stones are hematite-laden; the red color ensured prospectors that the rocks would produce good-quality iron. They were carted off to local blast furnaces, where molten pig iron flowed out of the bottom of the furnace into molds for pots and kettles and tools.

During the Civil War, blast furnaces shifted production. Out of mountain ironworks such as Elizabeth Furnace and Catherine Furnace came the bullets, cannons, and guns that supplied Confederate troops. General Stonewall Jackson stated, "If the Valley is lost, Virginia is lost," and embarked on the Valley Campaign of 1862 to ensure that wouldn't happen. Battles at Kernstown, McDowell, Cross Keys, and Front Royal kept the valley

View from Kennedy Peak HEATHER KUBICK

in Confederate hands until 1864, when Northern general Philip Sheridan began sweeping through the Shenandoah Valley, burning homes, looting supplies, and slaughtering livestock.

The best view from Kennedy Peak lies west, across the northern Shenandoah Valley. This is the valley traveled by Quakers and Scots-Irish from Pennsylvania and Maryland in the early 1700s. With their arrival, two Virginias evolved. In coastal regions, a few wealthy landowners controlled land and an economy based on tobacco and slave labor. Mountain Virginia reflected the religious fervor of German and Scots-Irish immigrants. Wheat fared better here than tobacco, due in part to limestone-rich soil. Nicknames for these two Virginians developed: Easterners were Tuckahoes, a term derived from the arum root that grows around marshes; western Virginians were Cohees, slang derived from "Quothe he," a reflection of the settlers' strong religious backgrounds.

From the Cohees' valley towns, Massanutten Mountain appears as a single, continuous ridge. At its northern reach, the bedrock divides into two ridges separated by a bowl-like depression called Fort Valley. In the 1700s, English colonists built a fort here for trading and protection against the French and Native Americans. The boast "Washington Slept Here" rings true in Fort Valley and neighboring towns such as Winchester and Front Royal. These mountains and valley were a proving ground for the young George Washington, who first visited as a surveyor for Lord Fairfax, and then as an officer in the Virginia militia.

The views off Kennedy Peak show that a century of human progress has erased physical signs of the destruction of the past. The whole of Massanutten Mountain appears separate from the valley that unfolds at its feet. In reality, it is just the opposite. You cannot remove the mountain from the valley. Nor would it seem right to do so.

MILES AND DIRECTIONS

0.0 Start at the parking lot just east of the entrance to Camp Roosevelt. Turn left onto the orange-blazed Massanutten East Trail. It climbs uphill past the white forest gate.

0.1 Enter a clearing, turn right, and climb on the Massanutten East Trail. The trail passes under a set of power lines several times and narrows from a dirt road into a footpath. **Note:** There is an equipment shed in the clearing. The trail that leads straight past the shed is Stephens Trail, the return leg of this loop.

0.7 The trail reaches VA 675. Turn left and walk 50 yards up the left side of the road, reentering the woods on a forest road. There is an impressive view over Fort Valley on the side of VA 675.

1.8 Massanutten East Trail branches right from the dirt road to circumvent a knob. In 0.2 mile, the trail repeats this pattern. There are nice views here, across Fort Valley to Massanutten Mountain's west ridge.

2.1 Pass a campsite on the right side of the trail. Kennedy Peak is visible at this point.

2.3 The trail switchbacks northwest amid a rock slide.

2.4 Where the trail bends right around the side of Kennedy Peak, there are good views west over Fort Valley. At shoulder height on your right side, thick slabs of sedimentized rock stick out of the hillside at a 45-degree angle.

3.1 Reach the spur trail to Kennedy Peak. Turn right and make the short, 0.2-mile uphill trek to a stone shelter/lookout tower constructed by the Civilian Conservation Corps stationed at Camp Roosevelt in the 1930s. Return to the Massanutten East Trail and hike north atop the ridge.

3.9 Where the trail drops briefly off the right side of a knob, look for exposed sections of rock that show the layered sandstone rock formations. This is Massanutten sandstone, light gray and highly resistant rock.

4.1 Stephens Trail branches left while Massanutten East Trail continues a northward route to Elizabeth Furnace. Turn left onto Stephens Trail and make a beeline through open hardwood forest. Where the downslope pitch steepens, the trail switches back to descend along the northwest flank of Massanutten Mountain. Watch for red flinty rocks underfoot, indicative of the iron ore deposits found in the mountain bedrock.

5.2 As you wrap around a shoulder ridge and begin a lateral descent on the wavy course of Stephens Trail, there are good views over Fort Valley west. For 2 miles, the trail will alternate between moist coves and exposed hillsides as it crosses the many unnamed tributaries of Passage Creek, which flows through Fort Valley, a basin formed by the east and west ridges of Massanutten Mountain.

8.2 Enter a clearing and hike straight past a junction with the Massanutten East Trail. The equipment shed is on your right.

8.3 Return to the parking lot on VA 675.

HIKE INFORMATION

Local Information

Shenandoah Valley Travel Association, New Market, (800) VISIT-SV, www.visit shenandoah.org

Local Events/Attractions

Edinburg Ole' Time Festival, held in Sept, (540) 984-7272, http://edinburgole timefestival.org

Camp Roosevelt was the site of the first Civilian Conservation Corps Camp, built in 1933.

Luray Caverns, Luray, (540) 743-6551, www.luraycaverns.com. One of several commercial caves in the Shenandoah Valley. Guided tours available.

Lodging

Camp Roosevelt has fee camping near the trailhead, open late May through Oct, operated by the Lee Ranger District of the national forest. Vault toilets, no water, no hookups. (540) 984-4104.

Fort Valley Lodge has camping, cabins, and horseback riding, (540) 9336633, www .fortvalleystable.com

Restaurants

Edinburg Mill Restaurant, (540) 984-8898, www.edinburgmillrestaurant, is located in a historic 1848 mill with a winery and cultural heritage museum on site.

Organizations

Potomac Appalachian Trail Club (PATC), Vienna, (703) 242-0315, www.patc.net
Civilian Conservation Corps Legacy, www.ccclegacy.org

19 LAUREL FORK AREA

Laurel Fork was proposed for wilderness protection in 2004, but dropped in 2011, due in part to opposition from inholders—private property owners inside national forest boundaries. Fortunately, most of it is managed as a Special Biological Area, offering a measure of protection, particularly from gas mining. The desire to keep this place forever wild is understandable. There's a whiff of spruce in the air. Songbirds trill and peep in the bushes. Pine needles pile thick on the forest floor. Streams wriggle around and over the deadfall and boulders strewn in their path by storms and hurricanes. Native trout swim the Laurel Fork. It has been a long 70 years since loggers cleared the red spruce and fir trees. Nature has reclaimed Laurel Fork fully, and for this, we're all better off.

Start: Locust Springs Day Use Area
Distance: 11.2-mile double loop
Hiking time: About 6 hours
Difficulty: Moderate due to numerous stream crossings and steep trails up Middle Mountain that merge with streambeds. Because of its elevation, Laurel Fork receives heavy snowfall in winter.
Trail surface: Dirt footpaths and old forest roads wind through high-altitude red spruce forests and stream coves.
Land status: National forest
Nearest town: Monterey, VA
Other trail users: Mountain bikers, equestrians, and hunters (in season)
Accessibility: None

Canine compatibility: Dogs permitted
Trail contact: Warm Springs Ranger District, Hot Springs, (540) 839-2521, www.fs.usda.gov/gwj
Schedule: Open year-round. Hunting is permitted in national forests, with deer season running from Nov through early Jan.
Fees/permits: None.
Facilities/features: The Locust Springs Day Use Area has a vault toilet, but no drinking water.
NatGeo TOPO! map: Thornwood, Snowy Mountain
NatGeo Trails Illustrated map: Staunton, Shenandoah Mountain

FINDING THE TRAILHEAD

From Monterey, drive west on US 250. In 22 miles, turn right onto WV 28 and drive north for 6.7 miles. Turn right onto FR 60/FR 106, following signs for Locust Springs Day Use Area. In 0.3 mile, bear left onto FR 60. At a second intersection in 0.3 mile, bear right and uphill, following signs for Locust Springs Picnic Area. The picnic area is on the right on FR 142 in 0.4 mile. **GPS:** N38 35.129' / W79 38.527'. *DeLorme: Virginia Atlas & Gazetteer*: Page 64 (inset), A1.

THE HIKE

Laurel Fork is a classic mountain stream, appreciation of which requires little effort. A big boulder helps. Sit on the rock and stare. In early morning hours a haze wraps around overhanging branches. Spray tossed up by the water sparkles. And just like that, an entire day watching birds flit from branch to branch seems a reasonable proposition.

It would, however, preclude exploration of the 10,000 acres in Laurel Fork Special Management Area. The steep west slope of Middle Mountain beckons. Up Christian

Laurel Fork area in the fall NATIONAL FOREST SERVICE

Run or Cold Spring Run, the narrow footpaths are overrun with rhododendron. Trails and creeks intermingle without regard. The moss is spongy. There's a dank smell of moist, decomposing leaves. When the trails widen, the earth buckles and ripples where railroad ties were once embedded. Laurel Fork was privately owned until 1922. Railroads chugged up and down the mountain slopes carrying workers in and logs out. Today's trail network follows these grades, and rusted cast-iron remains of old railroad engine parts lie near the junction of Bearwallow Trail and Laurel Fork Trail.

Loggers were after the red spruce that gives Laurel Fork a unique aura. Much of it went to pulp mills. The highest-quality boards, craftsmen used in musical instruments; they preferred spruce to other woods because of its consistent growth patterns. Consider that a felled tree exhibits growth rings of varying size. Thick rings indicate the salad years, when sunlight and water were plentiful. Narrow rings reflect leaner times. Spruce somehow avoids these highs and lows; its growth rings are almost always the same size and compact, two qualities favorable for musical instruments. (Another interesting aside: The older the instrument, the better it sounds—but that's only if it's played, not left under glass to age. Wood becomes elastic with vibration, so an old wood instrument can sound as poor as one made of "green" wood if left untouched.)

For a hiker whose exposure to needle-leaf trees extends from jack pine to hemlock, a spruce forest can seem like an altered state. Technically, Laurel Fork is an "Appalachian extension of a northern boreal forest." Nontechnically speaking, it's cold, snows like crazy in winter, and harbors animals normally found farther north. If you're lucky, a snowshoe hare might hop across the trail. The distribution map for this animal shows a shaded area over all of Canada and parts of Minnesota, Wisconsin, and New York. The map also shows fingerlike extensions reaching down the chain of Appalachian Mountains as far south as the Great Smoky Mountains in Tennessee. This sums up nicely the whole boreal forest effect. Glaciers never reached as far south as Virginia (as indicated by the dearth of natural lakes). But even if the ice never made it, the northern species of trees and animals suited for that environment did.

Buck Run Trail is a good introduction to the habitat. From Locust Springs Picnic Area the trail leads first past beaver dams. In the backwaters of all the major drainages—Buck Run, Slabcamp Run, and Bearwallow Run—you'll find sizable beaver populations.

Their handiwork is not confined to dams. Spring-time finds logs felled across trails; the gnawed pointed trunk gives away the culprit. The shallow ponds created by the dams are thick with salamanders and frogs and the shrill of spring peepers.

HEADS UP
The trail may or may not be maintained, and blazes may be sparse, so hike at your own risk.

One of the trees you'll see along with the red spruce is the Fraser fir. In 1784 the tree's namesake, John Fraser, a Scotsman, sailed into Charleston hoping to follow in the footsteps of his contemporaries, William Bartram and Andre Michaux, botanists who made names for themselves studying the flora and fauna of the Southern Appalachians. Fraser was an amateur, primarily concerned with making a fortune (why he chose botany as a career is a mystery). He roamed the Southern Appalachians collecting specimens for the highest bidder. His short list at times included the king of England, Catherine the Great of Russia, and her successor, Czar Paul. For a brief period, Fraser and Michaux traveled together, but their competing interest (Michaux was sending samples to Louis XVI of France) soon caused them to part company. Michaux let Fraser travel ahead, and, as a result, Fraser had the good fortune of being the first to discover the tree that now bears his name.

Nature is an exact science, down to the arrangement of needles on a red spruce branch. Clusters of needles minimize heat loss and keep the tree branch warm through the winter. The interlocking branches weave a canopy that blocks out sun and lends everything below a gloomy aspect. Thick piles of fallen needles mat the forest floor. Moist green sphagnum moss covers roots and rocks. Besides moss, little else grows under a mature spruce-fir forest canopy. It's a vicious little circle, whereby needles and moss give the soil a high acid content, and the acid soil in turn slows decomposition. The moss, especially, thrives by coating dead logs and whatever else will host it.

The red spruce that dominate in Laurel Fork are well suited for life here. The soil is thin, a product of years of logging and erosion. The tree spreads wide, shallow roots into this soil. Porcupines like to nibble on the sweet bark of these trees, while red squirrels seem adept at extracting seeds from cones. Berry shrubs sprout and survive to feed a host of birds and small rodents through the lean winter months. Bearberry and prickly gooseberry mingle with the more readily identified high- and low-bush blueberries.

When West Virginia seceded from Virginia after the outbreak of the Civil War, it took with it some of the roughest natural terrain on the East Coast. Virginia's valleys and ridges seem downright pastoral when compared to the jumble of peaks, cliffs, and ridges that form the Allegheny Mountains in West Virginia. Virginia can at least take some comfort in having kept this corner of Highland County and the Laurel Fork watershed.

LAUREL FORK AREA

MILES AND DIRECTIONS

0.0 Start at the Locust Springs Day Use Area. Walk up a dirt road at the east end of the picnic area. Almost immediately, look for a gated forest road on the right, marked with blue blazes and a hiker sign. This is the Buck Run trailhead. Turn right, pass by the gate, and follow the road.

0.4 Turn left off the grass road. Pass through a stand of red spruce. The ground is flat and the trail is now a dirt singletrack. There are several beaver dams in this area. **Note:** Buck Run Spur Trail is straight ahead on the grass road.

1.3 The trail descends off the side of Buck Knob and switchbacks five times as it drops to Buck Run.

1.6 Cross Buck Run and walk downstream following the left bank. In 0.1 mile, re-cross Buck Run to the right stream bank. **Note:** From now until the junction with Laurel Fork Trail, note how the slopes on either stream bank host starkly different plants: The left slope is covered with rhododendron, while the right supports more hardwoods, and sparse at that. Many exposed rock formations on this leg make it a geologist's delight, amateur or otherwise.

3.0 Buck Run Trail ends at a junction with the Laurel Fork Trail. Turn left onto Laurel Fork Trail and cross the stream. After crossing, turn left and hike downstream. (In the river floodplain, yellow sundrops may be in bloom. Pink lady slippers and the white bell-shaped flowers of Solomon's seal grow near the edge of the forest. Red elderberry displays its fruit in August.) **Note:** From the end of Buck Run Trail, Laurel Fork Trail also leads straight upstream and intersects Locust Springs Run Trail, Slab-camp Run Trail, and Christian Run Trail.

3.7 Turn right and ascend on the blue-blazed Cold Spring Run Trail. The trail joins the stream for a short stretch, then widens to show signs of an old railroad bed.

4.7 The ground levels on both sides of the trail as it enters a grassy meadow. **Note:** The fields on Meadow Mountain were cleared for grazing when the mountain was privately owned. Today, The Stamp, an inholding farther south on the mountain, remains the last piece of private property in the special management area.

4.9 Turn right onto Middle Mountain Trail, following blue blazes.

6.0 Pass a hunters' camp on the left, by a Forest Service gate. A large field opens up on your left. Turn right and walk through a meadow. Blue arrows on trees on the right fringe of the field will guide you to where the Christian Run Trail enters the woods.

6.7 The trail narrows and runs close to Christian Run. It crosses three times.

7.0 Christian Run Trail junctions with Laurel Fork Trail. Turn right and walk along the right stream bank.

7.4 Where Slabcamp Run Trail branches left and crosses Laurel Run, continue straight on Laurel Fork Trail. There are several good campsites on this stretch of trail, including one, just prior to crossing Laurel Fork, that overlooks a swimming hole.

7.6 Cross Laurel Fork and hike along the left stream bank.

7.8 Turn left onto Locust Spring Run Trail. The next 1.5 miles brings numerous stream crossings. In places, the stream and trail merge for some messy hiking.

9.9 Bear right and away from a left-branching trail, which is Locust Spring Run Spur Trail. It leads to FR 106.

11.2 Hike ends at the Locust Springs Day Use Area.

HIKE INFORMATION

Local Information
Highland County Visitor Center, 61 Highland Center Dr., Monterey; (540) 468-2550; www.highlandcounty.org

Local Events/Attractions
The Highland County Maple Festival, held in Mar, Monterey, (540) 468-2550, www.highlandcounty.org/maple-festival. Celebrates the opening of the trees with a festival and camp tours.

Lodging
Monterey Inn, (540) 495-0070, www.montereyinnva.com. Monterey's recently renovated historic hotel right on Main Street.

Restaurants
High's Restaurant, Main Street, Monterey, (540) 468-1700, www.highsrestaurant.com. This local institution serves lunch and dinner 7 days a week.

Organizations
Friends of Shenandoah Mountain, Mt. Crawford, (540) 234-6273, www.friendsof shenandoahmountain.org

In an inconspicuous corner of Botetourt County, seven peaks converge to form a backcountry nook where bears just may outnumber human visitors. The region's namesake, Roaring Run, pulses through a break in Rich Patch Mountain with force enough to have powered a blast iron furnace for half a century. Ruins of that furnace mark the beginning of a loop hike that takes you along the high, dry top of Pine Mountain, then down to headwaters of three small streams. Between ridgetop and riverbed spreads a forest that is as secluded as it is satisfying. For an easier, family-friendly hike, the 1.5-mile Roaring Run Falls Trail is well marked.

Start: Trail board next to the restrooms at Roaring Run Furnace National Recreation Area
Distance: 10.0-mile lollipop
Hiking time: About 5 hours
Difficulty: Moderate due to long climbs and length. The bushwhack up Pine Mountain requires skills in across-country hiking, including the ability to use a compass.
Trail surface: Dirt footpaths and old dirt roads lead along dry ridges, through extended fields of heath, boulder fields, and stream headwaters.
Land status: National forest
Nearest town: Clifton Forge, VA

Other trail users: Hikers only
Accessibility: None
Canine compatibility: Dogs permitted
Trail contact: Eastern Divide Ranger District, Blacksburg, (540) 552-4641, www.fs.usda.gov/gwj
Schedule: Open year-round, sunrise to sunset
Fees/permits: None
Facilities/features: Vault toilets and stream-side picnic sites; no drinking water
NatGeo TOPO! map: Strom
NatGeo Trails Illustrated map: Covington, Alleghany Highlands

FINDING THE TRAILHEAD

From Clifton Forge, drive west on I-64 to the Low Moor exit. Drive south on VA 696 and, in 0.1 mile, turn left onto VA 616. Drive 5.7 miles, then turn left onto VA 621 at Rich Patch Union Church. In 3.3 miles, turn right into the Roaring Run National Recreation Area. **GPS:** N37 42.400' / W79 53.594'. *DeLorme: Virginia Atlas & Gazetteer:* Page 52, C3.

THE HIKE

In 1804 William Clark, a man whose name would become synonymous with exploration, left the small town of Fincastle in Botetourt County, Virginia, for the unknown of the American frontier. He and friend Meriwether Lewis would lead the Corps of Discovery through the void of middle America to the Pacific Ocean, and back. Three years later, Clark returned to Fincastle a national hero. He settled and married the daughter of wealthy landowner George Hancock. Clark's journals from the Corps of Discovery expedition were stored and edited in Fincastle, in Hancock's home. In 1810 President Thomas Jefferson appointed him governor of the Missouri Territory, thus ending his Virginia residency. Clark departed for St. Louis and left behind a legend proudly guarded

On Roaring Run Trail to the falls

by Fincastlians, who are known to claim their town as the real point-of-embarkation for the Lewis and Clark expedition.

Fincastle, a town of roughly 300 souls, is as fitting a beginning for Clark's journey as any spot. For a brief period before the Revolutionary War, this town sat on the edge of the great unknown. The boundaries of Botetourt County, of which Fincastle was the county seat, stretched as far as the Mississippi and contained parts of seven present-day states. Standing atop Pine Mountain on a clear fall or winter day, you get a small sense of that vast landholding, where views stretch into West Virginia and in the imagination, if prodded, farther. And as is the case for all good explorations, getting to this secluded vista on Pine Mountain is as much a reason for going as the payoff.

The journey begins at Roaring Run Furnace, a national recreation area south of Clifton Forge in Botetourt County. The Iron Ore Trail climbs from the ruins of a blast furnace on old dirt roads and abandoned railroad grades. In a saddle between Shoemaker Knob and Iron Ore Knob, the trail turns and skirts the slope of Pine Mountain as a foot-path. If a hiker sticks to the blazed trails, the route eventually leads to a forested saddle of the Pine Mountain ridge. But there's an alternate route up Pine Mountain, a short, steep path—more a detour than a true bushwhack. Look for this route as you climb Hoop Hole Trail, less than 0.5 mile uphill from the T intersection with Iron Ore Trail. In a world of well-blazed, clearly defined paths, this side trail is a gift. Marked by infrequent plastic squares the size of a quarter, following it still requires hunt-and-peck skills. These are times a hiker falls back on basic skills: orientating; identifying telltale plants, deter-mining whether they are typical of a certain elevation or slope; and wondering who, or more precisely what, has walked here before you. (Lewis and Clark would be so proud.)

From Pine Mountain's first knob, a sight line carries southwest along the 3,000-foot-high ridge to a point where Pine Mountain buttresses against Rich Patch Mountain. Patches of stunted vegetation grow in thin shale soil on the upper slopes of the ridge. Berry bushes thrive here, where the larger, moisture-loving witch hazel will not. Wild grasses propagate in gaps of forest created by fire. Among the berry bushes, poverty oat grass grows in gray-green mats. Another grass, yellow sedge, is found on more gently graded slopes. Both grasses are present in early stages of forest recovery and may be

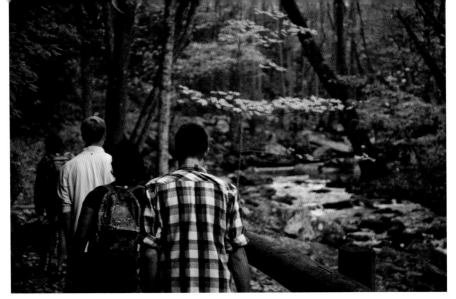

Autumn hikers on Roaring Run VTC/LUCAS MOORE

indicators of a recent fire. The shoots need only a thin soil cover and seem adaptable to the acidic, nutrient-deficient soil typical of dry, fire-ravaged areas.

So thick is the undergrowth at points, Hoop Hole Trail can become difficult to follow. At these times, it pays to watch for the red stone flakes that litter the trail; this color indicates the mineral hematite. Hematite is a principal iron ore mineral, and its presence, embedded in sandstone deposits formed 400 million years ago, helped catapult this region into a leading producer of iron ore during the second half of the 19th century.

Roaring Run Furnace, where this described loop begins, operated as a blast furnace for only 30 years. That's a short time in a region famous for iron production. The furnace's obscurity may explain, in a backhanded way, how it survived intact through the years. During the Civil War, Tredegar Iron Works leased Roaring Run as an insurance policy against losing its larger furnaces located in the Great Valley. Union forces eventually destroyed three of Tredegar's mines in an effort to disrupt the Confederate's supply of bullets, cannons, and gun parts. Tredegar, especially, held significance. From its Virginia furnaces, it produced the cannons at Fort Sumter, South Carolina, site of the first battle between North and South. And even Grace Furnace, an iron ore furnace 5 miles west of Roaring Run, fell to Union forces. It all points to a conclusion that Roaring Run survived because it wasn't producing iron ore. Tredegar's records show it blasted the furnace once, in 1865, just before the war ended. This inactivity made it an impractical target for Union forces.

Evidence of mining activity around Roaring Run Furnace is visible in the large depressions cut from the mountainside. In other spots, talus (rock piles) lie beneath gouged out chunks of hillside. For some unknown reason, the minerals around Roaring Run were never exploited to the extent they were elsewhere in Virginia. By 1870, Virginia iron furnaces were switching to a more efficient, coke-based fuel source. Charcoal-burning furnaces such as Roaring Run faded into obscurity. Given that a furnace consumed on average 750 bushels of charcoal in a single day—the equivalent of an acre of woodland—the furnace's inactivity once again held an unintended benefit. This time, it saved a beautiful corner of the forest from mining and logging—a benefit hikers can certainly appreciate.

MILES AND DIRECTIONS

0.0 Start from a trail board next to the restrooms at Roaring Run Furnace. Follow the wide, orange-blazed Iron Ore Trail under table mountain pines.

0.2 At a fork in the trail, bear left and climb on the Iron Ore Trail. Soon, the falls on Roaring Run are audible downhill on the right.

0.4 Pass under power lines.

0.7 At a T junction, turn left and follow the orange-blazed Iron Ore Trail, which is still a dirt road. **Note:** Avoid the road that leads straight from this intersection. It is marked with yellow blazes.

0.8 Pass a road that splits right and uphill away from Iron Ore Trail. In another 20 yards, Iron Ore Trail forks right onto a narrow trail leading uphill; bear right at this fork and follow the Iron Ore Trail uphill. It breaks from the woods to pass under power lines, then reenters the woods.

1.0 Switchback up the northeast slope of Iron Ore Mountain. Iron Ore Trail climbs steadily to a gap between Iron Ore (2,117 feet) and Shoemaker Knobs (2,429 feet).

Roaring Run iron ore furnace

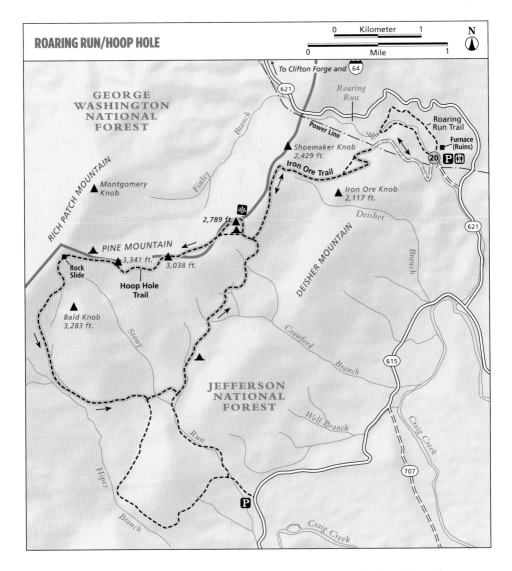

Iron Ore Trail is wide and well graded in sections where it follows old roads or railroad grades that date from a time in the 19th century when the blast furnace at Roaring Run was in operation.

1.7 At a double blaze, turn left and cross the dry creekbed of Deisher Branch.

2.0 Pass a campsite nicely situated in a large, flat clearing on the left side of Iron Ore Trail.

2.3 At a T intersection, turn right onto the yellow-blazed Hoop Hole Trail. **Note:** A left onto Hoop Hole leads along the lower elevations of Pine Mountain. It is the return leg of this loop hike.

2.5 Turn right on an overgrown path that leads sharply uphill. The route is marked with plastic yellow diamonds, about the size of a quarter, nailed into trees. Be alert: The trail is overgrown and hard to follow. Markers are small and infrequent. This route is a steep, 0.3-mile ascent of Pine Mountain's first knob (2,789 feet). In fall and winter, this peak provides the best views off the mountain into West Virginia. **Option:** The climb up Pine Mountain's first knob, while blazed, is difficult. A hiker can avoid it by continuing straight on the Hoop Hole Trail. A half-mile from this junction, Hoop Hole Trail enters a clearing in a saddle between Pine Mountain's first and second knobs. In this clearing, the route from Pine Mountain's first knob rejoins Hoop Hole Trail.

2.8   At the top of Pine Mountain's first knob, turn left onto an overgrown trail marked with faint yellow paint slashes. The trail descends. **Note:** This route description applies to hikers who followed the detour to Pine Mountain's first knob. Otherwise, see mileage cue 3.0.

3.0   Rejoin the Hoop Hole Trail in a saddle between Pine Mountain's first and second knobs. Hike straight on the Hoop Hole Trail along the top of the ridge as it climbs toward Pine Mountain's second knob.

3.5   Shale rock outcrops on the right mark the approach of Pine Mountain's second knob (3,038 feet). This stretch of trail is enveloped in waist-high berry bushes and mountain laurel.

3.8   Climb out of the gap between Pine Mountain's second and third knobs. Hoop Hole Trail stays left of the ridgetop.

4.1   Climb on Hoop Hole Trail to the spine of Pine Mountain. In a few hundred yards, reach a campsite. From this spot, Hoop Hole Trail drops gradually off the left side of Pine Mountain. **Note:** Another unmarked trail leads from this campsite up the spine of Pine Mountain and tops out on Rich Patch Mountain.

4.4   A mass of boulders marks the rocky joint of the Pine Mountain ridge and Rich Patch Mountain. Follow Hoop Hole Trail as it turns left and threads a gap between Rich Patch Mountain and Bald Knob.

5.7   Cross the headwaters of Hipes Branch.

6.4   Turn left at a T junction and follow Hoop Hole Trail. **Note:** A right turn at this T junction leads to parking on VA 615.

6.7   At a fork in the trail, bear left onto the yellow-blazed Hoop Hole Trail. **Note:** Bearing right at this fork leads to parking on VA 615.

8.0   Turn right onto Iron Ore Trail.

9.1   After descending along a section of trail with steep banks and a trough-like appearance, Iron Ore Trail bears right. Look straight into the woods for an ill-defined footpath marked with faint yellow-painted blazes. It descends to a power line cut in 0.1 mile. Follow the power line easement downhill to a T junction with a dirt road. Turn left onto this dirt road and, in 0.1 mile, turn left onto the Iron Ore Trail.

10.0   Hike ends at the trail board near the restrooms at Roaring Run Furnace.

HIKE INFORMATION

Local Information
Clifton Forge is a quaint, small town with several restaurants, shops, and B&Bs. www.visit cliftonforgeva.com

Roanoke is the closest large city, with lots of visitor amenities. Visit Virginia's Blue Ridge, (540) 342-6025, www.visitroanokeva.com

Local Events/Attractions
Clifton Forge Fall Foliage Festival, Oct, www.visitcliftonforgeva.com

Lodging
Firmstone Manor in Irondale was, appropriately for this hike, built by the ironmaster of the Irondale Furnace Company. (800) 474-9882, www.innatfirmstonemanor.com

HONORABLE MENTIONS: VALLEY & RIDGE

V. FRIDLEY GAP

Squeezed together accordion-like, the long, parallel ridges of First, Second, Third, and Fourth Mountains concentrate a number of different habitats. At the lower elevations, sunlight bathes stream valleys that attract deer to the water's edge. A half-mile away stands another world: the dry, barren ridgetops where views stretch for miles. Two different worlds, one hike. www.visitharrisonburgva.com/fridley-gap. **GPS:** N38 27.245' / W78 41.825'. *DeLorme: Virginia Atlas & Gazetteer.* Page 67, A6.

W. MASSANUTTEN MOUNTAIN WEST/SIGNAL KNOB

From Strasburg, drive east on VA 55 and then south on VA 678 to the Signal Knob Trail parking area on the right. This 17-mile hike climbs Signal Knob, then swings south down the western ridge of Massanutten and provides great views overlooking the Shenandoah Valley. Hike it as an out-and-back, or a point-to-point with a shuttle on VA 653 east of the village of Toms Brook. (540) 984-4101, www.fs.usda.gov/gwj. **GPS:** N38 56.119' / 78 19.197'. *DeLorme: Virginia Atlas & Gazetteer.* Page 74, A2.

X. MASSANUTTEN MOUNTAIN EAST/DUNCAN HOLLOW

Begin at Camp Roosevelt on VA 675. (See "Finding the trailhead" for Hike 18: Stephens Trail.) Duncan Hollow is a lesser-used portion of the Massanutten East Trail with great loop options using Peach Orchard Gap and Scothorn Gap. (540) 984-4101, www.fs.usda .gov/gwj. **GPS:** N38 43.819' / W78 31.073'. *DeLorme: Virginia Atlas & Gazetteer.* Page 73, C7.

Y. WILD OAK NATIONAL RECREATION TRAIL

This 25.4-mile loop trail begins near the North River Gorge area north of Churchville, off FR 95, 1 mile north of Stokesville. There are views off Little Bald Knob and difficult terrain past Todd Lake Recreation Area, a full-service national forest recreation area with a lake, campsite, and picnic area. The Wild Oak Loop intersects with trails leading into Ramsey's Draft Wilderness. (540) 432-0187. **GPS:** N38 20.361' / W79 12.446'. *DeLorme: Virginia Atlas & Gazetteer.* Page 66, B2.

Z. SHENANDOAH MOUNTAIN TRAIL/SOUTH

A 22-mile point-to-point hike that begins at the Confederate breastworks on VA 250, 17 miles west of Churchville. The southern end is on VA 627 (Scotchtown Draft Road), off VA 629. This difficult, high-ridge hike along the spine of Shenandoah Mountain is best done as a 2-day trip. (540) 885-8028. **GPS:** N38 18.675' / W79 23.053'. *DeLorme: Virginia Atlas & Gazetteer.* Page 65, B7.

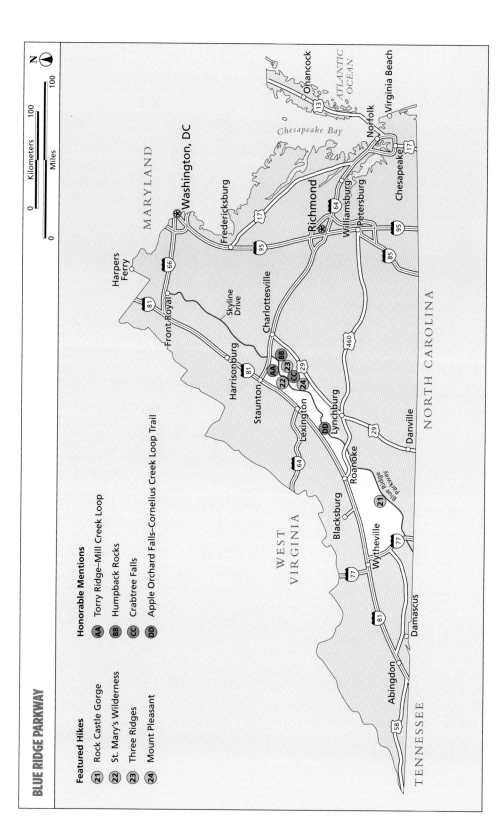

BLUE RIDGE PARKWAY

Featured Hikes

21 Rock Castle Gorge
22 St. Mary's Wilderness
23 Three Ridges
24 Mount Pleasant

Honorable Mentions

AA Torry Ridge–Mill Creek Loop
BB Humpback Rocks
CC Crabtree Falls
DD Apple Orchard Falls–Cornelius Creek Loop Trail

BLUE RIDGE PARKWAY

Climb the mountains and get their good tidings. Nature's peace will flow into you as sunshine flows into trees. The winds will blow their freshness into you, and the storms their energy, while cares will drop off like autumn leaves.
—John Muir, Our National Parks, 1901

Designer Stanley Abbott envisioned a roadway that "lay easy on the land," a route devoid of commercial traffic carrying motorists along six mountain ranges of the Appalachian chain, dropping into gaps and gracefully regaining the top of the Blue Ridge. Today, pull-offs link with more than 100 walking and hiking trails, from half-mile leg-stretchers to the great Georgia-to-Maine Appalachian Trail. The scene through the car window ranges from rolling pastures dotted with grazing cattle to dramatic granite domes.

One of the three Peaks of Otter, Sharp Top (milepost 83) was long revered as the state's highest peak at 3,875 feet. Its stone was used in DC's Washington Monument, which is inscribed: "From Otter's summit, Virginia's loftiest peak. To crown a monument to Virginia's noblest son."

The view from the top of Mount Pleasant

Sharp Top was once thought to be the highest peak in Virginia.

When geologists later measured Mount Rogers in southwest Virginia, they declared that 5,729-foot peak tallest. But mere numbers do little to diminish inspiring views from atop Sharp Top (unrivaled even by Mount Rogers, whose summit is tree-covered). A short, lung-busting climb ends at panoramic views of the surrounding peaks and valleys. Far below, dense forest is interrupted only by the Peaks of Otter Lodge on tranquil Abbott Lake, named for the Parkway's designer.

Sharp Top is a monument in itself, memorializing the sweat and talent of immigrant stoneworkers who fashioned elaborate steps to its peak. Out-of-work masons were given the task during the Depression. Their beautiful arched bridges, tunnels, retaining walls and paths, all using native stone, can be seen throughout the park.

Many other Parkway hikes are "top-down." Rock Castle Gorge (milepost 167) epitomizes this, beginning along the Parkway in quiet pastures and dropping into the deep, quiet world of an Appalachian cove forest. You can spend the night in one of the primitive campsites alongside Rock Castle Creek, a stream that powered six sawmills around 1910, when upwards of seventy families lived in this "holler."

Grazing cattle are still a common sight along the Parkway, with pastures leased out to approximately 500 families. There's intentionally a sense of "no boundaries" to the park, with farmland instead of fences at the Parkway's outskirts.

THE HIKES
21. Rock Castle Gorge
22. St. Mary's Wilderness
23. Three Ridges
24. Mount Pleasant

HONORABLE MENTIONS
AA. Torry Ridge–Mill Creek Loop
BB. Humpback Rocks
CC. Crabtree Falls
DD. Apple Orchard Falls–Cornelius Creek Loop Trail

21 ROCK CASTLE GORGE

This strenuous loop begins innocently enough: in the cow pasture and mountain balds that flank the Blue Ridge Parkway. Its true nature soon reveals itself as you descend some 1,800 feet in just 3 miles to the edge of bubbling, rock-strewn Rock Castle Creek. The hillsides and stream valley of this national recreation area harbored a sizable community of mountain settlers leading up to the Great Depression; evidence of their homes—vine-encased foundations, clearings, and fruit trees—are visible throughout the trip. After a walk along the lush streambed, the return to the Parkway will be sure to prompt that age-old hiker question: Which is more difficult, hiking uphill or downhill?

Start: Rocky Knob Campground, milepost 167 on the Blue Ridge Parkway

Distance: 10.6-mile loop

Hiking time: About 7 hours, with option of an overnight

Difficulty: Strenuous due to steep grades

Trail surface: Dirt footpaths, old fire roads, and streamside paths

Land status: National recreation area

Nearest town: Floyd, VA

Other trail users: Anglers and hunters (in season)

Accessibility: None

Canine compatibility: Leashed dogs allowed, but make sure they are in good shape for the steep and rocky portions.

Trail contacts: Blue Ridge Parkway Headquarters, (828) 348-3400, www.nps.gov/blri; visitor Information recorded message: (828) 298-0398; Rocky Knob Campground, (540) 745-9664

Schedule: The Blue Ridge Parkway and trails are open year-round, but trails and the Parkway may close in inclement weather.

Fees/permits: No entrance fee. A free permit is required to use the backcountry campsite along Rock Castle Creek. Obtain permit at the Rocky Knob Campground (540-745-9664) Memorial Day through Oct, call (540) 745-9660 for a permit Nov–May

Facilities/features: None on the trail. Rocky Knob Contact Center has a gift shop and restrooms. For Rocky Knob Campground (milepost 167), make reservations at www.recreation.gov. Half the campsites are available on a first-come, first-served basis.

NatGeo TOPO! map: Woolwine

Other maps: Rocky Knob hiking map is available in the hiking section of www.nps.gov/blri.

FINDING THE TRAILHEAD

From Floyd, drive south on VA 8 for 5.8 miles. At Tuggle Gap, turn left onto the southbound entrance of the Blue Ridge Parkway and go 1.8 miles to the entrance of the Rocky Knob Campground. Park along the roadside near the entrance to the campground; park with all four wheels of vehicle off the pavement. Alternate parking is available at Saddle Overlook, on the northbound side of the Parkway 0.9 mile south of the campground entrance. A leg of the Rock Castle Gorge Trail links Saddle Overlook with the trailhead described in this hike. If the Parkway is closed, hikers can access the streamside section of Rock Castle Gorge Trail via CC Camp Road off VA 8, 3.5 miles south of Tuggle Gap. **Rocky Knob Campground Trailhead GPS:** N36 49.878' / W80 20.658'. *DeLorme: Virginia Atlas & Gazetteer*: Page 25, B7.

Top: The author on a rest break
Bottom: A foggy day hiking among cattle on Rock Castle Gorge Trail

THE HIKE

Coves are some of the most sheltered, protected pockets of the Appalachian forests, found on steep mountain terrain and infused with rich flora. While famous for its profusion of spring wildflowers, by late summer the gorge's mesic habitat sports a single color—green—albeit with many subtle variations to be found between club moss, ferns, laurel, trees, and grass.

Add to this thick vegetation rain-dripping mistiness, and a journey up Rock Castle Gorge can take on a near Middle Earth quality. Combine this with the pastoral beauty of its mountain bald meadows, and you get the sense that the 10.6-mile loop has all the ingredients for a classic Blue Ridge adventure.

The hike off the ridge begins gently enough, but soon demands full attention. The slope to the left drops off with cliff-like severity and the trail narrows into a billy goat path. Tree roots become steps and handholds that help prevent hikers from tripping.

When it's over, treat yourself to a good, foot-numbing soak in Rock Castle Creek. Measuring about 15 feet wide, this stream in late summer doesn't show the strong flow that once enabled it to power six sawmills in the gorge. Around 1910, upwards of seventy families lived here along the creek or in smaller hollows up in the hills.

A locally published memoir, *Little Boy Blue,* recounts Robert Blue's years growing up in this gorge, or "hollow," as locals referred to it (the term *gorge* was tacked on by the US Park Service). Blue's family grew fruit trees on the hillside and sold the harvest in the surrounding towns. While lore and legend play up the famous Appalachian lawlessness of moonshiners and their ilk, I like Blue's stereotype-busting image of a hardworking family. Judging by the ruins we found, homes in the gorge were small, basically a place to sleep and eat, with time in between spent scraping out a living, or in the case of the young boy Blue, exploring nature in a beautiful hollow.

The gorge is a perfect place to spend a day with a good book, lying in a hammock slung up by the creek. Camping is limited to this one spot along the river, which leaves 2-night campers a whole day for exploring hillsides for specimens of the stream's namesake—quartzite rock formations that early settlers thought resembled rock castles. Rock Castle is a catch-and-release trout stream as well; two fly fishermen passed by camp and gave good reports from the small pools higher up.

The hike out of the gorge is all uphill. *Euphoria* wouldn't be too strong a description of how it feels to pass out of the cove environment into cow pastures that flank the Blue Ridge Parkway. The scene is reminiscent of the famous mountain balds along this same parkway in North Carolina's high country.

The final climb up Rocky Knob (elevation 3,572 feet) is a fitting ending to the hike, offering a majestic view of the gorge you've journeyed through. Rock Castle Gorge viewed from this height looks like a deep gash in the mountain, wrapped in clouds of mystery.

MILES AND DIRECTIONS

0.0   Start from the Rocky Knob Campground (milepost 167). Cross the Blue Ridge Parkway and pass through a fence stile. Turn left and follow signs for the green-blazed Rock Castle Gorge Trail. **Note:** If you are starting from alternate Saddle Overlook parking area (milepost 168), it is a 0.7-mile hike north to this start point.

2.3   After a long descent, begin paralleling Little Rock Castle Creek.

ROCK CASTLE GORGE

0 — Kilometer — 1
0 — Mile — 1

N

21
Fence
Stile

Rocky
Knob

Rock Castle Gorge Trail

Little Rock Castle Creek

?

ROCKY KNOB
RECREATION AREA

Blue Ridge Parkway

Rock Castle Gorge Trail

Floyd / Patrick

Grassy
Knoll

Private
Property

Rock Castle Creek

Rock Castle Gorge Trail

3.0 Your 1,800-foot descent off the Blue Ridge Parkway ends at Rock Castle Creek. Turn right on the green-blazed Rock Castle Gorge Trail, which now follows an old fire road up the stream valley.

3.2 Pass a backcountry camp on the right. ***Note:*** A permit is required to camp here. See "Fees/permits" in the hike specs.

4.5 Pass through a private inholding in the Rocky Knob Recreation Area. This is the site of an abandoned but well-cared-for two-story home.

5.6 Veer right off the fire road and descend a singletrack woods path to the water's edge. Cross Rock Castle Gorge Creek and begin a long ascent to the Parkway.

5.8 Pass through a boulder field of large, house-size rocks.

7.0 Pass through a fence and enter a cow pasture. The trail here is marked by posts with arrows.

8.7 Continue straight at a junction with the blue-blazed Black Ridge Trail on the left.

9.3 Veer right and follow green blazes as you begin climbing Rocky Knob. ***Note:*** The trail straight ahead at this junction returns to the Saddle Overlook parking area in 0.5 mile.

9.8 Reach the summit of Rocky Knob.

10.1 Pass the Saddle Overlook on the left.

10.6 Arrive back at the fence stile across from the entrance to Rocky Knob Campground.

HIKE INFORMATION

Local Information
The great little town of Floyd has a general store that doubles as a bluegrass venue, the Floyd Hotel, and many shops. Floyd County Tourism Office, 108 E. Main St., Floyd; (540) 745-4407; www.visitfloydva.com

Local Events/Attractions
The picturesque and historic Mabry Mill is a working gristmill with adjacent blacksmith shop and cabin, picnic area, and visitor center, just 9 miles north at milepost 176. There's also a restaurant and gift shop, (276) 952-2947, www.mabrymillrestaurant.com, open seasonally from Apr to early Nov.

Lodging
Rocky Knob Campground, milepost 167, has tent and RV sites, restrooms, but no hook-ups or showers. Open May through Oct. Reservations: (877) 444-6777, www.recreation .gov

Restaurants
Floyd Country Store, 206 Locust St., Floyd; (540) 745-4563; www.floydcountrystore .com. A true Appalachian experience of food, shopping, and live music.

Organizations
Friends of Blue Ridge Parkway, (800) 228-PARK, www.friendsbrp.org

Other Resources
Hiker registration and maps are available at Rocky Knob Contact Center, milepost 169, (540) 745-9660.

22 ST. MARY'S WILDERNESS

There are two types of Virginia hikers: those who have visited St. Mary's Wilderness and those who soon will; more people visit this 10,000-acre plot of protected wild land on the western slope of the Blue Ridge than any other Virginia wilderness. Easy access to the premier attraction, St. Mary's Falls, ensures this won't change any time soon. And a beauty this waterfall is—a wide, 15-foot drop into a deep, narrow gorge replete with massive river boulders and mountain laurel. Our route takes a lesser-known approach to the wilderness, where beauty of a subtler nature lies deeper into the folds of the Blue Ridge. Take the time to explore a bit farther.

Start: Gravel parking lot opposite Fork Mountain Overlook, milepost 23 on the Blue Ridge Parkway
Distance: 10.6-mile loop
Hiking time: About 7 hours
Difficulty: Moderate due to the hike length and the steep grades along Mine Bank Branch
Trail surface: Dirt roads and footpaths traverse steep mountain slopes, upland meadows, and waterfalls.
Land status: National forest and wilderness area
Nearest town: Steeles Tavern, VA

Other trail users: Cross-country skiers and hunters (in season)
Accessibility: None
Canine compatibility: Dogs permitted
Trail contact: Glenwood-Pedlar Ranger District, Natural Bridge Station, (540) 291-2188, www.fs.usda .gov/gwj
Schedule: Open year-round
Fees/permits: None
Facilities/features: None
NatGeo TOPO! maps: Big Levels, Vesuvius
NatGeo Trails Illustrated map: Lexington, Blue Ridge Mts

FINDING THE TRAILHEAD

From Steeles Tavern, drive east on VA 56. In the town of Vesuvius, the road turns left, crosses railroad tracks, and continues east. After a long stretch of winding road and switchbacks, VA 56 junctions with the Blue Ridge Parkway 5.6 miles from Steeles Tavern. Proceed north on the Blue Ridge Parkway for 3.8 miles. At the Fork Mountain Overlook (milepost 23), turn left into a gravel parking lot. There is room for eight to ten cars. **GPS:** N37 54.682' / W79 05.202'. *DeLorme: Virginia Atlas & Gazetteer*: Page 54, A2.

THE HIKE

People visit St. Mary's Wilderness for one overriding reason: waterfalls. The largest, on St. Mary's River, impresses not so much with height as with width and power. Farther upstream, smaller cascades await in the mountain gullies that feed the river. In these sheltered coves, rock and water interact in subtler ways, as on Mine Bank Branch, where the stream glistens and shines as it tumbles down step-falls. It's a small reminder why the path less traveled can sometimes be the most rewarding.

The hunt for waterfalls leads farther up into the wilderness. Small streams run off Mine Bank Mountain, Bald Knob, Big Levels, and Cellar Mountain. On them, cascades of

Left: Author and trail dog Coco hiking St. Mary's Wilderness
Right: Rewarded with a view along the Bald Mountain Trail

varying shapes and sizes spill water en route to St. Mary's River. There are 20-foot drops into small pools on Sugartree Branch. On Mine Bank Branch, water rolls like a slinky down the streambed. Small as they appear, each stream contributes volumes of water to St. Mary's River, which changes from a meandering stream near its headwaters into the frothing, churning powerhouse at St. Mary's Falls.

In late spring, the rash of mountain laurel blossoms along Mine Bank Branch serves as a timely reminder that waterfalls aren't the only attraction here. For a few days, the landscape looks as if a late-season snowstorm hit. The dusting of pink and white fills folds and faults where the stream cuts steeply through bedrock, as if Tinkerbell had brushed hills with a pixie dust. This is the Appalachian wake-up call that marks the end of spring blooms; mountain laurel is the last to flower, after the redbuds, apple blossoms, and dogwoods have shown their stuff.

The sheer volume of mountain laurel makes one consider how this tree reproduces. Stamens on the flower act like a spring. When triggered by bees, the pod-like fruit opens, the anther is released, and oblong pollen beads shake out. Leave the laurel's honey to the bees, though; if ingested, it'll cause cramps and chills—even vomiting in extreme cases.

Not to be outdone by the rush of pink and white laurel, June-blooming rhododendron adds its color a month later. Along the fire road that links Green Pond to the Bald Mountain Trail, pink blossoms are abundant. Lore has it that rhododendron hid the moonshiner's still. Growth is so dense, so high, and seemingly impenetrable, it's quite possible to pass within a yard or so of someone—or something—and never know it. The tree's spindly hardwood trunk is unyielding. Not surprisingly, rhododendron and laurel wood have never amounted to much commercially, outside of use in making briar pipes, a tobacco pipe shaped from the root burls, or knots, of heath plants. Manufacturers favored the burl—the hard, dense knots found on roots of these trees—for shaping the bowl of the pipes because it burned slowly.

In late July, mountain laurel and rhododendron flowers give way to the blueberry—the über-berry of its class. Trapped inside these little blue bombers are enough cancer-fighting antioxidants to rank the small blueberry number one among fruits and vegetables in this category. Health benefits don't stop there, either. Anthocyanin, a chemical that gives berries their blue color, is said to ease eyestrain and improve circulation. Other studies suggest blueberries may even slow the aging process, reason enough to toss another handful into your mouth.

Health is an appropriate subject to consider in light of the threats that face St. Mary's Wilderness. Here, direct human activity has only the slightest impact. Even scars from mining activity as recently as the 1950s fade as grass and trees overgrow the old railroad grades and mine camps. More insidious is acid rain, which has raised pH levels in St. Mary's River to a point where native brook trout are suffering—to say nothing of such small aquatic life-forms as salamanders and frogs. The issue put the Forest Service in a quandary: Wilderness areas, by their very definition, are exempt from the tinkering of forest rangers and land managers. These areas are meant to return to nature in whatever form that takes. There is an exception to this rule, however. In cases of fire, insect infestation, or disease, the Forest Service can intervene, as it has since done in St. Mary's. If one considers acid precipitation a disease, then liming the river (lime is a natural base that counterbalances the acid) is justified. Thus, in the past 20 years the Forest Service has limed the river three times—in 1999, 2005, and 2013—and native brook trout populations in the river have rebounded, to the great satisfaction of anglers who treasure the river as much as hikers.

MILES AND DIRECTIONS

0.0 Start from a trail sign for the Mine Bank Trail on the wooded side of the gravel parking lot. A few feet after starting the hike, turn left and follow the orange blazes of Mine Bank Trail. The Bald Mountain Trail that turns right at this junction is the return portion of this hike.

0.3 The trail switches back several times as it drops down the side of Mine Bank Mountain. The trail surface is loose pebbles. In fall, the views soar across the river valley below to Cellar Mountain.

0.5 After a steep descent, reach the headwaters of Mine Bank Branch. The trail bears left and descends with the stream to the right. Mountain laurel and rhododendron are plentiful here.

1.0 Cross the stream to the right bank. As you cross, the stream drops 20 feet or so on a series of steps cut into the bedrock. The trail descends steeply with the stream on the left.

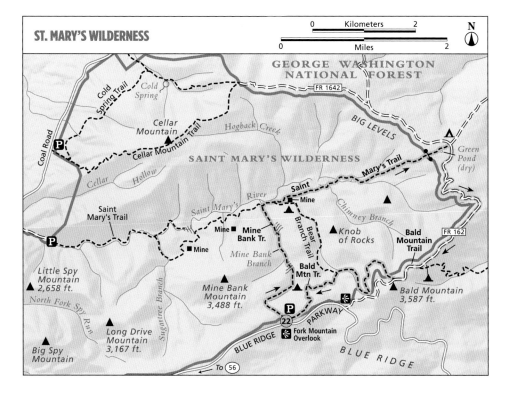

ST. MARY'S WILDERNESS

1.3 Cross back to the left stream bank. The trail continues to descend past rock outcrops on the left hillside. Take time to cut through the woods on the right for wonderful photo ops of the stream's many small waterfalls.

2.1 Mine Bank Branch takes the first of two steep plunges off the mountain slope. The trail, which has descended at a moderate rate, steepens at each waterfall.

2.6 The trail and stream part ways, with Mine Bank Trail arcing left through the oak-hardwood forest. *Note:* In spring, this is a muddy stretch of trail.

3.0 Turn right onto blue-blazed St. Mary's Trail. Follow St. Mary's River upstream. *Side trip:* St. Mary's Trail to the left leads 2.0 miles to a junction with St. Mary's Falls Trail. The trail passes first through an old mine operation and, farther downstream, rugged Sugertree Hollow. St. Mary's Falls Trail is a 0.5-mile hike to the 15-foot St. Mary's Falls. This detour adds 5.0 miles and several hours to the loop hike.

3.2 Cross Bear Branch as it enters from the right. Follow St. Mary's Trail upstream. *Option:* To shorten your trip, you can turn right onto the unmarked Bear Branch Trail as it follows Bear Branch for a return to the Bald Mountain Trail. This bushwhack requires you to follow the Bear Branch stream bank for about a mile, after which an old road leads another mile to Bald Mountain Trail.

3.3 Signs of old iron ore mining operations are visible off the trail. Dirt mounds cover rusted buckets, and an inspection of the tall grassy areas reveals twisted pieces of metal and concrete footings. The trail passes through some shallow mining pits and reenters the woods.

4.0 After crossing a much diminished St. Mary's River several times, the trail begins climbing on an old road. Several times, it dips into the woods for switchbacks to aid the steep ascent.

5.1 Enter Big Levels, a mountain plateau. Continue straight on St. Mary's Trail.

5.6 Reach Green Pond. Pass to the left of the pond. ***Note:*** Green Pond is a "pond" in name only. It dries up in drought conditions and should not be considered a reliable source of water.

5.9 Turn right onto FR 162. This wide dirt and gravel road with no markings climbs Bald Knob on switchbacks.

7.1 FR 162 levels as it crosses Flint Mountain.

7.4 Views open on the left side of the trail. Torry Ridge is visible to the north. To the east, Three Ridges looms beyond the Blue Ridge Parkway. The trail arcs southwest and climbs at a more gradual pace.

8.8 Turn right onto the yellow-blazed Bald Mountain Trail. Look for a wilderness boundary sign on the right as a guide mark. The trail drops down the slope through a young hardwood forest.

9.3 Continue straight past an unmarked road that descends downhill on the right. This is the upper end of the Bear Branch bushwhack.

9.6 Cross a small stream on a three-log bridge amid heavy growth of mountain laurel and rhododendron, with only a few majestic hemlock trees that have survived the woolly adelgid blight.

9.8 The trail arcs left and the climb, which has been gradual the last half-mile, steepens.

10.2 Cross several earthen embankments intended to block vehicle traffic on the trail, which is now an old roadway. There are campsites in this area.

10.5 Turn right onto a narrow footpath and walk several hundred yards to a junction with Mine Bank Trail.

10.6 Turn left onto Mine Bank Trail and arrive back at the gravel parking lot.

HIKE INFORMATION

Local Information
Staunton Visitors Center, Staunton, (540) 332-3971, www.visitstaunton.com
   Lexington Visitors Center, (540) 463-3777, www.lexingtonvirginia.com

Local Events/Attractions
Woodrow Wilson Birthplace & Museum, 24 N. Coalter St., Staunton; (540) 885-0897; www.woodrowwilson.org
   The Cyrus McCormick Farm & Workshop, Raphine, (540) 377-2255, www.arec.vaes
.vt.edu/shenandoah-valley. Site where McCormick invented the first mechanical reaper, with a blacksmith shop, gristmill, and museum. The annual McCormick Farm Mill Day is held in Oct.

Organizations
The Virginia Wilderness Committee has trail information and a downloadable map of St. Mary's Wilderness at www.vawilderness.org/st-marys-wilderness.html.
   Wilderness Connect, www.wilderness.net, also has good information on the nation's wilderness areas.
   Tidewater Appalachian Trail Club, Norfolk, www.tidewateratc.com. Maintains trails in the St. Mary's Wilderness.

23 THREE RIDGES

The term *wilderness* conjures visions of craggy peaks and untamed woodland far from the beaten track. Virginia's newest designated wilderness area, Three Ridges and The Priest region, isn't quite that. And that's not necessarily a bad thing. The Appalachian Trail (AT) traverses both peaks, and the two AT shelters on either side of Three Ridges suit an overnight hike perfectly. The link between them, the Mau-Har Trail, follows Campbell Creek past a 40-foot waterfall and numerous smaller cascades. The treacherous terrain, soaring views, and sheer elevation gain make this one of the most strenuous and dramatic hikes in Virginia.

Start: Swinging bridge over the Tye River, 0.1 mile downhill from VA 56
Distance: 13.8-mile lollipop
Hiking time: About 10 hours
Difficulty: Difficult due to the steep climb up Three Ridges via Chimney Rock, and rocky, eroded trail conditions along Campbell Creek
Trail surface: Dirt footpaths and old dirt forest roads run through steep mountain ridges, high-elevation rock outcrops, stream gorges, and sloping hardwood forests.
Land status: National forest and wilderness area
Nearest town: Lovingston, VA
Other trail users: Hunters (in season)

Accessibility: None
Canine compatibility: Dogs permitted on a leash.
Trail contact: Glenwood-Pedlar Ranger District, Natural Bridge Station, (540) 291-2188, www.fs.usda.gov/gwj
Schedule: Open year-round
Fees/permits: None
Facilities/features: None
NatGeo TOPO! map: Massies Mill, Horseshoe Mountain, Sherando, Big Levels
NatGeo Trails Illustrated map: Lexington, Blue Ridge Mts; Appalachian Trail, Bailey Gap to Calf Mountain

FINDING THE TRAILHEAD

From Lovingston, drive south on combined US 29/VA 56. In 4.6 miles, follow VA 56 west as it branches right, off US 29. In 4.9 miles, VA 56 merges with VA 151. Turn right and follow the combined VA 56/VA 151 north. In 2.7 miles, follow VA 56 west as it branches left off VA 151. Drive 6 miles on VA 56 as it crosses back and forth over the Tye River. Pass through the small communities of Massie Mill and Tyro. In 6 miles from the split from VA 151, turn left into a dirt parking area. **GPS:** N37 50.299' / W79 01.370'. *DeLorme: Virginia Atlas & Gazetteer*: Page 54, B4.

THE HIKE

The region surrounding the mountains of Three Ridges and The Priest packs gorgeous scenery and rugged terrain into a small area. Situated in Virginia's Blue Ridge Mountains and spread over 10 square miles, the two peaks boast an elevation gain of 3,000 feet and rank among the hardest climbs in Virginia. Approaching Three Ridges from the Tye River, the mountain soars 2,973 feet in 6 miles to an elevation of 3,970 feet. The Priest, visible from Three Ridges' southern cliffs and rock outcrops, offers an almost identical elevation gain. Standing at Harpers Creek and staring up the seemingly vertical ascent

The authors in Three Ridges Wilderness

up Three Ridges leaves you with a feeling not often encountered in Virginia—that is, a feeling of being completely dwarfed by the land.

Hikes that start with this kind of bang are prone to ending with a whimper. The return along Campbell Creek on the Mau-Har Trail happily defies this notion. (The odd-sounding name *Mau-Har* is derived from the features it links: Maupin Field Shelter and Harpers Creek.) The trail downhill from Maupin Field Shelter is a narrow footpath etched into the steep-sided stream banks traversing loose rocks. Footing in some areas is as dangerous as the ascent of Three Ridges is difficult.

In 2000 President Clinton signed a bill designating 11,000 acres in The Priest and Three Ridges area as Virginia's seventeenth wilderness area. The Forest Service and Appalachian Trail Conservancy (ATC) have, since 1993, treated the area as wilderness in anticipation of this move. (This includes, by the way, volunteers maintaining the AT by nonmechanical means. The ATC has held workshops on Three Ridges on the proper use of crosscut saws to fell trees 3 feet in diameter.) When they took their campaign for wilderness designation to Washington, DC, in 2000, Nelson County residents and wilderness advocacy groups cited development pressures as a reason for protection. The land itself is too rugged for timber management, but it protects headwaters of three rivers: the Tye, Piney, and Rockfish Rivers. Two other streams, Campbell and Harpers Creeks, source from the slopes of Three Ridges itself. (Lest anyone think designating wilderness is a regular occurrence, the Three Ridges–The Priest Wilderness was the first for Virginia in 13 years.)

Another view of why Three Ridges deserved wilderness protection comes on Chimney Rock, a well-placed rest and overlook on the AT along the south tip of the mountain. From this elevation of 3,204 feet, the rugged aspect of Virginia's Blue Ridge fills the horizon. Absent are long, parallel ridgelines that define Virginia's mountains to the west. Here, it appears a force punched the earth's crust from below, randomly pushing up steep-sided mountains etched with deep V-shaped gorges down their slopes. It's as clear a picture a hiker will receive of Virginia's dual mountain systems. The Blue Ridge

Mountains originated in prehistoric volcanic activity. The Allegheny Mountains to the west, by contrast, evolved into long ridges and valleys during extensive folding and faulting of layered rock.

The ruggedness of Three Ridges has given rise to an unusual variation on old-growth trees. You won't find the enormous trunks and towering heights normally associated with centuries-old stands of oaks and other ancient hardwoods here. Instead, it's small oaks—called Virginia orchard oaks—that qualify as old growth. They occupy the highest portions of Three Ridges, a factor that shaped both their appearance and their preservation. Why were they spared? They were simply too difficult to get to and remove.

Designation of Three Ridges as a wilderness completes a triumvirate of specially protected lands in the central Blue Ridge of Virginia that includes St. Mary's Wilderness and the special management area at Mount Pleasant. Special protection doesn't necessarily mean solitude, however. The 20-foot waterfall on Campbell Creek, 3 miles from VA 56 on the Mau-Har Trail, will likely ensure Three Ridges remains a popular destination for day-trippers. St. Mary's remains the most heavily used of all Virginia's wilderness areas—reports of hikers carrying coolers up to the falls on St. Mary's River persist. Thankfully, the ascent from Harpers Creek Shelter to the highest point on Three Ridges is so severe, a backpack is all the weight that can be safely transported. And that's the way it should be.

MILES AND DIRECTIONS

0.0   Start at a parking area on the south side of VA 56. Cross the highway and descend 0.1 mile to a hand-built cable suspension bridge (reconstructed in 1992 by AT club members). Walk across the bridge and follow the white-blazed AT as it climbs on switchbacks through a forest of mixed hardwoods.

0.3   The AT levels out atop a small knob. It eases across the knob and in 0.1 mile begins another steep climb through an oak forest. During the climb, the slope downhill to the right segues into a field and apple orchard.

1.7   Turn right and follow the AT at a junction of the AT and Mau-Har Trail. The next mile is a descent to Harpers Creek.

2.5   Cross Harpers Creek and hike upstream with the brook on your left. In 0.1 mile, turn right as the AT switches back and begins a steep ascent. **Note:** At this turn, a faded dirt road leads straight to the Harpers Creek Shelter in about 400 yards. The shelter sleeps six and there is room to pitch tents around it.

4.4   Pass Chimney Rock off the left side of the AT. This overlook, along with Hanging Rock on the north side of Three Ridges, offers the best views off Three Ridges. (The term *chimney* refers to the rock formation of solid, uniform blocks of granite beneath your feet.)

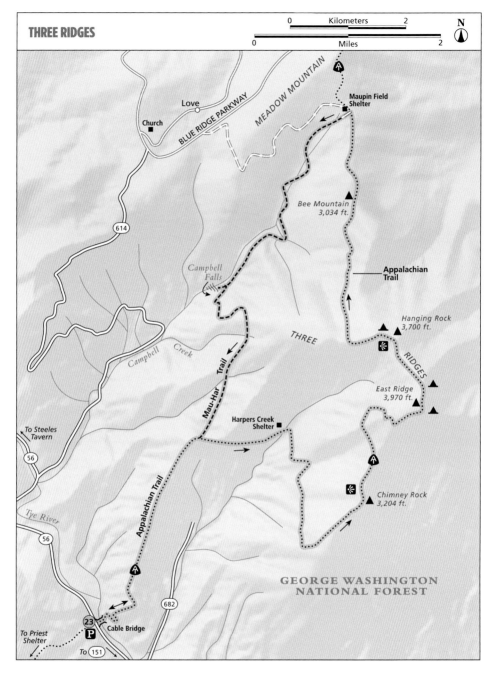

Kilometers

Miles

N

Love

Church

MEADOW MOUNTAIN

Maupin Field
Shelter

BLUE RIDGE PARKWAY

Bee Mountain
3,034 ft.

614

Appalachian
Trail

Campbell
Falls

Hanging Rock
3,700 ft.

THREE

RIDGES

Campbell Creek

East Ridge
3,970 ft.

Mau-Har Trail

Harpers Creek
Shelter

To Steeles
Tavern

56

Appalachian Trail

Chimney Rock
3,204 ft.

Tye River

56

GEORGE WASHINGTON
NATIONAL FOREST

682

23

To Priest
Shelter

P

Cable Bridge

To 151

5.8 Begin a traverse of the highest point on Three Ridges. The landscape is flat. The grassy forest floor and widely spaced maple and oak trees give this summit approach the appearance of a wooded meadow.

6.1 Turn left at a double white blaze and follow the AT over the top of Three Ridges. **Note:** There are some well-used campsites in this area. Farther up, off the right side of the trail, are more secluded spots with access to small rock outcrops with views north to the Blue Ridge Parkway.

6.8 The dirt AT turns to open rock face as the trail crosses Hanging Rock. Views to the south take in The Priest and the Harpers Creek stream valley. The view makes this one of the most coveted tenting spots on this stretch of trail.

8.4 Cross Bee Mountain. After this 3,034-foot knob, the AT continues its descent on a narrow, rocky footpath. In 0.3 mile, it widens and turns grassy.

8.8 Reach Maupin Field Shelter and turn left onto a wide road. Cross the headwaters of Campbell Creek at the shelter and, in 300 yards, turn right and descend on the blue-blazed Mau-Har Trail along Campbell Creek.

9.3 Cross Campbell Creek twice in the next 0.3 mile. *Note:* Use caution on this narrow section of trail; portions are eroded.

10.0 The trail climbs into and out of a gorge where a stream, tumbling off Three Ridges' steep slope, empties into Campbell Creek.

10.5 Mau-Har Trail bears left and uphill, departing the stream valley for a return to the AT. (There is a swimming hole here.) Downstream 0.1 mile is Campbell Falls, a 40-foot waterfall.

12.1 Turn right onto the AT for a return to VA 56 and the Tye River.

13.7 Cross the Tye River on the suspended bridge.

13.8 Hike ends at parking lot on VA 56. (Author recommendation: Ditch the pack, return to stream, and soak yourself in the icy cool of the Tye River.)

HIKE INFORMATION

Local Information
Nelson County Visitor Information Center, 8519 Thomas Nelson Hwy. (Route 29), Lovingston; (434) 263-7015; www.nelsoncounty.com

Local Events/Attractions
Waltons Mountain Museum, Schuyler, (434) 831-2000, www.walton-mountain.org. The school attended by Earl Hammer Jr., creator of *The Waltons*, preserves sets from this classic '70s television series. Open first Sun in Mar until first Sun in Nov.

The Nature Foundation at Wintergreen holds a Spring Wildflower Symposium in May.

Lodging
Wintergreen Resort, Wintergreen, (434) 325-2200, www.wintergreen resort.com. Lodging in ridgetop condos, a nature foundation, a wilderness school, and 30 miles of its own hiking trails.

Organizations
Tidewater Appalachian Trail Club, Norfolk, www.tidewateratc.com. Maintains the Mau-Har Trail.

Wilderness Connect, www.wilderness.net, has good national wilderness information.

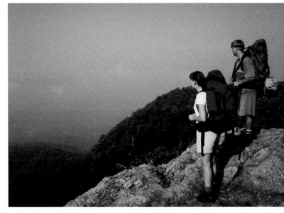

A backpacker's view in Three Ridges Wilderness

24 MOUNT PLEASANT

Mount Pleasant must rank as one of Virginia's most aptly named peaks. Few hikes, if any, offer so much for so little work. For the price of a small elevation gain, hikers can climb two of the Blue Ridge's highest peaks on a loop trail that is, for lack of a better phrase, quite pleasant. Steep, rocky climbs along the final miles to Mount Pleasant will appease the gung ho hiker. Otherwise, it's easy hiking on wide paths and old roads through thick masses of rhododendron and mountain laurel; forests of oak, hickory, and beech; and small pockets of high-grass open forest.

Start: Parking area on FR 48, 0.3 mile past a forest gate at Hog Camp Gap
Distance: 4.8-mile loop
Hiking time: About 4 hours
Difficulty: Moderate due to a long uphill approach along the Henry Lanum Loop Trail and a single, steep climb on Mount Pleasant Spur Trail
Trail surface: Dirt roads and forest footpaths lead through open rock formations, fields, open peaks, mountain meadows, remnant chestnut forests, steep cliffs, and along streams.
Land status: National Scenic Area
Nearest town: Buena Vista, VA

Other trail users: Hunters (in season)
Accessibility: None
Canine compatibility: Dogs permitted
Trail contact: Glenwood-Pedlar Ranger District, Natural Bridge Station, (540) 291-2188, www.fs.usda.gov/gwj
Schedule: Open year-round
Fees/permits: None
Facilities/features: None
NatGeo TOPO! map: Montebello, Forks of Buffalo
NatGeo Trails Illustrated map: Lexington, Blue Ridge Mts; Appalachian Trail, Bailey Gap to Calf Mountain

FINDING THE TRAILHEAD

From Buena Vista, drive east on US 60 for 8 miles to the town of Oronoco. Turn left onto VA 634 (Coffey Town Road) at a small general store. In 1.7 miles, turn right onto VA 755 (Wiggins Spring Road), which turns into a rough gravel FR 48 and veers right in 1.4 miles. Continue on FR 48 across the Appalachian Trail (AT) in 1.4 miles. Come to a fork and sign for Mount Pleasant in 0.2 mile. Turn right and go 0.2 mile to the parking area. **GPS:** N37 45.553' / W79 11.338'. *DeLorme: Virginia Atlas & Gazetteer*: Page 54, B2.

THE HIKE

The wind—you notice it first, and it never really goes away. Long gusts wrap around Mount Pleasant's highest point, a 4,090-foot exposed rock face with views in all directions. It chaffs cheeks and hands as you stare out to the low-lying Piedmont rolling east from the mountain. Falcons or some other raptor too far off to distinguish with certainty circle on the upward-spiraling currents. A blurry rush fills your ears, and soon after it chills your bones.

You descend off the peak, but the wind isn't done yet. In an under-grown forest gap below the Mount Pleasant summit, streaks of air rustle a thin forest canopy. Sunlight leaks through a patchwork of young oak and poplar, playing crazy angles with pole-size tree

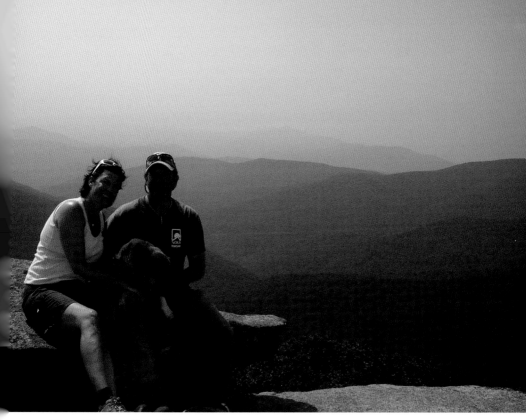

The authors atop Mount Pleasant

trunks. As the day lengthens, the wind picks up strength. Streaks of light and shadows interlace across the woodland. Grass bristles in the breeze. Here, a circle of light stretches halfway up a tree trunk. There, the setting sun alights on branch tips of an oak. In the darkness that drops suddenly, the wind remains, wrapping around you as it races through the trees.

Wind generates some of the Virginia mountains' most severe storms. As systems of high and low pressure move eastward across the mountains, the haphazard arrangement of steep-sided mountains and deep valleys creates small tempests. Under proper conditions, a storm pocket will wreak sizable damage. Far more common, however, are isolated windthrows (aka downbursts or microbursts), where a sudden, fierce storm has torn down, snapped, or uprooted a few acres of trees. These are the seemingly out-of-place gaps in an otherwise solid forest that appear suddenly as you approach Mount Pleasant from the southwest. These gaps lack the clear, defined lines of a meadow. A rash of sub-canopy vegetation, plants such as Virginia creeper or poison ivy, blur the line between forest and open space. Grasses that normally perish in the shadows of a forest canopy lend the subforest a pastoral look. To a bone-weary hiker, they appear as a perfectly peaceful spot to camp. Closer inspection, however, shows mounded soil where trees came uprooted, indicating a violent episode sometime in the past.

Disturbances, whether natural or man-made, have long been a part of the Mount Pleasant landscape. Meadows atop Cole Mountain, in the southern portion of the 7,580-acre Mount Pleasant National Scenic Area, date from a time when private landowners grazed livestock (indicated by place-names such as Cow Camp Gap and Hog Camp Gap). Maintaining the open fields through prescribed burns and timber management kept Mount Pleasant from being named a federal wilderness. Although much smaller, the fields inevitably invite comparisons to the high-country meadows of Mount Rogers National Recreation Area.

The southern slope of Cole Mountain drops into the North Fork Buffalo River, and from this stream rises Chestnut Ridge, a long ascending buttress that leads to Mount Pleasant's peak. Unfortunately, the ridge's name only reminds us of when the American chestnut tree blanketed the Appalachian forest. Here's a reminder that ecological disturbances come in many forms, not just wind. Consider as you descend along the trail that a forest canopy once rose 100 feet and higher overhead, that tree trunks measured 10 feet in diameter. "No greater catastrophe has ever befallen a tree in our time," Roger Tory Peterson wrote of the chestnut blight. That may well be an understatement. Imported from Asia, the blight—a fungus that appears as a black canker on the tree trunk—spread virulently down the Appalachian chain, destroying in a span of 20 years an estimated 3.5 million trees. (Look for signs of chestnut blight beyond Pompey Mountain as you hike the Henry Lanum Loop Trail away from Mount Pleasant.) It also deprived today's hiker the opportunity to see this once strong tree grow past head-height—the size at which, today, the blight destroys chestnut trees. This is a humbling status for a tree once considered North America's most productive.

Hope, however, is not lost. Biologists believe they now have an American chestnut that is 95 percent resistant to the blight. Here in Virginia, the American Chestnut Cooperator's Foundation is experimenting with grafting techniques in the Warm Springs Ranger District of the George Washington National Forest. This technique takes young American chestnuts with no signs of blight and grafts resistant chestnut stems onto them. The hope is that the tree will produce nuts with blight-resistant genetics. In the Lesesne State Forest in nearby Nelson County, American chestnuts are being backcrossed—a type of genetic altering—with highly blight-resistant Chinese chestnuts in the hopes of producing a blight-resistant American chestnut. A reason, perhaps, to hope.

MILES AND DIRECTIONS

0.0   Start from a trail board in the parking area on FR 51. Walk straight past the trail board and follow the blue-blazed Henry Lanum Loop Trail as it descends gently on a dirt road. **Note:** The Pompey Trail, which is the return leg of this loop hike, departs from this parking area. It climbs left from the trail board on a dirt road.

0.8   Cross two seasonal streams. The trail slowly arcs right and continues to descend.

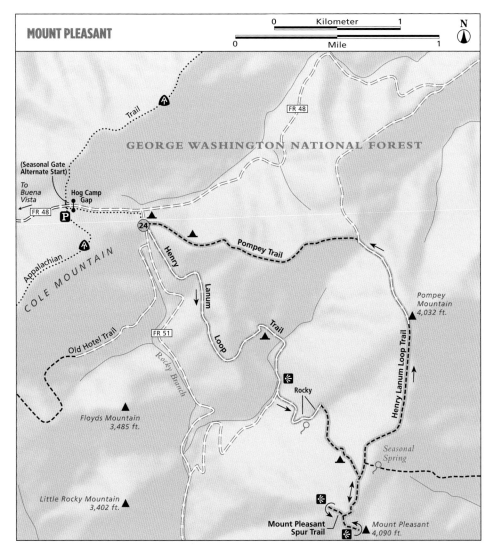

GEORGE WASHINGTON NATIONAL FOREST

1.5 Turn left at a double blaze and climb. The trail, a bit rockier, crosses a stream. A mature hardwood forest covers the slopes, replacing the fields and gaps at lower elevations.

1.7 Turn right at another junction with an unmarked forest road. The trail is now a footpath and crosses several seasonal drainages. **Note:** Do not count on water from these sources during summer or fall.

1.9 A relentless climb marks the approach to Mount Pleasant. The trail switches back several times. Large boulders along the trail make for convenient rest points.

2.3 Turn right onto the Mount Pleasant Trail and begin a final ascent of Mount Pleasant.

2.6 Reach the open rock face of Mount Pleasant's 4,090-foot summit. To return to the Henry Lanum Loop Trail, turn and descend 0.3 mile on the Mount Pleasant Trail. Before doing so, however, take time to soak in the views that encircle the mountain. Far eastward rolls the Piedmont. To the north is Pompey Mountain. Chestnut Ridge approaches the mountain from the south. Through the valley south of the mountain runs the Buffalo River.

2.9 Intersect the Henry Lanum Loop Trail and hike straight ahead. As you descend off the mountain, continue straight ahead.

3.0 The blue-blazed trail crosses a saddle between Mount Pleasant and Pompey Mountain. Several gaps in the forest open up as you walk through a grassy landscape.

3.2 The trail passes just to the left of Pompey Mountain. (Although only a few feet shorter than Mount Pleasant, Pompey Mountain is wooded with no views.) After passing the summit, the trail drops hard down the north slope.

3.6 Turn left onto a narrow footpath that wends its way through a spare forest notable for the waist-high grass. The trail climbs and reenters forestland, where rhododendron forms a brief tunnel. There are campsites off either side of the trail along this section.

4.1 Cross a small knob and begin a descent to the parking area.

4.8 Hike ends at the parking area on FR 51.

HIKE INFORMATION

Local Information
Lexington Visitor Center, Lexington, (540) 463-3777, www.lexingtonvirginia.com

Local Events/Attractions
Lime Kiln Theater, 607 Borden Rd., Lexington; www.limekilntheater.org

Other Resources
The Virginia Wilderness Committee has good information and a downloadable map of Mount Pleasant at www.vawilderness.org/mt-pleasant.html.

HONORABLE MENTIONS: BLUE RIDGE PARKWAY

AA. TORRY RIDGE–MILL CREEK LOOP

A long trek that departs from White Oak Campground at Sherando Lake. Reach the lake via the Blue Ridge Parkway, milepost 16. This Blue Ridge hike has it all: mountains and streams, blueberries, rhododendron, and the convenience of a base camp with showers and flush toilets. (828) 348-3400, www.nps.gov/blri. **GPS:** N37 55.226' / W79 00.382'. *DeLorme: Virginia Atlas & Gazetteer*: Page 54, A3.

BB. HUMPBACK ROCKS

A challenging day hike off the Blue Ridge Parkway 6 miles south of Rockfish Gap and I-64. Trailhead located at milepost 6. Humpback Rocks is a 3,080-foot outcrop of greenstone with wide views west to the Shenandoah Valley. The hike to the rocks is 1 mile on the Appalachian Trail. Humpback Mountain and more views await another mile down the trail. (828) 348-3400, www.nps.gov/blri. **GPS:** N37 58.101' / W78 53.781'. *DeLorme: Virginia Atlas & Gazetteer*: Page 55, A5.

CC. CRABTREE FALLS

Trailhead is 17 miles northeast of Buena Vista on VA 56. This 3-mile trail runs along a creek that has five major cascades, overlooks, and ends at a parking lot on VA 828. The cumulative 1,200-foot drop in elevation along Crabtree Creek makes this one of the highest waterfalls east of the Mississippi. There are steps and railings along the trail to aid with hiking over treacherous terrain. (828) 348-3400, www.nps.gov/blri. **GPS:** N37 51.071' / W79 04.749'. *DeLorme: Virginia Atlas & Gazetteer*: Page 54, B3.

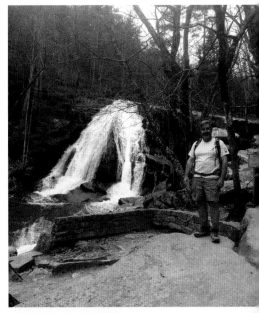

DD. APPLE ORCHARD FALLS–CORNELIUS CREEK LOOP TRAIL

Begin at Sunset Field Overlook near milepost 78 on the Blue Ridge Parkway for this 7.5-mile loop. Two-hundred-foot waterfalls and old-growth forest are the highlights of this National Recreation Trail. (540) 291-2188, www.fs.usda.gov/gwj. **GPS:** N37 30.458' / W79 31.420'. *DeLorme: Virginia Atlas & Gazetteer*: Page 53, D6.

Crabtree Falls EDDIE FORT

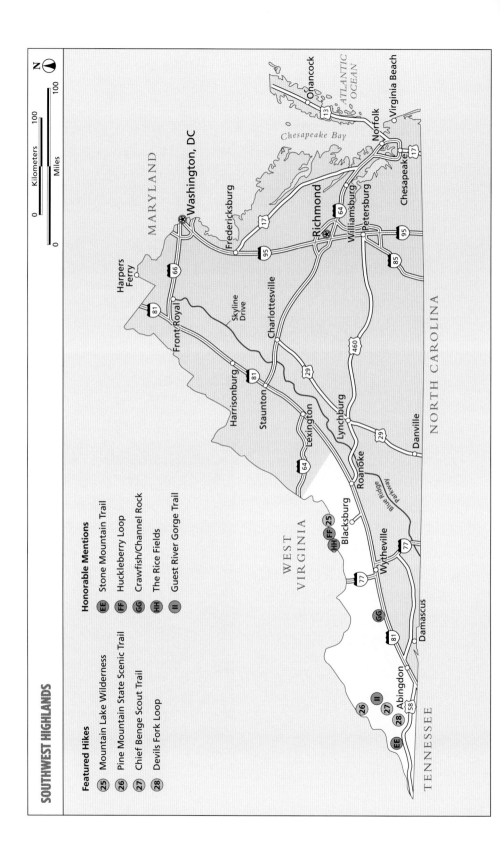

SOUTHWEST HIGHLANDS

Featured Hikes

25 Mountain Lake Wilderness
26 Pine Mountain State Scenic Trail
27 Chief Benge Scout Trail
28 Devils Fork Loop

Honorable Mentions

EE Stone Mountain Trail
FF Huckleberry Loop
GG Crawfish/Channel Rock
HH The Rice Fields
II Guest River Gorge Trail

SOUTHWEST HIGHLANDS

Southwest Highlands covers two distinct geological regions of the state: a southwest portion of the Valley & Ridge province, and the Appalachian Plateau of far southwest Virginia. This is the land of timber, iron ore, and coal—and more recently, natural gas production. The rugged terrain, coupled with its distance from metropolitan centers on the East Coast, gives the area a remoteness that adds to its allure as a destination.

Rivers shape and define this region as much as the mountains. The New River, the oldest flowing body of water on the North American continent, flows northwest out of the North Carolina hills. Moving in the opposite direction is the Roanoke River. Farther south, the Clinch and Powell Rivers flow along deep troughs between tall mountain ridges, their supply feeding the Tennessee River. Most spectacular of all is Russell Fork, viewed from atop the 1,000-foot cliff walls where it passes over the Virginia-Kentucky border.

The forces that wrought southwest Virginia's mountains are inseparable from those elsewhere in the state: volcanic activity along the Blue Ridge, sedimentary rock in the valley and ridge, forged by periods of heat, pressure, folding, and faulting. Amid this, one area stands apart. Pine Mountain, along the Virginia-Kentucky border, is a stellar example of thrust plate movement: one piece of the earth's crust ramped up onto another. This geologic borderline features a dramatic landscape where the mountain drops steeply into Kentucky, while to the east, the terrain rolls downhill.

For generations, southwest Virginia remained an isolated region, both from the state and the country as a whole. Even after timber and coal barons brought riches in the form of logging and mining, pockets of poverty persisted. The booms in economic and cultural life were grand times. Big Stone Gap lured vacationers from New York City and royalty from abroad. When busts hit, they hit hard. Throughout the 20th century, quality of life hinged on the price of coal. Since the 1970s, demand and price for Virginia coal have declined. That has forced leaders to find other economic stimuli; chief among them is outdoor recreation. Given the natural beauty of the region, this is a happy development for hikers and mountain bikers alike.

A shelter on the Pine Mountain State Scenic Trail

THE HIKES
25. Mountain Lake Wilderness
26. Pine Mountain State Scenic Trail
27. Chief Benge Scout Trail
28. Devils Fork Loop

HONORABLE MENTIONS
EE. Stone Mountain Trail
FF. Huckleberry Loop
GG. Crawfish/Channel Rock
HH. The Rice Fields
II. Guest River Gorge Trail

25 MOUNTAIN LAKE WILDERNESS

Geology lesson: Virginia did not have glaciers, hence there are really no natural lakes in the state. The largest lakes are actually man-made reservoirs. Virginia's only true mountain lake is quite small and was formed by a fluke incident. It sits just outside this, the largest of all Virginia wilderness areas. And most of your climbing is done in the car getting here. Which is just fine, really, because this saves your breath for exploring upland bogs on Lone Pine Peak, slabs of Tuscarora sandstone on Salt Pond Mountain, and a red spruce glade on Potts Mountain. Trails through Mountain Lake Wilderness are well marked and maintained (the Appalachian Trail is the most-traveled route).

Start: Parking lot for the War Spur Loop on the right side of VA 613
Distance: 10.2-mile loop
Hiking time: About 6 hours
Difficulty: Moderate due to distance, steep climbs, and poor trail markings on Potts Mountain
Trail surface: Narrow dirt woodland paths lead through fern glades, mountaintop swamps, and steep rock outcrops.
Land status: National forest wilderness
Nearest town: Blacksburg, VA
Other trail users: Hikers only
Accessibility: None
Canine compatibility: Dogs permitted

Trail contact: Eastern Divide Ranger District, Blacksburg, (540) 552-4641, www.fs.usda.gov/gwj
Schedule: Open year-round. Hunting is permitted on national forest property, with Nov through Jan the busiest season.
Fees/permits: None
Facilities/features: None
NatGeo TOPO! map: Waiteville, Interior
NatGeo Trails Illustrated map: Blacksburg, New River Valley; Covington, Alleghany Highlands; Appalachian Trail, Bailey Gap to Calf Mountain; New River Blueway

FINDING THE TRAILHEAD

From Blacksburg, drive north on US 460 for 10 miles and turn right onto VA 700. In 6.8 miles, pass through Mountain Lake Lodge. Here, VA 700 changes to VA 613 and wraps around the west side of Mountain Lake. The road turns to gravel 0.7 mile past the hotel. After another 0.9 mile the road forks; bear left. The parking area for the War Spur–Chestnut Loop is 3.5 miles past the resort. *Option:* If using a shuttle, drive a second car 2.1 miles up VA 613 to a parking area for Wind Rock and the Appalachian Trail (AT). **GPS:** N37 23.445' / W80 30.481'. *DeLorme: Virginia Atlas & Gazetteer*: Page 41, A5.

THE HIKE

Suddenly, after a long, sweaty day in pursuit of the almighty loop, you encounter the unusual. Maybe it's a great view. Maybe it's a morning mist rising off a wildlife pond, or a stream's song as it cuts through crowded woodland. Whatever form it takes, these are as unexpected and pleasant as a breeze on a hot day. They stir something deep within. The mellow you, the one who tugs at your conscience, says, *Hey, hold up. Stay here a while.*

The famous Mountain Lake Lodge, filming location for *Dirty Dancing*, is on the edge of the Mountain Lake Wilderness.

Because the experience is both unusual and infrequent, coming across an upland bog ranks as that type of special moment. The observant hiker finds upland bogs in small depressions on a flat mountaintop or in broad gaps. They often form the headwaters of streams—even when the stream doesn't appear to be in the immediate area. Steeped in water year-round, an upland bog hosts plants that wouldn't survive 10 feet away in dry, gray-brown soil of the deciduous forest. Animals converge on it as if it were a desert oasis, both to eat and sometimes to be eaten.

Salt Pond Mountain in Mountain Lake Wilderness holds the right ingredients for an upland bog. The highest point is a flat pan of forest stretching a half-mile in a northwest direction. The forest is mostly skinny hardwoods—oak, beech, poplar. As War Spur Connector Trail approaches a downhill stretch that will end at the Appalachian Trail (AT), trees on the left give way to a grassy patch. It looks at first glance like a nice campsite. One step into the clearing, the ground turns soft and wet. Perhaps, you think as you pull a foot from the mire, this is why there are no fire rings. Walking the perimeter of the bog, you see Indian pipe stem and Virginia chain fern. Unseen to the eye, the fern spreads long, thin rhizomes beneath the soil. New ferns grow off this rhizome while roots sink deep into the bog, with its layered leaf rot. Bogs hold water like a sponge, ensuring lush conditions even in drought.

After you've climbed to the summit of Lone Pine Peak, you'll notice another upland opening on the right side of the AT on Lone Pine Peak. Here, the ground is drier. Laurel

THE MYSTERY OF MOUNTAIN LAKE

The natural lake, one of a very few in all of Virginia, that gives the area and the famous hotel their names, remains a continuing mystery. How was it formed and why does it periodically drain and fill again? Scientists from nearby Radford University have concluded the Mountain Lake basin is a unique phenomenon not only in Virginia, but in the world. Not only is it an archaeological mystery, but an unsolved human mystery as well. In 2008 the lake drained almost completely, revealing human remains along with a pair of shoes, a ring, and a belt buckle with initials that linked to a New York City man who had fallen overboard in the lake in 1921.

and winterberry add a shrubby, dense appearance to the forest understory encircling the bog. Camouflaged and positioned carefully, you might see a deer pick its way through mountain maple and scrub oak, nibbling on the grass or ferns covering the wet, spongy earth. In August or September, the red or gray fox might approach a mountain winter-berry for a mouthful of red fruit. Long-stalked holly, similar in appearance to the win-terberry, grows exclusively in the moist conditions of upland bogs. The chief difference between these two deciduous shrubs is the flowers: Long-stalked holly's flowers are a yellow-green color; the flower of a mountain winterberry has white petals.

Sit next to either bog for a spell and the sound of busy birds calling and singing fills your ears. If it's early spring, it's a male songbird who has arrived early from southern environs to prepare a nest. You might hear black and white wrens, a solitary vireo, and robins. You might see a tufted titmouse flit from thin branch to ground for a quick forage among the leaf litter. But whether you can tell the song of an eastern wood-pewee (*pee-ah-wee*) from a white-breasted nuthatch's call (a rapid *wer-wer-wer*) isn't really the point. Purse your lips and make up your own song, then see what kind of bird comes to investigate.

The best of Mountain Lake Wilderness's bogs comes last. In the Southern Appala-chians, where you find red spruce, you'll find Fraser fir (like a married couple, they're always together, thus giving rise to the nicknames: he-balsam for spruce and she-balsam for fir). Not so on Potts Mountain, which lost its oak, chestnut, and red spruce in the first decade of the 20th century—all, that is, except for small patches now protected by federal wilderness. A red spruce bog grows in the headwaters of Stony Creek on Potts Mountain's south-facing slope; there are strong ecological ties between this spot and the highland wilderness of Mount Rogers. Despite a difference in elevation of about 1,000 feet, both Little Wilson Creek Wilderness at Mount Rogers National Recreation Area (NRA) and Mountain Lake Wilderness Areas protect old-growth red spruce. It's worth pondering, as you sit next to this rarest of upland bogs, why the red spruce, the most common of the native spruce trees in the East and a mainstay of northern forests, is rel-egated to isolated spots here in Virginia. No matter what answer you arrive at, their rarity makes listening to that inner voice—the one that tells you *Stay here a while*—a lot easier.

MILES AND DIRECTIONS

0.0   Start at the parking area on VA 613. Enter the woods and immediately turn right onto the War Spur Loop Trail.

1.0   Bear right on a short 0.2 mile detour to a rock outcrop with jaw-dropping views down into the War Spur stream valley and the formidable Potts Mountain ridge-line. After returning from the overlook rejoin War Spur Loop Trail, bear right, and descend to War Spur Branch.

1.8   Reach War Spur Branch. In this dark stream valley, turn left and follow the trail as it leads upstream beneath old-growth hemlocks. **Side trip:** Experienced hikers can bushwhack War Spur Branch downstream for 1.6 miles to the AT. Where War Spur Branch intersects with the AT, turn left onto the AT. In 75 yards, pass the War Spur Shelter on the right. The AT climbs steeply and, in 1 mile from the War Spur Shelter, intersects War Spur Connector Trail on the left. The first part of this side trip is a dif-ficult bushwhack with many stream crossings. War Spur Branch is overgrown with mountain laurel and rhododendron, which hinders passage.

2.2   Reach a T junction of War Spur Loop Trail and War Spur Connector Trail. Turn right onto the War Spur Connector Trail. **Option:** A left turn leads 0.2 mile to the parking area on VA 613.

2.5 Scrub oak, Allegheny chinquapin, and witch hazel open onto a grassy, fern-ringed upland bog on the left side of the trail. A few feet past this on the right, a boulder field is visible through the trees. Large slabs of Tuscarora sandstone lie scattered over 3 or 4 acres. There are no tall cliffs or rock ledges—just disrupted, disjointed chunks of rock.

2.9 Turn left onto the AT and begin a short, steep ascent of Lone Pine Peak. You'll climb 335 feet in less than 0.5 mile to reach the wooded 4,054-foot summit.

3.7 Another upland bog opens up on the right side of the AT.

4.0 Double white blazes mark a hard left turn onto the AT. Instead of following the AT left, continue straight into the woods on a faint, unblazed path. In 0.1 mile, emerge from the woods onto Potts Mountain Trail, a wide, grassy forest road. A tall oak tree in the middle of the road marks this spot. Turn right onto Potts Mountain Trail and walk along the gently sloping ridgeline. *Note:* There are several campsites within the next mile.

5.2 Reach White Rocks, an exposed rock formation on Potts Mountain with overlooks onto Little Mountain and beyond to Stony Run. To the east you will see Johns Creek Mountain and the War Spur drainage. Turn and retrace your steps along Potts Mountain Trail.

6.3 Pass the tall oak that marks the spur trail to the AT; continue straight on Potts Mountain Trail. You may see faint white blazes on trees, leftovers from days when the AT followed Potts Mountain Trail.

7.1 Enter a large, sloping field overgrown with tall grass. The trail climbs from the bottom of the field to a clearing in the grass in the middle of the field. The trail then arcs gently right and reenters woods at the top of the field. Stay alert: There are no blazes or trail markers through this field. Several roads branch off from the clearing in the middle of the field.

7.3 Potts Mountain Trail passes through another clearing. Concrete pilings off the left side of the trail are all that remain of the Stony Creek lookout tower.

7.7 Potts Mountain Trail junctions with the AT, which enters from the left side. Off the right side of Potts Mountain Trail is Wind Rock, another overlook across to Fork Mountain and the West Virginia state line.

8.1 The AT ends at a gravel parking lot on VA 613. If you're shuttling, the hike ends here. If not, turn left and hike 2.1 miles on gravel VA 613 to the hike starting point.

10.2 Arrive back at the gravel parking area for the War Spur Loop.

HIKE INFORMATION

Local Information

Visit Giles County, Pearisburg, (540) 921–2079, www.virginiasmtnplayground.com

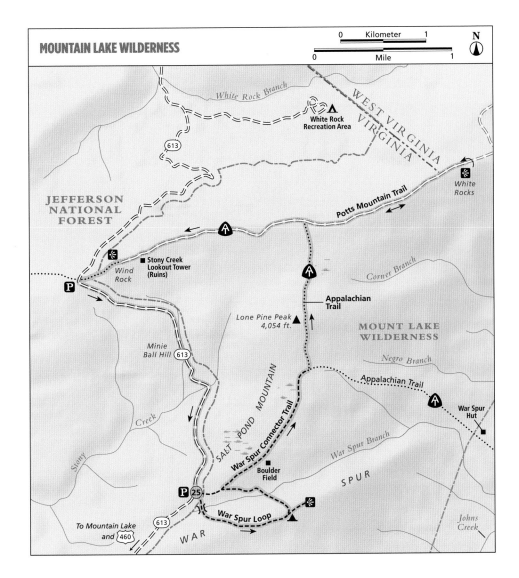

Labels within map:
White Rock Branch
White Rock Recreation Area
WEST VIRGINIA
VIRGINIA
613
White Rocks
JEFFERSON NATIONAL FOREST
Potts Mountain Trail
Corner Branch
Stony Creek Lookout Tower (Ruins)
Wind Rock
P
Appalachian Trail
Lone Pine Peak 4,054 ft.
MOUNT LAKE WILDERNESS
Negro Branch
Minie Ball Hill 613
Appalachian Trail
War Spur Hut
SALT POND MOUNTAIN
War Spur Connector Trail
Creek
Stony
Boulder Field
War Spur Branch
SPUR
P 25
War Spur Loop
613
To Mountain Lake and 460
WAR
Johns Creek

Lodging

Mountain Lake Lodge, Pembroke, (540) 626-7121, www.mountainlakelodge.com. The iconic hotel where *Dirty Dancing* was filmed.

White Rocks National Recreation Area Campground, Pearisburg, (540) 552-4641, open mid-May through mid-Oct

Claytor Lake State Park, Dublin, (540) 643-2500, www.dcr.virginia.gov/state-parks/claytor-lake

Organizations

Virginia Wilderness Committee, www.vawilderness.org/mountain-lake-wilderness.html

Mountain Lake Wilderness trails are maintained by volunteers with the Roanoke Appalachian Trail Club (RATC) and the Southern Appalachian Wilderness Stewards (SAWS), www.ratc.org.

26 PINE MOUNTAIN STATE SCENIC TRAIL

Pine Mountain State Scenic Trail traces a razor's edge along the Virginia-Kentucky border. You're walking a geological fault line known as an overthrust plate—a chunk of the earth's crust that buckled, broke, and ramped up over another chunk hundreds of millions of years ago. The resulting terrain slopes gently east to Virginia, while to the west, sheer drops of 500 feet or more fall away into Kentucky. The stunning views, combined with the rugged terrain, make this one of Virginia's most dramatic and scenic trails. The length of the trail and its remoteness make it one of the most challenging as well.

Author's note: When we first hiked the Pine Mountain Trail in 1998, it was a sparsely marked, pieced-together dream of a few dedicated volunteers to form a continuous trail from the Breaks Interstate Park to Cumberland Gap National Historical Park. Shad Baker, who helped us with route-finding, maps, and shuttling, was instrumental in getting the Kentucky legislature to bestow scenic trail designation nearly 20 years later.

Start: Highlands Section trailhead on US 23 in Pound Gap
Distance: 15.7 miles point to point
Hiking time: 8–10 hours
Difficulty: Strenuous due to length and rugged terrain
Trail surface: Dirt footpaths and dirt roads lead to high escarpments, upland forest, and spectacular vistas off exposed rock faces.
Land status: National forest
Nearest towns: Pound, VA; Whitesburg, KY
Other trail users: Hunters (in season)
Accessibility: None
Canine compatibility: Dogs permitted
Trail contacts: Pine Mountain Trail Conference, www.pinemountain statescenictrail.com; Clinch Ranger District, Norton, (276) 679-8370, www.fs.usda.gov/gwj
Schedule: Open year-round. Hunting is allowed on national forest property. Deer-hunting season in Wise and Dickenson Counties runs Oct through Jan. The national forest limits hiking groups to 10 people.
Fees/permits: None
Facilities/features: None
NatGeo TOPO! map: Jenkins West, Jenkins East, Clintwood, Hellier, Elkhorn City
NatGeo Trails Illustrated map: Clinch Ranger District
Other maps: Pine Mountain Trail Conference has excellent downloadable trail guides and maps at www.pinemountainstatescenictrail .com/maps.

FINDING THE TRAILHEAD

From Pound, drive north on US 23 for 3 miles. In Pound Gap, just before passing into Kentucky, turn left into the Stateline Food Mart. Parking for hikers is provided on the side and in the back of this convenience store and gas station.
GPS: N37 09.213' / W82 37.937'. *DeLorme: Virginia Atlas & Gazetteer*: Page 36, C2.
Shuttle point: Shuttle service is available at www.pinemountainstatescenictrail .com/guides/shuttles. From Pound Gap, drive north on US 23 for 1.3 miles to a junction with US 119 in Kentucky. Turn left onto US 119 and drive 10.8 miles to Whitesburg,

Kentucky. At a junction with KY 15 in Whitesburg, turn left and continue on US 119 as it climbs Pine Mountain. In 4.9 miles, turn right into a trailhead parking area for the Pine Mountain State Scenic Trail's Little Shepherd Trail section. There is parking for more than twenty cars and an interpretive sign. **GPS:** N37 04.581' / W82 48.644'. *DeLorme: Virginia Atlas & Gazetteer:* Page 37, B5.

THE HIKE

At its core, Pine Mountain is a geologic phenomenon called the Cumberland Overthrust Block. The mountain range formed when a piece of the earth's crust buckled and broke. The southeast chunk of rock (the Virginia piece) moved between 6 and 11 miles west and slid up and over the northwest rock (the Kentucky piece) at an angle of 30 to 40 degrees. The highest bits of rock on Pine Mountain are sandstone normally found 2,000 feet underground. And here's a kicker: It's thought that the Pine Mountain we see today is half its original size.

There is another story about Pine Mountain, one of settlers and generations that followed them. The first settlers moved to southwest Virginia seeking isolation—from people, politics, and/or culture. Most settlers worked hard in the logging and mining industries. They were fiercely independent, to the point of suspecting any kind of authority. Some turned outlaw; others ran moonshine. Doc Taylor, aka "Red Fox," a notorious local outlaw, hid amid the caves and hollows of Pine Mountain. He was later hanged in Big Stone Gap for murder. In the gaps of Pine Mountain, settlers eked out a living—barely. Their cows grazed on rocky slopes. Cornfields cheapened already thin soil. Crop rotation simply meant clearing a few more acres and planting anew. Wherever they set roots, settlers guarded their holdings closely, often to protect their stills. For a time, moonshine was the cash crop of the region.

Knowing a bit of this history made meeting Henry Mullins special. Dusk had settled on our second day of hiking when Mullins stepped from the shadow of Birch Knob and introduced himself. He and his girlfriend had driven up to Birch Knob to catch the sunset. Together, the four of us climbed the final rocky upthrust. Sitting atop the second-highest bump in the long Pine Mountain ridge, Henry pulled out a beverage and lit a cigarette. I figured this was as good a time as any to ask if he knew the Henry Mullins killed on Pine Mountain.

The Henry Mullins I had read about lived at Dutton Bottom Farm. As the story goes, deputized Virginians came upon Mullins's cabin while hunting for stills in the mountains. They had, earlier that day, found a still and partook in some of the spoils. Drunk and ornery, they found a bottle of moonshine on Mullins's front porch—which was located on the Virginia side of the Virginia-Kentucky border—and confronted

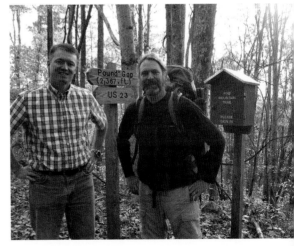

The author with Shad Baker, one of the trail's pioneers

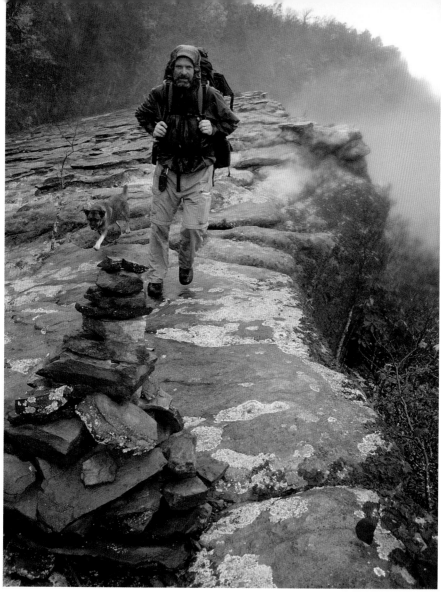

The author walks the ridge that forms the boundary between Virginia and Kentucky.

him. Mullins protested his innocence. A scuffle broke out and a deputy shot and killed Mullins. Local authorities decided jurisdiction lay with Kentucky, and the deputies were tried and convicted, although they served minimal time.

As the sun slipped behind the Kentucky mountains, modern-day Henry Mullins confessed never having heard the story. In the lingering twilight, we climbed down off the peak and parted ways as darkness settled in, Mary and I to our tent, Henry and his girl to civilization in a Ford Bronco.

The latest chapter in Pine Mountain's rich history is being written as you read this. Dedicated and enthusiastic organizers and hikers in Virginia and Kentucky, working under the guidance of the Pine Mountain Trail Conference, have rebuilt and re-blazed 42 miles of trail from Breaks Interstate Park to Cumberland Gap Historical Park. When we first hiked the northern section of Pine Mountain Trail in the 1990s, Shad Baker—now the trail conference president—assisted with route planning, water sources, and local contacts. Nearly 20 years later, as we prepared to hike a new section of the trail, there again was Shad with a smile and lending hand.

The strong commitment to building this trail and maintaining it—while still preserving and interpreting the rich history of the region's people—places Pine Mountain in the ranks of other great long trails, like the Bartram in North Carolina, Allegheny in West Virginia, and Tuscarora in Virginia, in offering some of the best long-distance trekking in the East.

Pine Mountain's past rests easy with homesteaders, coal miners, and outlaws. Its future looks to be in good hands, too. Without fail, when a fellow hiker asks which hike in Virginia we find most beautiful yet most challenging—the answer is always "Pine Mountain." End of story.

MILES AND DIRECTIONS

0.0 Start at a set of stone steps leading up a grass embankment next to the Stateline Food Mart. Climb the steps and bear left (south) on a mowed path through a grass field.

0.1 Pass through a fence stile that keeps out horseback riders and motorized vehicles and continue downhill on the Pine Mountain State Scenic Trail, which is blazed with fluorescent green markers.

0.7 Veer left onto an old forest road, a junction marked by a double blue blaze, and hike around a small knob in the Pine Mountain ridgeline. This pattern—the trail swerving south to work around the south side of small knobs—repeats itself numerous times in the first 5 miles along this hike.

0.8 Veer right and uphill at a double blaze as Pine Mountain State Scenic Trail splits off the old forest road and climbs to a saddle as a singletrack woods path.

1.5 Reach the Jack Sautter Campsite and a turnoff for the Old Meade homesite. There is a fire ring and four established tent sites here. **Note:** There is a water source at the Old Meade homesite, a 0.2-mile hike off the trail via an old mountain road.

2.4 Pass through a stone cleft in the mountain ridge at Twin Cliffs. **Side trip:** Turn left and scale open rock to reach a perch atop one of the Twin Cliffs in less than 0.1 mile. Views from this high point stretch south and east into Virginia.

2.8 Stay alert as a double blaze marks a hard left turn and then skirts another knob.

2.9 Pass through Cold Spring Gap.

3.0 Stay alert for a hard left turn as the trail skirts another knob.

3.5 Turn left as Pine Mountain State Scenic Trail merges with a forest road. Follow the wide two-track road downhill.

PINE MOUNTAIN STATE SCENIC TRAIL

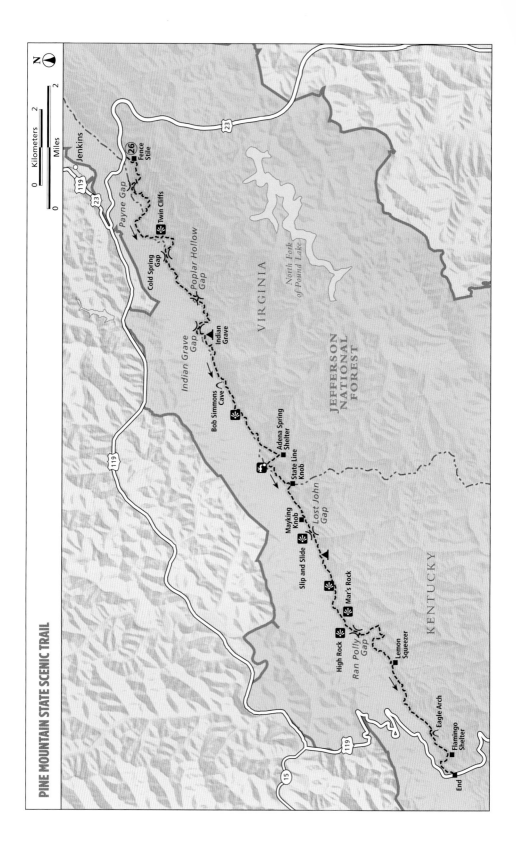

N

Kilometers 2

0

Miles 2

0

Jenkins

119

23

Payne Gap

26

Fence Stile

Cold Spring Gap

Twin Cliffs

Poplar Hollow Gap

VIRGINIA

North Fork of Pound Lake

Indian Grave Gap

Indian Grave

Bob Simmons Cave

119

Adena Spring Shelter

State Line Knob

JEFFERSON NATIONAL FOREST

Mayking Knob

Lost John Gap

Slip and Slide

Mar's Rock

KENTUCKY

High Rock

Ran Polly Gap

Lemon Squeezer

119

15

Eagle Arch

Flamingo Shelter

End

3.6 Stay straight on Pine Mountain State Scenic Trail as the forest road forks. The trail climbs the ridge as a wide two-track dirt road.

3.8 Turn left off the dirt road and follow the Pine Mountain State Scenic Trail as it passes through rock outcrops. Where the trail briefly rejoins the dirt road, stay alert: Within a few feet, turn left again and follow the trail downhill to slip around another knob that rises uphill on the right. *Note:* This work-around is meant to avoid private property.

3.9 A double blaze and a wood sign with an arrow mark a sharp right turn in the trail. Turn right and climb up to Poplar Hollow Gap. In the gap, the trail reverts to an ATV trail.

4.7 In Indian Grave Gap, veer left off the ATV track and follow the trail as a footpath as it skirts another knob on Pine Mountain's ridgeline.

5.4 Reach Indian Grave campsite. (This is a primitive campsite with a seasonal water supply—no water flow in fall and winter months.) After the campsite, the trail rises to the ridgeline, finally offering views north into Kentucky.

5.9 Follow the trail as it drops left off the ridgeline to skirt Bob Simmons Cave, a small cavity in a large rock outcrop uphill on the right. After working around the exposed rock, regain the ridge and enjoy nice views off to the right (north) down into Kentucky.

6.4 After a steep descent through a tunnel of rhododendron, pass through Bear Track Gap (2,910 feet).

6.6 Finish the climb out of Bear Track Gap by turning right and uphill on a forest road. For the next mile, the trail follows a narrow two-track path.

7.5 Double blazes mark a right turn off the narrow two-track path onto a woods path as you begin a descent to Adena Spring shelter.

7.7 Reach Adena Spring shelter. Follow the trail as it swings right and downhill. In 0.1 mile, pass a natural spring. *Note:* Adena is an AT-style covered shelter with room to sleep six to eight people. There is a fire ring, a privy, and a bear pole to hang food.

8.5 Pass through State Line Knob (3,206 feet). From this point south, Pine Mountain State Scenic Trail runs entirely within the state of Kentucky.

9.2 At a USGS benchmark, turn left and head downhill on an old forest road. After a short descent, the trail climbs steeply to another benchmark that marks the high-point of Mayking Knob (3,273 feet), the highest point on Pine Mountain.

9.3 Just past a power substation, descend a tall ledge on a set of iron rungs drilled into the rock. The next 2 miles showcase Pine Mountain's famous cliff-lines and views west into Kentucky at places like Slip and Slide Rock, Box Rock, Mar's Rock, and High Rock.

9.9 Reach the Swindell campsite, a primitive camp with no water sources. Continue south on Pine Mountain State Scenic Trail.

10.0 Follow the trail as it turns left off the ridgeline and descends.

10.5 Cross over The Cliff, an exposed rock face with steep dropoffs off the trail to the right.

10.9 Continue on the green-blazed Pine Mountain State Scenic Trail at a junction with the High Rock Loop Trail on the left. *Option:* High Rock Loop Trail descends into a hemlock grove around the headwaters of Bad Branch and rejoins Pine Mountain State Scenic Trail at mile 12.0 below. The trail and land is protected as the Bad Branch State Nature Preserve.

11.1 Cross Mar's Rock, another exposed rock face with ample views off the right side of the trail into Kentucky. Continue south on Pine Mountain State Scenic Trail and begin a descent into Ran Polly Gap.

11.5 A house-size boulder marks Ran Polly Gap. Hikers can find shelter or shade in a rock overhang. In 0.1 mile beyond Ran Polly Gap, Pine Mountain State Scenic Trail reverts to a wide graded forest road as it follows Bad Branch.

11.9 Turn right at a double green blaze, where the trail leaves the graded road and enters the woods as a footpath. Orange blazes are visible on the trail for 0.1 mile as Pine Mountain State Scenic Trail shares the footpath with High Rock Loop Trail.

12.0 Continue straight on Pine Mountain State Scenic Trail as High Rock Loop Trail splits left and downhill. ***Note:*** It is 1.9 miles on the High Rock Loop Trail to a parking area. En route, the trail passes by a 60-foot waterfall on Bad Branch.

13.0 "Squeeze" through the Lemon Squeezer, a narrow passage between tall rock outcrops.

14.7 Descend a set of stairs and pass a trail sign-in box.

15.1 Enter a clearing for the Flamingo Shelter. Pass straight through and continue on the Pine Mountain State Scenic Trail.

15.3 Enter a wide clearing where two forest roads intersect. Bear left to follow a dirt road, avoiding the hard left turn as well as any road that branches right, or south.

15.5 Veer right off the dirt road and follow a set of stairs downhill. At the foot of the stairs, cross US 119 and climb the roadside embankment via another staircase.

15.7 Hike ends at the Little Shepherd Trail trailhead of Pine Mountain Trail State Park.

HIKE INFORMATION

Local Information
Heart of Appalachia, St. Paul, (276) 762-0011, www.heartofappalachia.com
Wise County Tourism, (276) 328-2321, www.visitwisecounty.com
Letcher County Tourism, Whitesburg, KY, www.discoverletcher.com

Local Events/Attractions
Hills of Home Bluegrass Festival, Aug and Memorial Day weekend, 131 Hills of Home Park, McClure; www.drralphstanleyfestival.com
Virginia Highlands Festival, July/Aug, Abingdon, www.vahighlandsfestival.org
Carter Family Memorial Music Center, weekly live music shows, Hiltons, (276) 594-0676, www.carterfamilyfold.org

Lodging
Breaks Interstate Park, (276) 865-4413, www.breakspark.com, camping, cabins and restaurant. Reservations: www.reservevaparks.com

DINING
Pine Mountain Grill & Gifts, Jenkins, KY, located at the base of Pine Mountain. www.pinemountaingrill.com

Organizations
Pine Mountain Trail Conference (PMTC), www.pinemountainstatescenictrail.com, shadjbaker@gmail.com

Mountain Fork and Little Stony Creek thread the mountains of Wise and Scott Counties in wild and unpredictable fashion. Sticking with them faithfully is the 15-mile Chief Benge Scout Trail, a trek that links the cool waters of High Knob Lake with 30-foot falls, rapids, and small pools on the Little Stony. The trail follows old railroad grades at river level but makes several steep climbs up the ridges that make southwest Virginia such a rugged, wonderful place to hike. There is real variety of plants along this trail, from big-leaf magnolia to the huckleberries on the dry ridges. Bring a fishing pole and test stream waters or the wide Bark Camp Lake. With reliable water sources and only a few steep climbs, this hike is a highlight of any southwest trip.

Start: Parking lot for High Knob Lake in High Knob National Recreation Area (NRA)
Distance: 15.3 miles point to point
Hiking time: About 8 hours
Difficulty: Moderate due to the length and a number of unaided stream crossings
Trail surface: A combination of dirt footpaths, grassy forest roads, and gravel forest roads leads along streams and fern glades, through hardwood forests to 2 lakes and a craggy river gorge with 3 tall waterfalls.
Land status: National forest
Nearest town: Norton, VA
Other trail users: Hikers and bikes only. Motorized use, including e-bikes, is prohibited. Trail may not be suitable for horseback riders.
Accessibility: The Lakeshore Trail at Bark Camp Lake is paved.
Canine compatibility: Dogs permitted
Trail contact: Clinch Ranger District, Norton, (276) 679-8370, www.fs .usda.gov/gwj

Schedule: Open year-round. Hunting is permitted on national forest land. Deer-hunting season in Wise and Scott Counties runs Oct through Jan. Bark Camp Lake Campground is open late May through late Sept. Day use open year-round.
Fees/permits: High Knob Recreation Area day-use and camping fees; Bark Camp Lake Recreation Area day-use and camping fees.
Facilities/features: There are restrooms, picnic areas, and camping at High Knob Recreation Area, open May 15–Sept 15, at the beginning of the hike. Bark Camp Lake, about midway on the trail, has camping, restrooms, and drinking water but only during open season late May–late Sept. Hanging Rock at the eastern terminus of the trail has restrooms, water, and a picnic area.
NatGeo TOPO! map: Wise, Fort Blackmore, Coeburn, Dungannon, Norton, East Stone Gap
NatGeo Trails Illustrated map: Clinch Ranger District

FINDING THE TRAILHEAD

To High Knob, start of Chief Benge Scout Trail: From Big Stone Gap, take VA 23/Alt US 58 East to exit 1. At a stop sign, turn right on VA 619 (good signage for High Knob). It's a curvy, uphill, hairpin road. At 1.9 miles, pass the Flag Rock Recreation Area. At 3.1 miles, enter the national forest (signed). At 3.8 miles, turn left on FR 238. At 4.2 miles, make a sharp, hairpin right to go up to High Knob. A sign says gate is closed 10 p.m. to 6 a.m. (straight would take you to the camping area). Go 0.1 mile to the parking area and sign for trails. Before you head out, walk up the stairs a few hundred feet to the panoramic view from High Knob. **GPS:** N36 53.621' / W82 37.710'.

To Bark Camp Lake (the midway point, if want to break hike into 2 days): From Alt US 58 in Tacoma, take VA 706 South (Stone Mountain Road) and cross a railroad track almost immediately. There is a sign for Bark Camp Lake. At 7.5 miles is a national forest sign. At 8.2 miles, turn left on FR 699 (Pine Camp Road). At 8.5 miles, turn right on VA 822 (good signage). At 10.2 miles, turn right into Bark Camp Lake Recreation Area. Pay Station is at 11 miles. **GPS:** N36 52.017' / W82 31.446'.
To Hanging Rock (end of Chief Benge/Little Stony Falls hike): From Coeburn, take VA 72 south 8.8 miles and turn right into Hanging Rock National Recreation Area. **GPS:** N36 51.681' / W82 26.769'. *DeLorme: Virginia Atlas & Gazetteer*: Page 20, A3-A4.

THE HIKE

Mountain Fork Creek swallows the sunlight with each step along the Chief Benge Scout Trail, as hills on either side steepen and the valley narrows. Thick patches of laurel, small trees, and an earthy smell fill the valley. Downed trees force water into narrow channels that spill over small rock ledges. Rushing water is always audible, even when the stream itself is obscured by vine and shrub entanglements. Soon trail and stream meet, cross, meet again, and cross again—before the wide, flat trail narrows and climbs the left hillside.

At this point, where mountain laurel gives way to oak and maple, we part ways with Mountain Fork—and the spirit who's been stalking silently behind since High Knob Lake. The ghost of Chief Bob Benge won't be following us up Bark Camp Branch; instead, he'll steer right along Big Stony Creek. Painted in warrior colors and traveling by night, he'll head south to the Livingston Farm on the North Fork Holston. He'll return this way, with prisoners and booty, evading militia by traveling obscure mountain passes. Eleven miles north of here, in a gap overlooking the city of Norton, he'll die as he did in 1794, of a bullet to the head.

Chief Benge entered southwest Virginia in April 1777 leading a band of Cherokee and Shawnee, marking the start of an 18-year reign of terror. A man who had, in his youth, lived with his Native American mother and English stepfather at Dorton's Fort on the Copper River, would kill between forty to fifty settlers as retribution for their encroachment on Native American land. Hunting parties fell prey to his ambushes. Farmers looked up from work to find him standing over them. Women peered from their homes, saw nothing . . . looked again . . . and saw Benge. Like a ghost, he materialized, murdered, plundered, and moved on.

What caused a man with an English father, trader John Benge, and Cherokee mother, Elizabeth Watts Dorton, to strike out so?

Benge came of age in the 1770s, a tense time in the colonies. City folk on the Eastern Seaboard were ruffled by such concepts as taxation without representation. In southwest Virginia, a more tangible threat occupied settlers. Local Native American tribes were lashing out against settlers' land gains down the Clinch, Powell, and Holston Valleys. When the American Revolution broke out in 1776, British-instigated Cherokee and Shawnee war parties returned to southwest Virginia for revenge. Virginia's Holston Militia retaliated by burning Cherokee towns in Tennessee. Bob Benge, who had run away from Dorton's Fort as a teenager to live out his days as a Cherokee, lost his home twice in these raids. Neighbors from his childhood years helped pillage his village.

With his red head and fair complexion, Benge could pass as a settler. He spoke flawless English and knew the mountains of the Clinch, Holston, and Powell Valleys like few others. His discovery of a pass between Stone and Powell Mountains enabled him to move in and out of the region undetected.

The view from High Knob near the trailhead for Chief Benge Scout Trail

The morning of April 6, 1794, found Benge at the Livingston family home near Mendota on the North Fork Holston River. A daughter of Elizabeth Livingston later described the scene:

> One bright morning after the sun had risen and the men had gone to the clearings and the women were busy at their wheels and looms, all joyous and jovial amid the fragrance of wild flowers and the music of songbirds, and not dreaming of coming danger, Benge and his painted warriors stealthily approached and surrounded the cabins.

In short order, Benge's band killed a woman and three children, burned the house, and carried off eight prisoners, including the wife of Henry Livingston, Susannah.

Runners carried the alarm northeast to Castlewood (then Castle's Wood) and northwest to Yoakum's Station near present-day Dryden. Militias moved to predetermined mountain passes Benge might use. A small group started out after Benge and tracked him down the North Fork Holston River to Hilton, across Clinch Mountain at Hamilton Gap, and north to the Clinch River. Yet as hours slipped past, the Cherokee's trail grew faint.

At the Clinch River just south of present-day Dungannon, Benge's raiding party made a fateful misstep—literally. Author Lawrence Fleenor recounts in his book *Benge!* how a wet moccasin print on a dry stone tipped pursuers to his route. Benge moved downstream to the confluence of Big Stony Creek near Fort Blackmore, turned upstream, and followed Big Stony up Powell Mountain, his pursuers closing ground.

In late afternoon, the sun slips behind Powell Mountain, shrouding one entire side of the Mountain Fork stream valley in dusk. The opposite bank remains bathed in warm light, although the hiker still feels vulnerable to ever-encroaching shadows. At this point, Chief Benge Scout Trail climbs up the left hill, first gradually, then at a steeper grade. Mountain Fork is 200 feet below you. Sunlight bathes a large fern glade on the valley floor. It's tempting to imagine Benge walking here on April 7, 1794. He would have kept one prisoner, Susannah Livingston, wife of Henry Livingston, out in front. The remaining prisoners would have been behind him. In single file, the party would have passed out of the light into the shadows of the stream valley, picking their way upstream to High Knob and spending the night at Camp Rock.

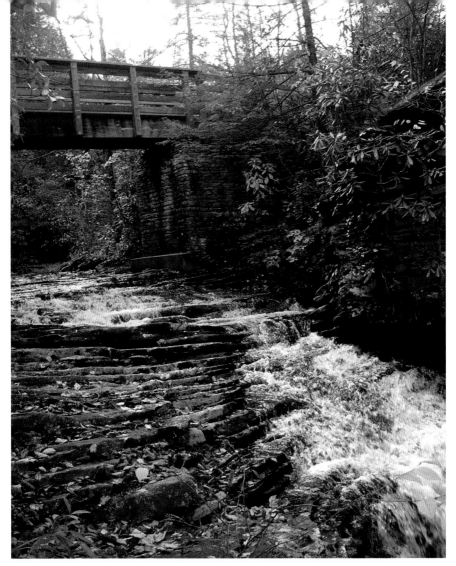

Falls at Little Stony

Benge did spend his last night alive at Camp Rock, but best evidence shows he followed a more direct route up Powell Mountain, one roughly approximated by VA 619. He was headed for a gap in the mountains overlooking a town called Prince's Flats (present-day Norton). At this pass, now called Benge's Gap, the party turned west and entered Hoot Owl Hollow.

Benge's pursuers set an ambush in Little Stony Gap, a deep mountain pass flanked by steep ridges and a valley floor covered with large rocks. Militiamen watched as Benge hustled his prisoners up the trail. One man took aim, but noise in lifting his rifle alerted Benge to danger. The Cherokee ran and, as he fled, stepped in a hole. The bullet intended to hit him square in the back lodged in his head.

Benge's death is a watershed event in southwest Virginia; raids on settlers ceased with his passing. The Cherokee, already pushed far beyond their homelands, never threatened the region again in any material way.

The Chief Benge Scout Trail touches only briefly on its namesake. Still, the warrior lingers with you on the 15-mile trek to the falls at Little Stony. The trail is a fitting tribute to a Native American whose hidden paths along dark mountain stream valleys enabled him to make a statement, however destructive, against the expansion of white settlers into Cherokee land.

MILES AND DIRECTIONS

0.0 Start at the High Knob Lake parking area. Walk 0.2 mile downhill, turn left in front of a shower house, and cross a small bridge spanning Mountain Fork (on USGS topo quadrant Wise, this stream is labeled Stony Creek but has been renamed). **Note:** There is a water spigot near the shower house. Stock up on water here. The trail follows streams almost its entire route, but this is the only treated water source for 9.5 miles.

0.5 Cross a concrete dam at the top of High Knob Lake and turn right on Chief Benge Scout Trail, a wide, flat dirt trail along the left bank of Mountain Fork. Through this ever-deepening stream valley, you'll hop the rough-and-tumble creek five times in the next 2 miles.

1.9 Pass a nice campground amid hemlocks on the right side of the trail.

2.4 Cross FR 704 and drop down the opposite bank. The trail keeps its wide, flat course while Mountain Fork runs through some wild stretches, obscured by rhododendron, other times nearly dammed by tree debris.

3.5 Climb out of the stream valley up the left slope and wrap around a small hill. (Mountain Fork takes a much longer route around the base of this hill.) The climb, at first gradual, steepens considerably as a drainage forms downslope on the right.

4.2 Cross Bark Camp Branch and climb out of this stream gully to a large field within 0.5 mile.

4.6 Pass by a natural gas well and enter a young hardwood forest. The trail, ascending on a gentle slope, is wide, grassy, and dry.

5.2 Turn left onto a gravel road (FR 2570). Within twenty paces, turn right and hike along a wide grassy road.

5.8 The trail reverts to a singletrack woods path as it descends off a small hill, crossing by the headwaters of Little Stony Creek.

6.1 Cross VA 706 and descend on another grassy woods road. Between here and Little Stony Creek, two trails branch right off this road. Stay left each time.

6.9 Cross Little Stony Creek and hike along the left stream bank. After a short distance, the trail climbs the hill on your left to meet a forest road.

7.3 Cross a gravel road (FR 2560) and reenter woods directly opposite on a narrow woods path. Ferns line the trail and there are several large specimens of big-leaf

CHIEF BENGE SCOUT TRAIL

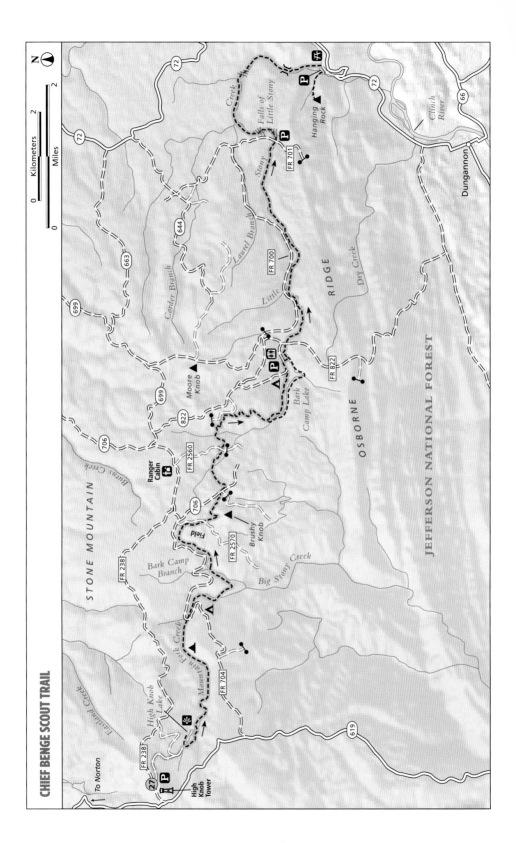

magnolias. From here, the trail drops back to Little Stony Creek and you'll follow the right stream bank for a short distance, then hop it to follow the left streamside.

8.4 Reach the Lakeshore Loop Trail encircling Bark Camp Lake. Signs show the Chief Benge Trail turns right and traces the backside of the lake. Turn left for a nice respite at Bark Camp Lake Recreation Area.

9.5 After wrapping in and out of the lake's marshy fingers, enter the picnic area. (There are bathrooms, a water spigot, and picnic tables.) Reconnect with the Chief Benge Trail by following the Lakeshore Loop Trail to a dam on the lower end of Bark Camp Lake. Cross the concrete portion of the dam, then immediately turn left and follow the right stream bank of Little Stony Creek. This is a difficult stretch of trail, obscured by tall shrubs and poorly marked. Cues for the turnoff include several rusted metal posts and a rotted stump slashed with double yellow blazes found on the earthen embankment just after the concrete portion of the dam.

9.7 Reach FR 822, a gravel road. Turn right and walk along the road for less than 0.1 mile. A sign on the left side reads "Falls of Little Stony, 4.9 Miles." Turn left and drop back into woods. The river is on your left side. Seven stream crossings follow in quick succession.

10.4 After the ninth stream crossing, look for a nice campsite on the right side of the trail. Ahead, the trail skips across Little Stony eight more times.

12.2 Look right immediately after crossing Little Stony Creek. There is a campsite under hemlocks on a small bluff at a bend in the river. Large stream boulders are ideal for lounging.

12.5 Reach FR 701. Follow the gravel road right, enter a vehicle turnaround, and look for the trailhead for Little Stony National Recreation Trail at a signboard at the back of the parking lot.

12.7 Cross over the top of a spectacular 25-foot waterfall. Two other falls (10 feet and 30 feet) follow in quick succession. After this, the trail drops to stream level and passes through hemlock and cove forests.

15.3 Reach Hanging Rock Picnic Area and the southern terminus of the Chief Benge and Little Stony Trails.

HIKE INFORMATION

Local Information
Scott County Tourism, www.explorescottcountyva.org

Wise County Tourism, (276) 328-2321, www.visitwisecounty.com

Heart of Appalachia, St. Paul, (276) 762-0011, www.heartofappalachia.com

Local Events/Attractions
Carter Family Memorial Music Center, weekly live music shows, Hiltons, (276) 594-0676, www.carterfamilyfold.org

High Knob Recreation Area, Norton, (276) 679-1754. Camping May 15–Sept 15.

Bark Camp Lake, Coeburn, (276) 328-2931. Camping May 15–Sept 15.

Natural Tunnel State Park, Duffield, (276) 940-2674, www.dcr.virginia.gov/state-parks/natural-tunnel. Camping and cabin reservations: www.reservevaparks.com.

Jessie Lea RV Park, Big Stone Gap, (276) 523-0055, www.jessielearv.com

Other Resources
Benge! by Lawrence J. Fleenor Jr., biography of Chief Benge

28 DEVILS FORK LOOP

Devils Fork is a luxuriant streamscape of rocks, cliffs, and small cascades that grow in size and frequency as you hike. It all comes together at the Devils Bathtub, where a long waterfall trips step by step over shale bedrock and crashes in a swirl of currents into a bowl-like pool—the bathtub. Framed by tall hemlocks and rhododendron, this scenery is as lush and abundant as the landscape a few hundred feet upslope is simple and unadorned.

Start: Forest gate at the end of FR 2631
Distance: 7.1-mile loop
Hiking time: About 4 hours
Difficulty: Strenuous due to the more than 10 unaided stream crossings, a narrow ledge, and 1 steep climb
Trail surface: Dirt footpaths and dirt roads lead through hardwood forest slopes and hemlock groves along streams.
Land status: National forest
Nearest town: Norton, VA
Other trail users: Hikers only
Accessibility: None
Canine compatibility: Dogs permitted

Trail contact: Clinch Ranger District, Norton, (276) 679-8370, www.fs .usda.gov/gwj
Schedule: Open year-round. Hunting is allowed on national forest land. Deer-hunting season in Scott County runs Oct through Jan. The national forest limits hiking groups to 10 people.
Fees/permits: High Knob Recreation Area day-use and camping fees; Bark Camp Lake Recreation Area day-use and camping fees.
Facilities/features: None, not even drinking water
NatGeo TOPO! map: East Stone Gap, Fort Blackmore
NatGeo Trails Illustrated map: Clinch Ranger District

FINDING THE TRAILHEAD

From VA 72 North near Fort Blackmore, turn left on VA 619 (Big Stoney Creek Road). Go 3.6 miles to the community of "Ka." In 0.6 mile, turn left on "High Knob SC" (it is still VA 619). In 0.3 mile, see an abandoned house on the left, surrounded by a chain-link fence, and a very rough dirt road to the left of the house. There are No Trespassing signs, so no parking here. You can drive this forest road, but 4WD or high-clearance is recommended. Go 0.2 mile to a clearing to park. Look to the right of the clearing for the trail sign, concrete steps up an incline, and yellow tree blazes. **GPS:** N36 49.107' / W82 37.602'. *DeLorme: Virginia Atlas & Gazetteer*: Page 20, B3.

THE HIKE

The trip up Devils Run hollow is 3 miles of tricky hiking. At each stream crossing, shrubs and ferns hide where the trail might climb the opposite bank; however, the trail is very well marked, with brown trail markers every half-mile as well as yellow tree blazes. The deeper into the hollow, the more damp and shaded the scenery. The rocky, uneven trail creeps up in elevation until stream banks become small cliffs, and the river froths 20 feet below your feet.

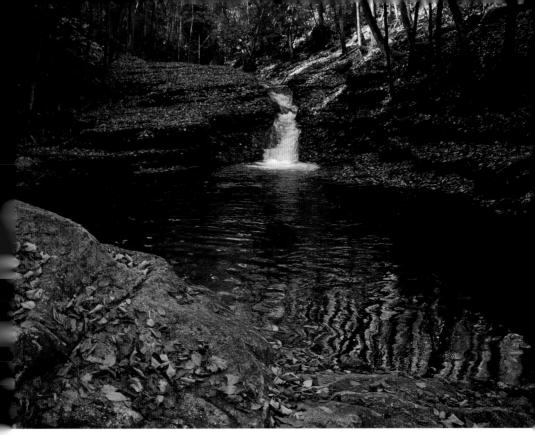

A stream cascades into a shady pool, nicknamed the Devils Bathtub.

This ruggedness makes it hard to fathom how a railroad once ran along this stream. It's been 80 years or more since private landowners carted oak, beech, chestnut, and poplar trees off the mountain slopes around Devils Fork. These were old-growth trees, described by one 19th-century traveler as "walls and buttresses, square structures like the titanic ruins of castles." As had been the case throughout much of southwest Virginia, companies from New York and Philadelphia owned the timber. A sawmill could produce 12,000 board feet from just three of these trees. (A small home uses about 6,000 board feet of timber—which means three of these trees could supply the lumber needed for two homes.) At the other end of the scale, Singer Manufacturing Company bought and removed all black walnut of a certain size in neighboring Wise County for their sewing machine cabinets and base plates.

HEADS UP
This trail is very popular, and parking is limited. The access road to the small trailhead may require a high-clearance vehicle. Additional parking is available at Scott County's Stony Creek Park, approximately one-half mile from the trailhead. Trail is subject to flash flooding during heavy rain. Exercise caution, and check weather prior to your visit. With more than ten stream crossings, prepare to get wet. Best done in warmer weather.

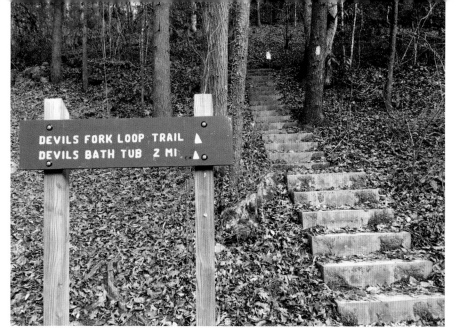

Signboard at the start of the trail MICHELLE DUFFOURC

Halfway between Straight Fork and Devils Bathtub, a rusted coal car lies half-buried in trailside brambles. Uphill from this, speculators dug a mining prospect in search of coal. These were "punch mines," small dents dug out of hills in hopes of finding a vein. Coal's era has passed, while natural gas production is rising. The return leg of Devils Fork Loop crosses a dirt road high on Stone Mountain. Embedded in the dirt road path are signs of modern prospecting. Exploratory drilling for natural gas produces long pieces of smooth, round stones—as large as a silver dollar and broken into 2- or 3-inch pieces.

When coal miners worked this area, they did so exclusively on the north bank of Devils Fork. The stream follows a geologic fault between sandstone on the north stream bank, which holds coal deposits, and limestone on the south bank. On its north stream bank, acid soil supports the hemlock and rhododendron that lend the hollow its lush setting. There are few, if any, of these type of plants on the south stream bank, where the soil is less hospitable.

The hemlocks along Devils Fork are second- and third-growth. Rhododendron, which seems to grow hand in hand with hemlock, fills the gaps in the forest floor. A spring hike here, while certain to net you wet feet, also leaves a lasting impression of both these evergreens. As you climb, the hemlock and rhododendron decrease in number until, on well-drained mountain slopes, white oak and hickory trees form the forest canopy. Off the slope run five streams and numerous seasonal runoffs, all of which feed Devils Fork. A century ago, when chestnut trees grew tall and wide, loggers would range throughout this forest, cutting rings around the trunk at certain intervals. Using tools called spuds, they ripped bark from the tree in sheets, piled it high onto wagons, and hauled it to tanneries. Before railroads and on-site sawmills, the trees were too difficult to remove. More often than not, they were left to rot.

At times, the route across Stone Mountain's slope pitches sharply downhill and right. This pitch is what, in part, led Appalachian Power in the mid-1970s to propose flooding Devils Fork and creating a reservoir out of the stream valley. Using a pipeline, the company could have generated electricity by directing the flow of water between the proposed reservoir and Big Cherry Reservoir on Long Mountain. Opposition from local residents was swift, and Appalachian Power abandoned the plan. The idea of protecting Devils Fork persisted, however. When the national forest proposed a road up the side of Little Mountain, a local trail club rose to the cause. Roadwork progressed to the point where a survey crew cut a first pass through the forest, but then the project was dropped. Sensing an opportunity, the trail club made use of the crew's work. Today, the road that would have opened the Devils Fork watershed up for timber harvest and natural gas production is one section of this loop.

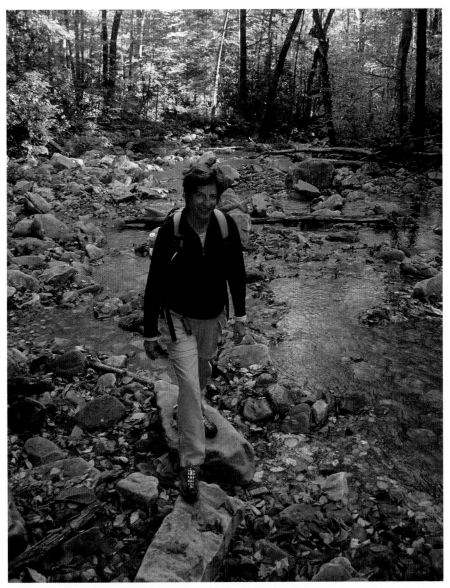

The author on one of the many stream crossings on Devils Fork Trail

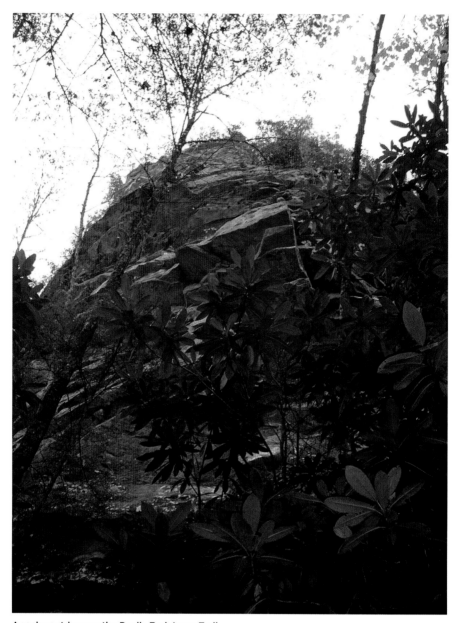

A rocky outdrop on the Devils Fork Loop Trail

MILES AND DIRECTIONS

0.0 Start at a parking area on FR 2631. Depart the parking area by walking up a flight of tall stairs and turning left on the dirt and gravel forest road.

0.1 Cross Straight Fork. In a few feet, bear left at a double yellow blaze, avoiding a trail that branches right. ***Note:*** The yellow-blazed dirt road that arcs right and uphill from this clearing is the return leg of this loop.

0.3 Cross Devils Fork, the first of numerous crossings in the next 2 miles. The trail alternates between wide, flat stretches and narrow, eroded footpaths. Sections of trail often merge with the streambed itself. After spring floods, parts of the trail may be washed out or blocked by downed trees.

0.6 After crossing Devils Fork several times, stay alert for ruins of a small railcar on the right side of the trail. (A narrow-gauge railroad once ran alongside Devils Fork, used to haul out lumber from the stream valley.)

1.4 Arrive at a scenic crossing of Devils Fork. Just downstream, the river bends and the stratified layers of bedrock are visible where the stream has eroded and undercut the stream bank.

1.5 In an area of fallen rocks strewn around the trail, a tall cliff face rises five stories high on the left side of the trail. Descend along the trail to the stream and the first of the "tubs" that comprise the "Devils Bathtub." (Devils Bathtub's name derives from the way the stream pours down a V-shaped cut in the shale streambed and swirls in whirlpool fashion into a round "tub," or basin at the foot of the falls.)

2.1 The trail takes a sharp right turn and heads northwest out of the Devils Fork gorge. Deep Hollow forms below on the right.

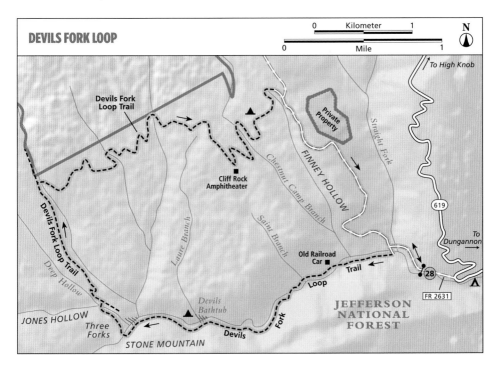

DEVILS FORK LOOP

2.3	After a steep climb on a woods path, the trail merges with an old roadbed, which is a wide, graded, and grassy path. In 0.1 mile after this merge, turn right at a double yellow blaze and descend into Deep Hollow on a footpath. Cross the small stream and climb the opposite hillside.
2.8	Switchback over a shoulder ridge separating Deep and Corder Hollows. The footpath will climb, then drop off this ridge into Corder Hollow.
3.6	Cross a streambed (dry in late summer) and begin a traverse of Little Mountain's undulating slope. A number of streams run down this hill to Devils Fork.
4.1	Veer left and downhill at a double yellow blaze on the trail.
4.6	Crest a small knoll and note the six-trunked tree. (Trees with two or more trunks are common in woodlands that were once logged. It is evidence of *girdling*, or removing a ring of bark between knee and waist high. This kills the tree above the girdle mark but not below. The still-living trunk will often sprout two or more trunks as it grows again.)
4.8	Turn right at a double blaze and descend right off the hillside into a gully. There is a natural rock amphitheater here along the right side of the trail.
4.9	Bear right as the trail merges with a faint road trace.
5.5	Straight Fork Ridge Trail enters from the left. Turn right and begin a descent to Straight Fork. Tree blazes become much less frequent, but it's easy to follow the wide old logging road.
6.0	Bear right as the trail merges with another grassy road. Uphill is private property.
7.0	Enter a clearing alongside Straight Fork. Cross the stream and hike up a small knoll on the dirt/gravel forest road.
7.1	Arrive back at the parking area on FR 2631.

HIKE INFORMATION

Local Information

Scott County Tourism, www.explorescottcountyva.org

Wise County Tourism, (276) 328-2321, www.visitwisecounty.com

Heart of Appalachia, St. Paul, (276) 762-0011, www.heartofappalachia.com

Local Events/Attractions

Carter Family Memorial Music Center, weekly live music shows, Hiltons, (276) 594-0676, www.carterfamilyfold.org

Lodging

High Knob Recreation Area, Norton, (276) 679-1754. Camping May 15–Sept 15.

Bark Camp Lake, Coeburn, (276) 328-2931. Camping May 15–Sept 15.

Natural Tunnel State Park, Duffield, (276) 940-2674, www.dcr.virginia.gov/state-parks/natural-tunnel. Camping and cabin reservations: www.reservevaparks.com.

Jessie Lea RV Park, Big Stone Gap, (276) 523-0055, www.jessielearv.com

HONORABLE MENTIONS: SOUTHWEST HIGHLANDS

EE. STONE MOUNTAIN TRAIL

From Cave Springs Recreation Area and campground, climb 2.5 miles to dramatic rock outcrops and overhangs atop Stone Mountain. A longer option is to follow Stone Mountain Trail one way 12.5 miles down Roaring Run to the town of Appalachia (shuttle required). From High Butte, it's possible to see the bumpy profile of Kentucky's Black Mountains to the west, while eastward run Virginia's narrow ridges and valleys. At approximately the halfway point (7 miles), you can take a 1-mile detour on the blue-blazed Olinger Gap Trail to Lake Keokee for a primitive camping overnight. **GPS:** N36 53.015' / W82 47.276'. *DeLorme: Virginia Atlas & Gazetteer*: Page 20, A1.

FF. HUCKLEBERRY LOOP

The 8-mile Huckleberry Loop encircles Locust Knob and Huckleberry Ridge in the Peters Mountain Wilderness Area. The trail down Dismal Branch on the eastern slope of Peters Mountain is as rough as they come, overrun with rhododendron, blocked by blowdowns, and often lost altogether in the streambed. This trail sums up everything a wilderness should be: beautiful, difficult, and, in the end, extremely satisfying. **GPS:** N37 25.597' / W80 33.331'. *DeLorme: Virginia Atlas & Gazetteer*: Page 41, A5.

GG. CRAWFISH/CHANNEL ROCK

From the flat bottomland and old fields of Crawfish Valley, Crawfish/Channel Rock Trail ascends Brushy Mountain on steep, narrow footpaths. En route, you'll cross the Tennessee Valley Divide, where Reed Creek and Bear Creek flow off opposite sides of the ridge. Each enters separate, ever-expanding stream networks that eventually reach the Ohio River, albeit 100 miles distant from one another. Deer and raccoons forage along the stream edges; turkeys and ruffed grouse hunt for acorns on the slopes of Brushy and Walker Mountains. Beavers leave the most lasting impression: a two-stage dam you'll traverse on Bear Creek. **GPS:** N36 57.916' / W81 18.916'. *DeLorme: Virginia Atlas & Gazetteer*: Page 23, A6.

HH. THE RICE FIELDS

From Blacksburg, take VA 460 west to VA 641; make a right onto VA 641 and follow to a parking lot (within 0.5 mile of where the Appalachian Trail [AT] crosses the road). The Rice Fields are beautiful open meadows on top of Peters Mountain accessed via the AT. For 10 miles along this stretch, the AT follows the Virginia–West Virginia border. Where it intersects the Allegheny Trail, the AT descends back into Virginia. This is an out-and-back hike with no loop possibilities. (540) 552-4641. **GPS:** N37 21.306' / W.80 45.944'. *DeLorme: Virginia Atlas & Gazetteer*: Page 40, B3.

II. GUEST RIVER GORGE TRAIL

A 5.8-mile point-to-point on a former railroad grade along the Guest River west of St. Paul. Starting at the northern end, this pleasant walk is a gradual and scenic descent into the gorge. The railway hauled the coal and saltpeter mined in the gorge, leaving behind sheer cliffs. The area harbors several threatened and endangered animals and plants. (540) 328-2931, www.dgif.virginia.gov/vbwt/sites/guest-river-gorge-trail. **GPS:** N36 55.378' / W82 27.053'. *DeLorme: Virginia Atlas & Gazetteer.* Page 20, A4.

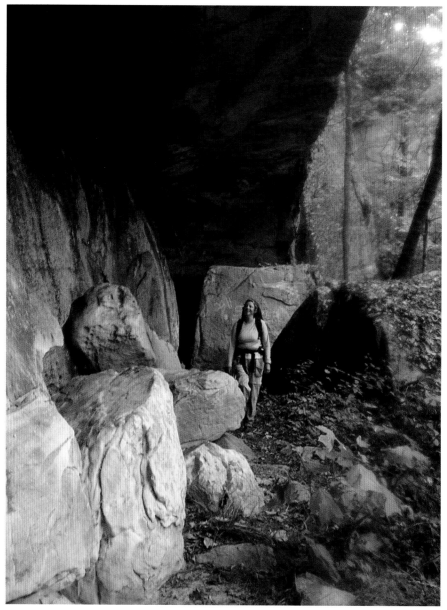

The author walking beneath the Stone Mountain overhang

MOUNT ROGERS NATIONAL RECREATION AREA

In Virginia, the Blue Ridge escarpment culminates in a large concentration of peaks and ridges near the North Carolina border. Here, Mount Rogers pokes a tree-shrouded summit above neighboring mountains to lay claim as the state's highest point. Competition is stiff, with only a 200-foot difference between it and nearby Whitetop Mountain. Striking about both—other than their size—is how little these peaks and the rural landscape around them resemble the more dramatic and sharply etched mountains in the northern Blue Ridge. The difference reflects forces that have shaped each. Folding and faulting characterized late-era mountain-building activity to the north. Here in southwest Virginia, the Blue Ridge's sweeping mountain slopes and rounded stream valleys resulted from hundreds of millions of years of erosion.

Little about Mount Rogers's high country resembles Virginia's other mountain regions. The spruce-fir forest at the highest elevations contains plants and animals typical of northern boreal forests, a result of the last ice age, which pushed plants and animals southward in its path. Mount Rogers's volcanic bedrock contains rhyolite, a mineral found nowhere else in Virginia. Even views seem otherworldly. Looking west from a wide meadow between Cabin Ridge and Mount Rogers appears more Big Sky, Montana, than Southern Appalachian.

In the high-mountain meadows that slope away from Mount Rogers, horses graze in knee-high grass. A hiker's approaching footsteps may stir a foal that lies hidden in the overgrowth on Wilburn Ridge. Hawthorn trees and large, house-size boulders are scattered randomly across the fields above. Scales break up the smooth lines of these meadows. The fields here are entirely man-made, created after clear-cut logging and since maintained, first by grazing and now through periodic burning done by the Forest Service.

Given the popularity of climbing Mount Rogers, visitors would do well to disperse their activity over as wide an area as possible. In a recreation area of 117,000 acres, it's easy to find other attractions, be it the laurel-choked streams on Iron Mountain or the rugged backcountry in Little Dry Run Wilderness, in the often-overlooked eastern section of Mount Rogers National Recreation Area.

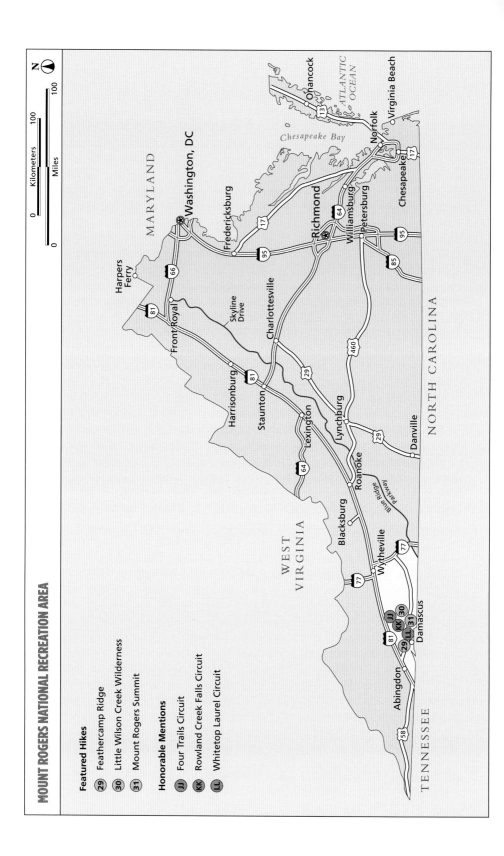

MOUNT ROGERS NATIONAL RECREATION AREA

Featured Hikes

- (29) Feathercamp Ridge
- (30) Little Wilson Creek Wilderness
- (31) Mount Rogers Summit

Honorable Mentions

- (JJ) Four Trails Circuit
- (KK) Rowland Creek Falls Circuit
- (LL) Whitetop Laurel Circuit

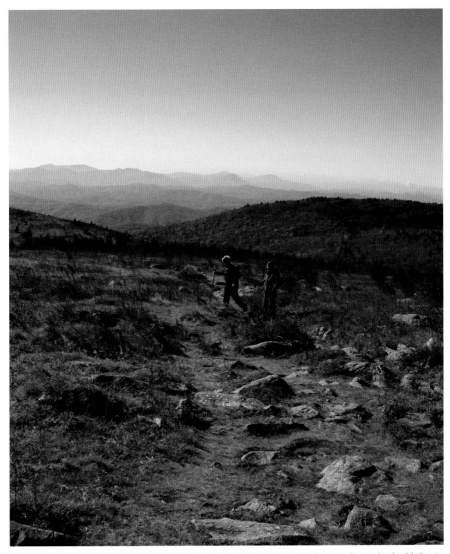

The author, Mary Burnham, and friend Jodi Urban, hiking to Mount Rogers Summit, the highest point in Virginia

THE HIKES
29. Feathercamp Ridge
30. Little Wilson Creek Wilderness
31. Mount Rogers Summit

HONORABLE MENTIONS
JJ. Four Trails Circuit
KK. Rowland Creek Falls Circuit
LL. Whitetop Laurel Circuit

29 FEATHERCAMP RIDGE

If Mount Rogers's summit is the heart, then Iron Mountain is the backbone of southwest Virginia's mountain playground. Its breadth, 80 miles from the Tennessee-Virginia state line to the New River, makes it one of Virginia's longest ridges. The natural resources it holds made it a target of mineral and timber industries in earlier times. Now it simply offers miles of uninterrupted hiking and access to remote, less-visited parts of Mount Rogers National Recreation Area. On Feathercamp Branch, the scenery rivals any along Virginia's many mountain streams. As it ducks under thick rhododendron, it gathers speed between the steep shoulders of Iron Mountain and drops into shallow pools deep enough to wade.

Start: Appalachian Trail (AT) at US 58
Distance: 8.1-mile loop
Hiking time: About 5 hours
Difficulty: Moderate due to well-graded trails, good signage, gentle ascents, and only a few steep sections of trail
Trail surface: Dirt woodland paths and old roads lead to dry ridges, cove forests, and streams.
Land status: National recreation area
Nearest town: Damascus, VA
Other trail users: Mountain bikers and equestrians
Accessibility: You can access the accessible Virginia Creeper Trail at Straight Branch.
Canine compatibility: Dogs permitted
Trail contact: Mount Rogers National Recreation Area, Marion, (276) 783-5196 or (800) 628-7202, www.fs

.usda.gov/gwj. The visitor center is 10 miles north of Troutdale on VA 16.
Schedule: Open year-round. Hunting permitted, with the busiest season between Nov and Jan.
Fees/permits: No permits required. Free backcountry camping.
Facilities/features: Toilet and parking at trailhead
NatGeo TOPO! map: Konnarock
NatGeo Trails Illustrated map: Mount Rogers High Country; Mount Rogers National Recreation Area; Appalachian Trail, Damascus to Bailey Gap
Other maps: Mount Rogers High Country & Wilderness map available at Mount Rogers Visitor Center; Appalachian Trail Map 1: Mount Rogers National Recreation Area available from Appalachian Trail Conservancy, Harpers Ferry, WV. Maps and guidebooks available at Mt. Rogers Outfitters, Damascus.

FINDING THE TRAILHEAD

From Damascus, take VA 91/US 58 east. At 0.6 mile, VA 91 splits to the right. Turn left to stay on US 58. Go 3.1 miles and turn right into the Straight Branch NRA parking area (there's a sign for Virginia Creeper Trail parking), with a restroom and access to the AT and Virginia Creeper Trail (the Iron Mountain Trailhead is across the highway.)

From Grayson Highlands SP, take US 58 west 22.7 miles to the Straight Branch NRA parking area on the left. **GPS:** N36 38.639' / 81 44.405'. *DeLorme: Virginia Atlas & Gazetteer*: Page 22, D2.

THE HIKE

As mountain ridges go, Iron Mountain is classic—undulating and, as you huff up and over your umpteenth knob, seemingly never-ending. Small peaks punctuate the long ridgeline. Hikers know a day spent "up on the ridge" is both an exhilarating and exasperating experience. The latter emotion results, unfortunately, from sheer monotony. Woods-covered ridges lack the glamour of a peak, or the drama, say, of a canyon. After the sixth knob (was it the sixth or was that last one the sixth?), they start to resemble a popular television rabbit: They keep going and going and going . . .

The Iron Mountain Trail would suffer this unkind judgment, if not for some key redeeming features. Among them, in my humble opinion, are blackberry thickets near Clark Mountain. One hundred yards of trailside thickets hold blackberries so juicy and plump, a mere touch stains the fingers with dark juice. No one should ever become so busy walking that she ignores the fruits of her labor.

Iron Mountain's other treasure lies in the many coves formed by ridge spurs that intersect it from all directions. Streams, torturous in their route, cut down these narrow, lush valleys. In the shade of tall trees, layers of leaf rot make a fertile bed for an array of mushrooms. The scaly vase chanterelle is an eye-catcher. Orange or yellow in color, its shape looks suspiciously like a waffle cone. Unlike waffle cones, however, tasting this mushroom is not recommended. It's not poisonous, but has a bitter flavor and may cause indigestion. Other mushrooms pop up unexpectedly as you hike: slickners (poisonous), American Caesars (edible, but not choice), and yellow and violet corals, as well as milky mushrooms.

The abundance of mushrooms on the Iron Mountain section of the Appalachian Trail makes it worth a closer look. Technically, mushrooms are plants. Unlike green plants, however, they do not contain chlorophyll; their food source is organic material. Where a mushroom grows not only helps identify the type, but also the food source. The thick, pink beefsteak polypore grows on dead trees and extracts food from the rotting wood. The largest and most-studied mushroom type, the mycorrhizal, has a symbiotic relationship with their host plant. Out of sight, beneath the earth, a mycorrhizal mushroom coats root stems of plants with threadlike strands; this helps the host plant grow. In exchange, the mushroom receives food. Of course, most people identify a mushroom by its cap—technically the fruit of a mushroom. And while tracking edible wild mushrooms is a booming hobby (remember, never eat a wild mushroom unless absolutely sure it is edible), their plentiful shapes and colors on Iron Mountain approach the beauty of wildflowers in spring.

The wildflowers on Feathercamp Branch emerge in April. The white blossom of mayapple hides away beneath umbrella-shaped leaves on a single, delicate stem (only plants with two leaves produce a flower). Appearances notwithstanding, this small wildflower is cousin to barberry, a thorny bush favored by professional landscapers—the link between them is berries. Anyone familiar with the orange and yellow barberry fruit will see a resemblance in the mayapple, which bears a single, red fruit 3 months after the flower blossoms. Herbalists use crushed barberry root for treating pink eye, diarrhea, and giardiasis (which hikers know as the infection contracted from drinking untreated stream or spring water). The unripe mayapple fruit isn't poisonous, but it will give you a stomachache.

Feathercamp Branch is a beauty of a stream, decked out in rhododendron, mountain laurel, and shrubby trees. After a rainstorm, shrubs and thickets fairly burst with chirps

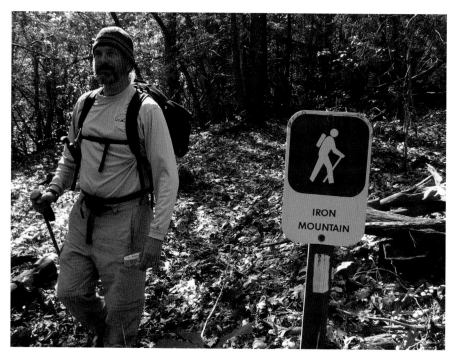

The author on the Iron Mountain Trail

and peeps of warblers and songbirds. The stream sings as well, running a gentle grade between two steep ridges. An impenetrable thicket of rhododendron camouflages the stream near its headwaters. Farther downstream, you can sit on boulders and watch buds fall from rhododendron and float past. If they were seaworthy, they'd eventually reach the Gulf of Mexico via Laurel Creek, the New River, the Kanawha River, the Ohio River, and, finally, the great Mississippi. Across Iron Mountain, Rush Creek flows off in the opposite direction of Feathercamp Branch; it empties into the South Fork Holston River. It, too, will reach the Gulf of Mexico someday, but because the ridge of Iron Mountain marks the Tennessee Divide, these two streams follow very different routes. That's the effect of the divide: Streams that begin a mere 2,500 feet apart empty into the Ohio River more than 100 miles distant from one another.

The Ohio and Mississippi Rivers and the Gulf of Mexico are distant thoughts as you nestle into your sleeping bag on Feathercamp Ridge. Leaves rustle, twigs crack, tree branches sway. If you're straining your ears, trying to attach size and shape to the noises (Feathercamp Ridge is home to deer, turkeys, a host of other animals, and a good number of bears as well), take comfort that you're not alone. Somewhere above you, in the trees, a great horned owl swivels its head. The owl's eyes are encased in bone. To compensate for little eye movement, they turn their heads on very flexible necks, with a rotation range of 270 degrees in some species. The great horned owl is among the largest of owls, and streamsides such as Feathercamp Branch make ideal hunting ground for live prey. But before you ever hear it swoop for a mouse or frog, you'll hear its signature call: three to eight hoots, the second and third rapid and doubled. Superstition labels owls as harbingers of ghosts and omens of death—in part due to their silent flight and stalking nature. It's also true, however, that when salted and eaten, the owl was thought to cure gout. I prefer to think of them as sentinels, sitting stock-still on a branch. If I'm feeling spooked, I mimic their call. There's a good chance the owl will respond.

MILES AND DIRECTIONS

0.0 Start from a pull-off on US 58 at the confluence of Laurel Creek and Straight Branch. Cross US 58, enter the woods, and hike upstream following white AT blazes. **Note:** The Forest Service built a large earthen mound where the trail enters woods to block off-road vehicles.

0.1 The blue-blazed Feathercamp Branch Trail continues straight. Turn left and follow the AT for a 2-mile climb to Iron Mountain Trail through rich hardwood forests.

0.6 The AT intersects with a dirt road (FR 4552). Cross the road and continue straight along the AT. (**Option:** A right turn on FR 4552 will take you up to the top of Iron Mountain, making for a shorter hike.) The trail is nicely constructed to dip in and out of Iron Mountain's folds. You'll pass under white oak, chestnut oak, hickory, and dogwood. The ground is covered with several types of mosses and numerous mushrooms.

2.0 Turn right onto an unnamed blue-blazed trail that connects the AT and Iron Mountain Trail. In 0.1 mile, turn right onto yellow-blazed Iron Mountain Trail. **Note:** Iron Mountain Trail skirts a knob to the right, passing by the wavy fronds of black snakeroot.

3.1 Enter a clearing where the trail becomes a wide, grassy road. There are blueberry thickets on your left. Follow the road straight. Ahead on the right you'll find a fire ring that sees frequent use.

3.4 Iron Mountain Trail reenters woods, climbing amid bear oak, poplar, and table mountain pine to skirt right of another knob. There are lots of mountain laurel here and a large dogwood tree.

5.0 Arrive at a fork in the trail; bear right and continue on Iron Mountain Trail up a small knob. **Side trip:** If you bear left at the fork, you can take Feathercamp Ridge Trail 0.2 mile to FR 90 and Feathercamp Lookout Tower.

FEATHERCAMP RIDGE

JEFFERSON
NATIONAL
FOREST

MOUNT ROGERS
NATIONAL
RECREATION AREA

5.9 Take a hard right and follow Iron Mountain Trail downhill through a grove of hemlock. Within 0.1 mile, it drops you onto blue-blazed Feathercamp Branch Trail, which begins as a doubletrack dirt road. Turn right to return to US 58. **Side trip:** Sandy Flats Shelter is 0.3 mile up Iron Mountain Trail.

6.0 Pass through a clearing with a fire ring. As you reenter the woods, Feathercamp Branch Trail reverts to a singletrack woods path.

7.0 The stream on your left, Feathercamp Branch, has gained enough strength at this point to create nice toe-dipping pools at the bottom of small cascades.

7.6 Cross a feeder stream that enters Feathercamp Branch from the right. This marks the start of a series of stream crossings between here and the AT.

8.0 Feathercamp Branch Trail merges with the AT trail. Follow the white-blazed AT trail straight.

8.1 Arrive back at US 58.

HIKE INFORMATION

Local Information

Town of Damascus Tourism, (276) 475–3831, www.visitdamascus.org

Grayson County Tourism, Independence, (276) 773–8002, www.graysoncountyva .com

Abingdon Visitor Center, Abingdon, (800) 435–3440, www.visitabingdonvirginia.com

Local Events/Attractions

Appalachian Trail Days, third week in May, Damascus, (276) 475-3831, www.visitdamascus.org/traildays.html. Annual gathering of AT thru-hikers in the town dubbed "friendliest town on the AT."

Virginia Creeper Trail is a 34-mile rail-to-trail from Abingdon to Damascus. Outfitters will transport you and their rental bikes (or yours) to the top of Whitetop for a 17-mile downhill ride to Damascus. www.vacreepertrail.org

The Mt. Rogers Volunteer Fire Department holds three great festivals each year: Maple Festival in Mar, Ramp Festival in May (ramp is a wild onion), Molasses Festival in Oct. More information on the department's Facebook page.

Lodging

Grayson Highlands State Park, Mouth of Wilson, has hiking trails, a museum/visitor center, store, cabins, and campground for both tents and RVs. (276) 579-7092, www.dcr.virginia.gov/state-parks/grayson-highlands. Reservations: www.reservevaparks.com

Damascus Old Mill Inn, Damascus, has dining and lodging overlooking a beautiful stream. (276) 475-3745, www.damascusinn.com

A wide range of lodging from inns to campgrounds to vacation rentals are listed at www.visitdamascus.org.

Restaurants

Damascus Old Mill Inn, (276) 475-3745, www.damascusinn.com. A renovated 1912 mill turned restaurant, with a craft beer and bourbon bar and outdoor seating on the banks of Laurel Creek.

Cowboys Market & Deli, Damascus, (276) 475-5444. Great southern breakfast located inside a service station.

Damascus Brewery & Tap Room, (276) 469-1069, www.thedamascusbrewery.com

Organizations

Friends of Mount Rogers, Chilhowie, www.facebook.com/FriendsOfMountRogers

Outfitters

Mount Rogers Outfitters, Damascus, (276) 475-5416, https://mt-rogers-outfitters.ueniweb.com. Located "on the AT" at 110 W. Laurel Ave., Damascus's main street. Great gear, hostel, and shuttle services.

Other Resources

Appalachian Trail Guide to Southwest Virginia, Appalachian Trail Conservancy, Harpers Ferry, WV, (304) 535-6331, www.appalachiantrail.org

30 LITTLE WILSON CREEK WILDERNESS

Most hikers enter Little Wilson Creek Wilderness on trails out of Grayson Highlands State Park. Scales, an area named for the livestock scales once located here, makes a great alternate starting point. You not only avoid crowds but get a high-country fix that much faster. Scales sits smack-dab in the midst of Mount Rogers's crest zone, flanked by Stone Mountain and Wilburn Ridge. Huckleberry bushes bloom profusely (there are reports of folks carrying 3 gallons or more out of thickets along Scales Trail). On Stone Mountain, wild horses graze. As you approach them, young foals bolt from cover of tall grass and dart behind their mothers. In the words of a passerby, "It's as wild as it gets up here."

Start: Corralled campground at Scales
Distance: 7.6-mile loop
Hiking time: About 5 hours
Difficulty: Moderate due to some long climbs and several muddy, eroded sections of trail
Trail surface: A combination of dirt footpaths, old dirt wagon roads, and railroad grades lead through high-altitude meadows, mountain balds, and mixed hardwood forests.
Land status: National recreation area
Nearest town: Troutdale, VA
Other trail users: Equestrians
Accessibility: None
Canine compatibility: Dogs permitted
Trail contact: Mount Rogers National Recreation Area, Marion, (276) 783-5196 or (800) 628-7202, www.fs.usda.gov/gwj. The visitor center is 10 miles north of Troutdale on VA 16. Grayson Highlands State Park, (276) 579-7092, www.dcr.virginia.gov/state-parks/grayson-highlands.
Schedule: Open year-round. Hunting permitted, with the busiest season between Nov and Jan. Forest rangers conduct prescribed burns outside the wilderness in fall and spring.
Fees/permits: No permits required. Free backcountry camping. Day-use fee if entering from Grayson Highlands State Park. Backpackers Lot there is open for overnight parking, but reservations are required. Visit www.reservevaparks.com to make reservations until midnight the day prior to arrival.
Facilities/features: None
NatGeo TOPO! Map: Trout Dale
NatGeo Trails Illustrated map: Mount Rogers High Country; Mount Rogers National Recreation Area; Appalachian Trail, Damascus to Bailey Gap; New River Blueway
Other maps: Mount Rogers High Country & Wilderness map available at the Mount Rogers Visitor Center; Appalachian Trail Map 1: Mount Rogers National Recreation Area available from Appalachian Trail Conservancy, Harpers Ferry, WV. Maps and guidebooks available at Mt. Rogers Outfitters, Damascus.

FINDING THE TRAILHEAD

Four-wheel-drive vehicles with high clearance: From Troutdale, take VA 603 west from its intersection with VA 16. In 2.8 miles, turn left onto FR 613, a dirt road. (Look for a sign on the right-hand side of the road.) Road conditions are rocky, rutted, and sometimes wet. Once on FR 613, you'll pass a fork at 0.7 mile. Turn left. Turn left at the second fork at 2 miles. At 2.8 miles, turn right at the fork. In 3.8

miles, pass through a metal gate (the gate may be closed, but not locked). In 0.2 mile past the gate, enter the campground at Scales. **GPS:** N36 40.165' / W81 29.224'. *DeLorme: Virginia Atlas & Gazetteer*: Page 23, C5.

Two-wheel-drive or low-clearance vehicles: From Troutdale: Drive south on VA 16. In 7 miles, turn right onto US 58. It is another 7.6 miles on US 58 to the Grayson Highlands State Park entrance road, VA 362. Turn right onto VA 362 and, in 3.1 miles, turn right onto the Grayson Highlands State Park campground access road. It dead-ends at the campground in 1.3 miles. The Wilson Creek trailhead is clearly marked near the ranger station. Follow it downhill and, in 1.8 miles, turn right onto Scales Trail, which is an old road. Reach the Scales area in 1.3 miles (for a total trip of 3.1 miles from the state park campground). **GPS:** N36 38.404' / W81 29.227'. *DeLorme: Virginia Atlas & Gazetteer*: Page 23, C5.

THE HIKE

They stare at you from a black-and-white photograph, fourteen men in dirty overalls wearing brimmed hats, saws and poles gripped firmly in hand. Remember them as you soak in the high-country meadows around Scales, a swale in Pine Mountain tucked between Wilburn Ridge and Stone Mountain. If not for loggers like them, this landscape wouldn't exist.

Transformation of Scales, once a weigh-in site for livestock, took a mere 20 years. Starting around 1900, lumber companies and private landowners stripped virgin spruce and fir, chestnut, maple, and oak from the hillsides. What's developed since is a product of man and nature. Erosion carried away fertile soil and exposed portions of volcanic bedrock. Livestock grazing and periodic fires set by the Forest Service keep the forest at bay. From this, Virginia's most striking landscape evolved: miles of meadow awash in green, orange, red, and purple cresting against a horizon filled with Virginia's highest peaks, fading into the haze of North Carolina's Blue Ridge.

First Peak Trail climbs through just this type of landscape en route to Little Wilson Creek Wilderness, a 3,900-acre tract protecting three peaks and five creek watersheds, including the dual headwaters of Little Wilson Creek. As you pass just under the summit of Third Peak, isolated clumps of hawthorn, buckeye, and beech grow increasingly thick and dense. This is how all of the Mount Rogers's crest zone—land 4,000 feet or more above sea level—would look if left to nature. Huckleberry grows in ever-larger thickets. Scrubby witch hazel (the divining rod of choice for modern-day dowsers), flame azaleas, and mountain laurel grow head-high. Small American chestnut intersperse with beech and chinquapin oak.

A blight has stunted the chestnut from growing even big enough to produce its burr-like fruit. Only 100 years ago, it grew so large, residents of Troutdale, a boomtown at the foot of Pine Mountain, cut 12-by-12-by-2-inch-thick pieces for stepping-stones across their muddy roads. C. P. Greer, a Troutdale resident, logged trees so big in this wilderness

Hawthorn, identifiable by its thorny branches, is a common tree sprouting from the thin soil of Mount Rogers high country. There are at least 165 species of hawthorn. Of them, thirty are native to the eastern region of the United States. Around Mount Rogers, you can narrow the search to cockspur, fanleaf, dotted, red plum, and fleshy hawthorns, all of which grow at elevations of 5,000 feet or higher.

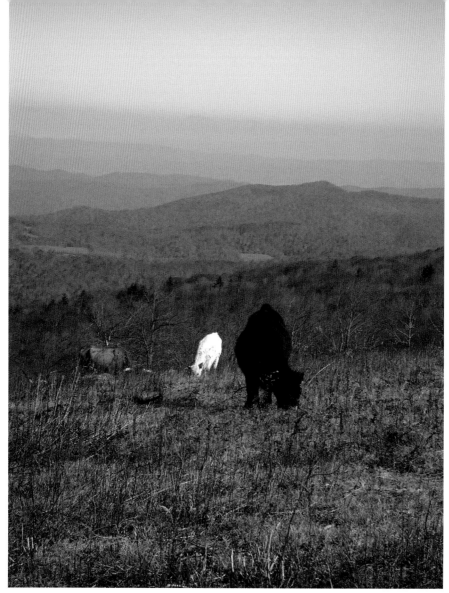

Cattle grazing

that, with his daughter perched on his shoulders, the base of a felled tree dwarfed them both. Greer is the man responsible for the faint trace of railroad grades visible on High-tree Rock Trail, one of the wilderness's less-traveled footpaths. He built a small-grade railroad on his own land to carry logs to his mill on Fox Creek, where he processed it for furniture and building material. (Ever the entrepreneur, Greer later converted the mill into a dynamo, or power plant, and supplied Troutdale's first electricity.) It was in the vicinity of Hightree Rock that Greer felled his largest trees. A mile and a half past where it splits from First Peak Trail, the Kabel Trail takes on the appearance of an old railroad grade: wide and flat with high banks. What might have been a rail spur angles left and peters out in thick woods. Rocks buttress the underside of the trail here, the masonry work visible by looking downslope off the left side.

Locomotives crossed grades like this daily during the boom years on Pine Mountain, traveling from Fairwood, a company town on FR 613. Before a fire destroyed it in 1911, Fairwood served as base of operations for the U.S. Spruce Lumber Company's Pine Mountain operations. Life there and in nearby Troutdale hummed along with the lumber business. Two furniture manufacturers employed any able-bodied man not working in timber. Farmers traveled the dirt roads between their homes and town, carrying livestock and produce to a rail depot at Troutdale. On their return trip, they were loaded with chairs from the factory for their wives and children to cane. Passenger trains ran twice a day from Troutdale south to Sugar Grove and Marion. For a time, Troutdale families rode the rails to Fairwood every Fourth of July for an annual baseball game, since the Spruce Lumber Company had built the finest baseball diamond in the valley.

It was for Spruce Lumber Company that engineer Kent Steffey worked on the fateful September day he took a Shay Locomotive No. 9 up Pine Mountain. After uncoupling a boxcar and reversing the engine, he started downhill. The train gathered speed and Steffey blew two sharp whistles, signaling for brakes. Nothing happened. The train careened on. Steffey's repeated whistle blows pealed across the mountain. The conductor and

Little Wilson Creek tumbles over rocks.

fireman jumped, but Steffey stayed aboard. Workers later found his body under the smoking wreckage of the 65-ton Shay. All that's left today is his tombstone in Rural Retreat, Virginia, and a ballad, "The Wreck of Ole Number Nine."

> *Still on the rails the bell / Began its pondering clang / And out upon the mountain air / the mourning whistle rang / "Farewell, farewell," it seemed to say / And the wheels like death did sing / It struck the curve with an awful shock / And from the rails she sprang.*

They stare at you, men in dirty overalls and brimmed hats sitting atop Steffey's wrecked Shay No. 9. Say what you will about habitats destroyed, species lost, trees gone forever. But don't forget their faces.

MILES AND DIRECTIONS

0.0 Start from the trail board at Scales, an enclosed campground on Pine Mountain. Past the trail board, exit the corral via a pass-thru in the fence. Turn left, keep the fence to your left, and round the next corner of the corral. Bear right and uphill at a signboard for First Peak Trail. **Note:** Avoid the Appalachian Trail (AT), which also ascends through these fields. The AT is clearly marked with white blazes.

0.8 Pass a junction with Third Peak Trail; continue straight.

1.0 Pass a campsite on the left side of the trail. This is an ideal spot for anyone looking for a sheltered evening under red spruce and hardwoods.

1.1 Pass to the right of 4,920-foot Third Peak.

1.8 Near the top of Second Peak, look out for several footpaths, unblazed, that branch left and disappear into the low forest cover. These trails lead a few hundred feet to a rock outcrop with views. Continue straight on First Peak Trail.

2.3 Enter a clearing. A fire ring marks this as an established backwoods campsite and there are signs of heavy use. Pass straight through the clearing on the First Peak Trail. **Note:** Bearpen Trail departs this clearing to the right. It descends to Little Wilson Creek before climbing to a junction with Big Wilson Creek Trail.

3.0 Reach a T junction and turn right onto Kabel Trail. **Note:** Hightree Rock Trail leads left from this T junction to an overlook in 2 miles.

4.8 After passing over some wet ground, climb on Kabel Trail as the route widens from a footpath into a dirt road.

4.9 Turn sharply left and downhill, still on the Kabel Trail.

5.2 Cross a fork of Little Wilson Creek. There's a prime camping spot on the left in a grassy meadow before you cross.

LITTLE WILSON CREEK WILDERNESS

0 Kilometer 1

0 Mile 1

N

To 603
FS 613 suitable for 4X4 only
FR 613
30
Third Peak Trail
Third Peak 4,920 ft.
PINE MOUNTAIN
(Muddy)
Second Peak 4,857 ft.
LITTLE WILSON CREEK WILDERNESS
Hightree Rock Trail
Hightree Rock
Scales Trail
STONE MOUNTAIN
Bearpen Trail
First Peak Trail
Bearpen Trail
First Peak 4,600 ft.
Little
Wilson
Creek
Kabel Trail
Kabel Trail
Creek
Big Wilson Creek Trail
Appalachian Trail
Little Wilson Creek Trail
Little Wilson
BEARPEN RIDGE
Brier Run
Bushwhack
740
Alternate Start
GRAYSON HIGHLANDS STATE PARK

5.5 Kabel Trail ends at Big Wilson Creek Trail. Turn right onto Big Wilson Creek Trail.

6.2 Leave the Little Wilson Creek Wilderness. Just beyond the wilderness sign, Big Wilson Creek Trail intersects Bearpen Trail at a T junction. Turn left onto Bearpen Trail. *Note:* A right turn onto Bearpen leads back to First Peak Trail. Hiking on this portion of Bearpen Trail is not advisable in wet weather because of eroded and muddy trail conditions.

6.4 At a four-way intersection, turn right onto the AT and climb. The trail crosses a barbed-wire fence on a step-up and enters high-country meadows. The grass is waist-high in spots, tall enough to hide young foals resting on the ground. This stretch of the AT is one of the best to see the wild horses of Mount Rogers high country, in part because it is less traveled than trails near the Mount Rogers summit.

7.6 Hike ends at Scales. *Note:* If your hike began in Grayson Highlands State Park, it's another 3.1 miles on the Scales Trail and Wilson Creek Trail to the campground and parking area.

HIKE INFORMATION

Local Information
Town of Damascus Tourism, (276) 475-3831, www.visitdamascus.org

Grayson County Tourism, Independence, (276) 773-8002, www.graysoncountyva.com

Abingdon Visitor Center, Abingdon, (800) 435-3440, www.visitabingdonvirginia.com

Local Events/Attractions
Appalachian Trail Days, third week in May, Damascus, (276) 475-3831, www.visitdamascus.org. Annual gathering of AT thru-hikers in the town dubbed "friendliest town on the AT."

Virginia Creeper Trail is a 34-mile rail-to-trail from Abingdon to Damascus. Outfitters will transport you and their rental bikes (or yours) to the top of Whitetop for a 17-mile downhill ride to Damascus. www.vacreepertrail.org

The Mt. Rogers Volunteer Fire Department holds three great festivals each year: Maple Festival in Mar, Ramp Festival in May (ramp is a wild onion), Molasses Festival in Oct. More information on the department's Facebook page.

Lodging
Grayson Highlands State Park, Mouth of Wilson, has hiking trails, a museum/visitor center, store, cabins, and campground for both tents and RVs. (276) 579-7092, www.dcr.virginia.gov/state-parks/grayson-highlands. Reservations: www.reservevaparks.com

Damascus Old Mill Inn, Damascus, has dining and lodging overlooking a beautiful stream. (276) 475-3745, www.damascusinn.com

A wide range of lodging from inns to campgrounds to vacation rentals are listed at www.visitdamascus.org.

Restaurants
Damascus Old Mill Inn, (276) 475-3745, www.damascusinn.com. A renovated 1912 mill turned restaurant with a craft beer and bourbon bar. Outdoor seating on the banks of Laurel Creek.

Cowboys Market & Deli, Damascus, (276) 475-5444. Great southern breakfast located inside a service station.

Damascus Brewery & Tap Room, (276) 469-1069, www.thedamascusbrewery.com

Organizations
Friends of Mount Rogers, www.friendsofmountrogers.org

Outfitters
Mount Rogers Outfitters, Damascus, (276) 475-5416, https://mt-rogers-outfitters.ueniweb.com. Located "on the AT" at 110 W. Laurel Ave., Damascus's main street. Great gear, hostel and shuttle services.

Other Resources
Appalachian Trail Guide to Southwest Virginia, Appalachian Trail Conservancy, Harpers Ferry, WV, (304) 535-6331, www.appalachiantrail.org

Dispense with the suspense right off: This 5,729-foot monolith of volcanic rock—third-loftiest mountain in the Southern Appalachians—is not hard to climb. Yes, you must hike 9 miles to reach it from Grayson Highlands State Park and, yes, the elevation change hovers around 1,000 feet. This elevation gain-loss, however, ranks lower than climbing Flat Top Mountain at Peaks of Otter and Three Ridges near Lexington, both mountains 4,000 feet or smaller. In other words, there are tougher climbs out there. But what Mount Rogers lacks in mountaineering derring-do, it easily compensates for in sheer presence, the diversity of its plant and animal life, the breathtaking views across high-country meadows, and, of course, its wild ponies. And to those eager for bragging rights, it affords the modest claim: "I climbed the highest mountain in Virginia."

Start: From the Massie Gap parking area on VA 362 in Grayson Highlands State Park

Distance: 9.0 miles out and back

Hiking time: About 5 hours

Difficulty: Easy to moderate due to open rock face and uneven footing along Wilburn Ridge

Trail surface: Dirt footpaths and open rock lead to Virginia's highest peak, grassy highlands, cove forests, and wooded slopes.

Land status: Federal wilderness and national recreation area

Nearest town: Troutdale, VA

Other trail users: Equestrians

Accessibility: Grayson Highlands State Park has some accessible facilities.

Canine compatibility: Dogs permitted

Trail contacts: Mount Rogers National Recreation Area office, 3714 Hwy. 16, Marion; (276) 783-5196 or (800) 628-7202; www.fs.usda.gov/gwj. Grayson Highlands State Park, (276) 579-7092, www.dcr.virginia.gov/state-parks/grayson-highlands

Schedule: Open year-round. Grayson Highland State Park is open daily 8 a.m. to 10 p.m. The park office is open Mon through Fri from 9 a.m. to 4 p.m. The visitor center is open daily from 10 a.m. to 5 p.m. Hunting permitted, with the busiest season between Nov and Jan.

Fees/permits: No permits required. Free backcountry camping and in AT shelters. Day-use fee to enter Grayson Highlands State Park, which has a campground near the trailhead with tent and RV hookups. Backpackers Lot is open for overnight parking, but reservations are required. Visit www.reservevaparks.com to make reservations until midnight the day prior to arrival.

Facilities/features: Grayson Highlands State Park has restrooms, picnic areas, and overnight parking. Full-service campground is open May through Oct; primitive camping only Nov, Mar, and Apr.

NatGeo TOPO! Map: Whitetop Mountain

NatGeo Trails Illustrated map: Mount Rogers High Country; Mount Rogers National Recreation Area; Appalachian Trail, Damascus to Bailey Gap; New River Blueway

Other maps: Mount Rogers High Country & Wilderness map available at the Mount Rogers Visitor Center on VA 16 north of Troutdale; Appalachian Trail Map 1: Mount Rogers National Recreation Area available from Appalachian Trail Conservancy, Harpers Ferry, WV

FINDING THE TRAILHEAD

From Troutdale: Drive south on VA 16. In 7 miles, turn right onto US 58. It is another 7.6 miles on US 58 to the Grayson Highlands State Park entrance road, VA 362. Turn right onto VA 362 and, in 3.3 miles, turn right into the Massie Gap parking area. There is parking for fifty cars, picnic tables, and interpretive signs. If you are backpacking in the high country, park in a separate lot accessed via the campground road. **GPS:** N36 38.404' / W81 30.541'. *DeLorme: Virginia Atlas & Gazetteer:* Page 23, D5.

THE HIKE

You reach a point climbing Mount Rogers's north slope where nature gets a little giddy. A relatively tame, wooded mountainside slips into a jumble of cliff and rock outcrops. In a short span of trail, large boulders appear. Down a steep grade on the right is a cliff and, at the base of the cliff, a shallow cave formed by the overhanging rocks. A birch tree grafts on exposed roots of another birch. A cleaved rock exposes the entire root system of a hemlock growing out its top side. The trail becomes more streambed than dirt footpath. On rainy days, runoff will trickle underfoot. All that's missing, really, is a big sign: "Welcome to 5,000 Feet. Enjoy Your Stay."

That's a magic number, 5,000. In the whole Blue Ridge chain, from southern Pennsylvania to north Georgia, only seven peaks exceed that threshold. Two of them stand in Virginia. One, Whitetop Mountain, has a road leading to the top. It's tempting to say the same about Mount Rogers, judging by the number of people who climb it every year. In truth, Mount Rogers, namesake for the 117,000-acre national recreation area, harbor for remnant boreal forests and threatened species, is in a class all its own.

Mount Rogers hasn't always enjoyed fame. For two centuries after colonial settlement in Virginia, it was just another obstacle to westward travel. During his 1728 survey of the "dividing line" between Virginia and North Carolina, Colonel William Byrd never reached the peak, thwarted as he was by the Blue Ridge Mountains, which he described from afar as "ranges of blue clouds." Byrd's group turned for home, frustrated by slow progress through "troublesome thickets and underwood," and the Southern Appalachians remained the "back of the beyond," as Horace Kephart described them, until a series of scientific explorations in the early 1800s. Not that the mountains remained unsettled. Pioneers were followed by mining and logging, but the region as a whole remained a place where people in neighboring hollows could pass a lifetime meeting only once or twice.

As it happens, the honor for mapping Mount Rogers goes to William Barton Rogers, Virginia's first state geologist. Rogers climbed the mountain during his geologic survey of Virginia in 1836, a mission ordered by the state legislature. These first decades of the 1800s were a busy time for scientists. States up and down the East Coast were interested in exploiting their mineral, plant, and animal resources. Rogers's brother, Henry Darwin Rogers, had conducted a geologic survey for Pennsylvania. Based on information gathered, the Rogers brothers published their famous theory on the Appalachian Mountains, a theory that generated some controversy for its assumption that the earth was at least several million years old. It's a notion few question today, but in the 1800s, the scientists who believed in creationism—that God created the world in a single moment— condemned Rogers's work. As it turns out, the criticism proved merely a warmup for Charles Darwin's *The Origin of Species,* published in 1859, and the work of biologist Asa Grey, who wrote of similarities between plants found in East Asia and North America.

A waterfall in Grayson Highlands State Park EDDIE FORT

Rogers didn't need to span continents in search of similar flora among regions far-removed from one another. Atop Mount Rogers, the fir-spruce forest indicates a mixing of temperate and cold-weather plants. At its highest points grow northern hardwoods, red spruce, and mountain wood sorrel wildflower. There are northern flying squirrels and birds such as the chestnut-sided warbler (its call: a slow *please, please, pleased to meet*

A wild pony on Mount Rogers Trail

A stunning mountain in Grayson Highlands

you) and Swainson's thrush (its call: a *whit* and a *heep*). These species, normally associated with northern forests, arrived with the last ice age in North America, when encroaching ice and cold weather pushed habitats south into Virginia. Eventually, the ice receded and so did the flora and fauna—except on high peaks such as Mount Rogers. Naturalists like to describe this peak as a southern sentinel for plants and animals more common to America's Northeast. The summit also supports stands of Fraser fir, an evergreen that grows no farther north than the crest zone of Mount Rogers.

Mount Rogers, then, stands as a link in a north–south chain of ecosystems, those typically found on cool, moist mountaintops such as Mount Mitchell in North Carolina and the 6,000-foot-plus peaks of the Great Smoky Mountains. It's a stepping-stone, especially for such birds as the magnolia warbler (its call: *weetee weetee weeteo*), which has extended its range out of New York and Pennsylvania and into North Carolina and Tennessee.

Mount Rogers is a threatened ecosystem. Many people worry about air pollution, which weakens a tree's resistance to disease. Survival of Mount Rogers's spruce-fir trees is fiercely debated, given the almost total obliteration of Fraser fir on Mount Mitchell, 75 miles to the south. The firs on Mount Rogers show resistance to the balsam woolly adelgid, a microscopic pest that coats the crowns of fir trees, leading to defoliation and eventually death. Nonetheless, eerie parallels exist between the trees on Mount Rogers and the hemlocks in Ramsey's Draft Wilderness and Shenandoah National Park, where the hemlock woolly adelgid is defoliating eastern hemlock at such a rate that park rangers predict virgin stands will soon disappear.

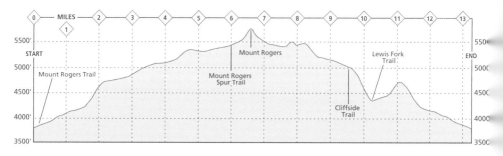

It's worth looking back over your shoulder as you hike up the Appalachian Trail (AT) toward Wilburn Ridge, savoring another view of a special mountain. Colonel Byrd, the surveyor who never made it this far west, couldn't help but do so. His reaction rings true today.

> We could not forbear now and then facing about to survey them (the mountains), as if unwilling to part with a prospect which at the same time . . . was very wild and very agreeable.

MILES AND DIRECTIONS

0.0 Start at Massie Gap parking area in Grayson Highlands State Park. Follow the blue-blazed Rhododendron Trail through an open field. The route is initially a mowed grass path. Within a few hundred yards, cross straight over a graded dirt and gravel path, which is the Virginia Highlands Horse Trail, pass through a gate in a fence, and continue walking north on the Rhododendron Trail. ***Note:*** For the first 1.2 miles, this route crosses the horse trail and, very briefly, merges with it.

0.4 Veer left onto the Virginia Highlands Horse Trail, which remains a wide dirt and gravel trail.

0.6 Turn left onto the white-blazed Appalachian Trail. ***Note:*** There is a wooden trail sign with mileage for Mount Rogers summit, Rhododendron Gap, and Thomas Knob Shelter.

1.2 Cross a fence stile and enter the Mount Rogers National Recreation Area. Immediately, cross straight over the Virginia Highlands Horse Trail and continue north on the Appalachian Trail. There is a primitive campsite in this area.

1.5 Turn left onto Wilburn Ridge Trail. ***Note:*** The AT continues straight and both trails will merge in 0.8 mile, just prior to Rhododendron Gap.

1.8 Cross over Rhododendron Gap Trail and continue north on Wilburn Ridge Trail.

2.3 Wilburn Ridge Trail merges with the AT. Continue straight on white-blazed AT. ***Note:*** Between here and Rhododendron Gap, there are numerous primitive campsites.

2.7 Cross over Crest Trail and continue straight on the AT. Within a few hundred feet, reach Rhododendron Gap, a trails crossroads marked by a house-size rock outcrop. Bear left and continue following the AT. ***Note:*** Keep a sharp eye out for white blazes marking the AT; avoid the Crest Trail and Pine Mountain State Scenic Trail.

3.2 Cross a fence that marks the boundary of the Lewis Fork Wilderness Area.

3.8 Cross another fence and approach Thomas Knob shelter on the left. ***Note:*** A blue-blazed trail leads 0.1 mile to a spring.

4.2 Turn right onto the Mount Rogers Spur Trail.

4.7 Reach the tree-shrouded summit of Mount Rogers, Virginia's highest point (5,729 feet elevation). Turn around and retrace the trail to Massie Gap.

6.9 ***Option:*** Continue straight on the AT to cross Wilburn Ridge for an alternate return route to Massie Gap.

9.0 Hike ends at Massie Gap parking area.

HIKE INFORMATION

Local Information
Town of Damascus Tourism, (276) 475-3831, www.visitdamascus.org

Grayson County Tourism, Independence, (276) 773-8002, www.graysoncountyva.com

Abingdon Visitor Center, Abingdon, (800) 435-3440, www.visitabingdonvirginia.com

Local Events/Attractions
Appalachian Trail Days, third week in May, Damascus, (276) 475-3831, www.visitdamascus.org. Annual gathering of AT thru-hikers in the town dubbed "friendliest town on the AT."

Virginia Creeper Trail is a 34-mile rail-to-trail from Abingdon to Damascus. Outfitters will transport you and their rental bikes (or yours) to the top of Whitetop for a 17-mile downhill ride to Damascus. www.vacreepertrail.org

The Mt. Rogers Volunteer Fire Department holds three great festivals each year: Maple Festival in Mar, Ramp Festival in May (ramp is a wild onion), Molasses Festival in Oct. More information on the department's Facebook page.

Lodging

Grayson Highlands State Park, Mouth of Wilson, has hiking trails, a museum/visitor center, store, cabins, and campground for both tents and RVs. (276) 579-7092, www.dcr .virginia.gov/state-parks/grayson-highlands. Reservations: www.reservevaparks.com

Damascus Old Mill Inn, Damascus, has dining and lodging overlooking a beautiful stream. (276) 475-3745, www.damascusinn.com

A wide range of lodging from inns to campgrounds to vacation rentals are listed at www.visitdamascus.org.

Restaurants

Damascus Old Mill Inn, (276) 475-3745, www.damascusinn.com. A renovated 1912 mill turned restaurant with a craft beer and bourbon bar. Outdoor seating on the banks of Laurel Creek.

Cowboys Market & Deli, Damascus, (276) 475-5444. Great southern breakfast located inside a service station.

Damascus Brewery & Taproom, (276) 469-1069, www.thedamascusbrewery.com

Organizations

Friends of Mount Rogers, Chilhowie, www.facebook.com/FriendsOfMountRogers
Virginia Wilderness Committee, www.vawilderness.org/little-wilson-creek-wilderness .html

Outfitters

Mount Rogers Outfitters, Damascus, (276) 475-5416, https://mt-rogers-outfitters .ueniweb.com. Located "on the AT" at 110 W. Laurel Ave., Damascus's main street. Great gear, hostel and shuttle services.

Other Resources

Appalachian Trail Guide to Southwest Virginia, Appalachian Trail Conservancy, Harpers Ferry, WV, (304) 535-6331, www.appalachiantrail.org

HONORABLE MENTIONS: MOUNT ROGERS

JJ. FOUR TRAILS CIRCUIT

Located near Hurricane Campground. Head south of Sugar Grove on VA 16, turn right onto VA 650, and then left onto FR 84 to Hurricane Campground. This moderately difficult 9.6-mile loop uses a portion of the Appalachian Trail (AT) and three other trails. Terrain varies from the dry ridgetop of Iron Mountain to cool waterfalls on Comers Creek. (800) 628-7202. **GPS:** N36 43.319' / W81 29.243'. *DeLorme: Virginia Atlas & Gazetteer.* Page 23, C5.

KK. ROWLAND CREEK FALLS CIRCUIT

Located west of Sugar Grove. From VA 16, turn right onto VA 601, which after 3.5 miles turns into VA 670 in Teas. Continue on VA 670 for 4.4 miles and then fork left onto VA 656. (If you pass the Butler Fish Culture Station on the right, you've missed this left turn. Go back 1 mile and look for the turnoff.) Stay on VA 656 for 1.7 miles, then turn left onto VA 668, which turns into dirt FR 643. Park at the first trailhead on the right-hand side. After following Jerry's Creek Trail to Iron Mountain, hikers can return via Rowland Creek or head west and explore Skulls Gap for a total hike of 11.8 miles. Rowland Creek Falls is a highlight of this trip. (800) 628-7202. **GPS:** N36 43.986' / W81 33.675'. *DeLorme: Virginia Atlas & Gazetteer.* Page 22, B4.

LL. WHITETOP LAUREL CIRCUIT

From Damascus, take US 58 east and turn right onto VA 728 to Creek Junction parking lot. This 11.5-mile loop uses portions of the Appalachian Trail (AT) and the Virginia Creeper Trail, and includes a number of crossings over the cascading Whitetop Laurel Creek. (800) 628-7202. **GPS:** N36 38.876' / W81 40/328'. *DeLorme: Virginia Atlas & Gazetteer.* Page 22, C3.

THE APPALACHIAN TRAIL THROUGH VIRGINIA

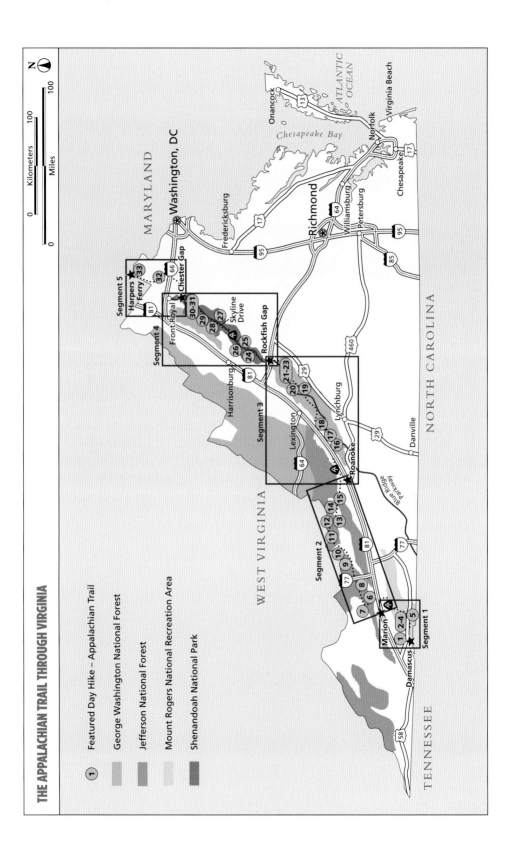

Featured Day Hike – Appalachian Trail

George Washington National Forest

Jefferson National Forest

Mount Rogers National Recreation Area

Shenandoah National Park

THE GREAT ESCAPE: THE APPALACHIAN TRAIL THROUGH VIRGINIA

It takes a northbound thru-hiker about 6 weeks to reach Virginia on the Appalachian Trail. Once here, there are another 6 weeks of difficult and rewarding trail ahead before the hiker exits Virginia at Harpers Ferry. The Old Dominion holds nearly a quarter of the AT's 2,173 miles—more miles than any other state along the trail. A half-million day hikers hit Virginia's portion of the AT each year. Most follow the south–north direction we've chosen to feature. Since hiking the entire length of the trail is a luxury most of us cannot afford, we've included a list of suggested day hikes or short overnight trips that capture Virginia's greatest natural highlights. And so, whether you choose one long trip, or small bite sizes, plan on a showcase of some of the East's most beautiful mountain scenery.

GREAT RESOURCES FOR HIKING THE AT

Appalachian Trail Guides, available for purchase from the ATC at (800) AT-STORE or at www.atctrailstore.org

Appalachian Trail Thru-hikers' Companion, available for purchase from the ATC at (800) AT-STORE

Story Line: Exploring the Literature of the Appalachian Trail, by Ian Marshall, University Press of Virginia

A Walk in the Woods, by Bill Bryson, Broadway Books (also a 2015 motion picture starring Robert Redford and Nick Nolte)

A Walk for Sunshine, by Jeff Alt, Dreams Shared Publications

TRAVELING GREEN: PUBLIC TRANSPORTATION TO THE AT IN VIRGINIA

The "leave no trace" ethic goes beyond the trailhead. Choosing not to drive farther reduces the footprint you leave on the environment. Taking a bus or train, or using ride-share and shuttle services, eliminates the hassle of shuttling two cars at opposite ends of the trail. Remember that these services are infrequent and subject to change, so it's best to call ahead and plan carefully. The Appalachian Trail Conservancy (ATC) provides general information and links to ride-share and shuttle services. For more information contact the ATC at (304) 535-6331 or visit www.appalachiantrail.org.

The major transit carriers that access towns all close to Virginia's AT are Greyhound Bus Lines, (800) 229-9424 or www.greyhound.com, and Amtrak, (800) 872-7245 or www.amtrak.com. Often you may want to use a combination of the two. Amtrak can get you to Roanoke, Lynchburg, Staunton, Charlottesville, Culpepper, and Harpers Ferry—all of which provide access, whether by bus, ride-share, or shuttle, to the AT.

The following towns are accessible by bus or by train and lie within a reasonable walking distance of the AT. This is not a complete list, but it is the most practical.

Marion and Wytheville (accesses Segment 1 and 2)

Greyhound services Marion and Wytheville. From Marion it is 7 miles west to the AT at VA 16. Wytheville is 16 miles south of the AT crossing at US 52.

Roanoke (accesses Segment 2 and 3)

Greyhound and Amtrak service Roanoke. From the Greyhound station, it's 10 miles to the AT trailhead at the US 220 crossing. The McAfee Knob Trail Shuttle runs between the I-81 exit 140 Park & Ride and the AT trailhead parking lot on VA 331.

Buena Vista (accesses Segment 3)

The Maury Express provides bus service between Roanoke and Buena Vista and Lexington.

Waynesboro (accesses Segment 4)

Waynesboro Tourism provides information about shuttles to and from Rockfish Gap, (540) 942-6512. Staunton is serviced by Virginia Breeze bus service, and its bus stop is 15 miles west of Rockfish Gap.

Harpers Ferry and Front Royal (accesses Segment 5)

Amtrak services Harpers Ferry, with connections to Washington, Pittsburgh, and Chicago. From Washington, DC, hikers can take the more frequent (and cheaper) MARC commuter rail, (866) RIDE-MTA or www.mtamaryland.gov. From the train station in Harpers Ferry, take a left onto Potomac Street and head down to Shenandoah Street, where you'll find the AT. Front Royal is serviced by Virginia Breeze bus service, with a bus stop 7 miles west of the AT at US 522. The Front Royal Trolley offers services to and from the AT at US 522 May through July.

SEGMENT 1. DAMASCUS TO MARION

As an introduction to Virginia, it's hard to top Mount Rogers National Recreation Area. The Appalachian Trail passes near the tallest mountains in the state. Close to the summit of Mount Rogers, wild ponies graze in the high-country meadows. There are steep climbs up Iron Mountain, past small waterfalls and tunnels of rhododendron. The hike seems over too soon. Longer lasting are memories of wide-open sky, jagged rock outcrops, and a refreshing dip below the falls on Comers Creek.

Start: Damascus Town Hall

Distance: 63.8 miles point to point

Difficulty: Difficult

Trail surface: Using dirt footpaths and abandoned dirt roads, hike along rocky peaks, cliffs, and steep ridges; through deep valley hollows; and across high-altitude meadows.

Nearest towns: Damascus, VA (south access); Marion, VA (north access)

Canine compatibility: Dogs permitted (must be on a leash in the Mount Rogers National Recreation Area)

Trail contacts: Appalachian Trail Conservancy, Harpers Ferry, WV, (304) 535-6331, www.appalachiantrail.org; Piedmont Appalachian Trail Hikers, www.path-at.org; Mount Rogers Appalachian Trail Club, Damascus, http://mratc.org

Maps/guides: AT Guide Set #9 covers the AT from the Virginia/Tennessee state line to Pearisburg, VA. www.atctrailstore.org

---

FINDING THE TRAILHEAD

To the Damascus Trailhead: In Damascus, locate the Damascus Town Hall, 208 W. Laurel Ave., between Smith Street and Reynolds Avenue. You can use on-street parking or park at Mount Rogers Outfitters, 110 W. Laurel Ave. Begin walking east on Laurel Avenue (US 58). *DeLorme: Virginia Atlas & Gazetteer*: Page 22, C2. **To Marion Trailhead:** See Segment 2: Marion to Roanoke.

THE HIKE

A few miles north of the Tennessee-Virginia border, the Appalachian Trail (AT) wraps around Holston Mountain, part of the Iron Mountain range, and descends into Damascus. The small town, first visible from an overlook high atop the ridge, bills itself as the "friendliest town on the AT." Its downtown strip, Laurel Avenue, doubles as the trail route. Shopkeepers and restaurants welcome AT hikers as friends. The hospitality really shows itself each May during the Appalachian Trail Days festival, when hundreds of hikers converge on Damascus and swap stories about the 2,173-mile trail.

Surrounding Damascus is scenery unlike any you've seen in Virginia. In Mount Rogers National Recreation Area (NRA), herds of wild ponies roam expansive mountain meadows. A strong spruce-fir scent lingers around the tree-capped Mount Rogers (5,729 feet), Virginia's tallest peak. Colorful mushrooms and large patches of wild berries brighten the slope and crest of Iron Mountain. Rhododendron's pink and purple blooms seem ever-present in June. Turk's cap lily, orange and delicate, is one of an array of wildflowers seen spring through fall.

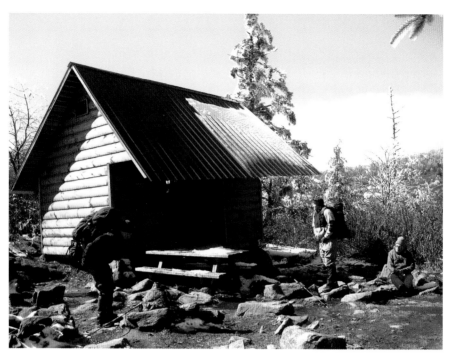
The Thomas Knob Shelter near Mount Rogers

The route north from Damascus begins with a 1,000-foot ascent of Feathercamp Ridge. The next 14 miles of AT bring two more steep climbs up Straight Mountain and Lost Mountain. Between each ridge, rhododendrons choke stream valleys cut by Straight Branch and Whitetop Laurel Creek. As the AT climbs and descends each ridge, flashes of yellow and red amid the drab-colored leaf rot signal mushroom colonies. Chanterelles, waxy caps, and a host of other types grow along the trail. Occasionally, a view of the rooftop of Virginia, as the high country is nicknamed, breaks out through the heavy oak forest atop the ridges.

From Elk Garden, the AT begins an ascent past Virginia's three tallest mountains—Mount Rogers, Whitetop, and Pine. All three peaks exceed 5,000 feet, and the AT slips past without actually crossing any of them. Whitetop Mountain (5,520 feet) has a road leading to its top. When the Virginia Creeper Railroad operated 100 years ago, the Whitetop station had the distinction of being the highest railroad depot east of the Rockies. Past Whitetop, the AT enters Lewis Fork Wilderness, which surrounds and covers Mount Rogers. Elevation is above 5,000 feet, and the forested summit of Mount Rogers appears a mere bulge in the high ridge. A spur trail leads 0.5 mile from the AT up to Rogers's summit area. It's a cool, moist woodland that covers Mount Rogers, with dangling bunches of moss and rotted logs everywhere. Many of the trees, plants, and animals at the summit are vestiges of a northern forest environment that developed here during the last glacial period in North America some 10,000 years ago.

Pine Mountain, the third in Mount Rogers NRA's triumvirate of 5,000-foot peaks, is a series of rocky promontories rising sharply from the sweeping meadows. This gray-purplish rock is rhyolite, formed 800 million years ago when the Blue Ridge was volcanically active. The trail passes several jagged piles of rock on Wilburn Ridge, then disappears into tunnels of rhododendron. When the AT reenters meadows, stunted hawthorn trees offer shade and a rest spot for watching wild horses graze. Meadow grass grows knee-high. Wildflowers wash the fields with orange and red. The meadows are burned regularly by the Forest Service in order to hold back total reforestation, creating conditions ideal for fireweed. Were it not for the fires, a new forest of hardwoods would reclaim the meadows.

A descent from Scales (an old cattle-weighing station dating back over 100 years) to Fox Creek signals the end of the Mount Rogers high country. From Fox Creek, the AT climbs again to the crest of Iron Mountain (4,200 feet). Yellow blossoms of the Indian cucumber root put on a spring show along streams. Absent its blooms, which appear in May and June, the cucumber root is identified by a distinct double-decker whorl of leaves. The tuber is edible, but should only be collected if they're found in abundance. As it crosses Iron Mountain Trail (which used to be the AT until it was relocated), the AT follows sections of old logging roads. There's little in the way of forest canopy, but the constant exposure to sunlight makes the blackberries that grow along the trail especially plump and juicy, much like the huckleberries that grow off the trail in the high-country meadows.

AT SHELTERS/HUTS
(MILEAGE ON THE AT NORTH FROM DAMASCUS TO VA 16)

Mile 9.4   Saunders Shelter

Mile 15.8   Lost Mountain Shelter

Mile 28.0   Thomas Knob Shelter

Mile 33.1   Wise Shelter

Mile 39.0   Old Orchard Shelter

Mile 43.9   Hurricane Shelter

Mile 53.2   Trimpi Shelter

Mile 63.7   Partnership Shelter

The route north from Iron Mountain might seem anticlimactic when compared with the high country; that is, until the AT crosses Comers Creek. As it runs down Hurricane Mountain, the stream forms a 10-foot waterfall. There's a small swimming hole here that is popular with hikers. It's a nice spot to tarry, dip your feet in cool water, and contemplate the remaining 483 miles of Virginia's AT.

HIKE INFORMATION

Local Information
Town of Damascus website, www.visitdamascus.org
   Abingdon Visitor Center, Abingdon, (800) 435-3440, www.abingdon.com/tourism

Local Events/Attractions
Appalachian Trail Days, May, Damascus, www.visitdamascus.org

Lodging
A list of lodging options in and around Damascus, ranging from campsites to inns to vacation rentals, can be found at www.visitdamascus.org.

SEGMENT 2. MARION TO ROANOKE

The Appalachian Trail through southwest Virginia forsakes the Blue Ridge for the valley and ridge region, but loses none of the beauty or steep climbs. Open cliffs on Tinker Mountain and overlooks from McAfee Knob and Dragons Tooth are popular day hikes. More remote is Wind Rocks in Mountain Lake Wilderness or a perch on Angels Rest, near Pearisburg, with views of the New River. It's been 80-plus years since volunteers moved this leg of the AT off the Blue Ridge in hopes of saving the trail's remote character. It's safe to say they succeeded.

Start: Mount Rogers Visitor Center
Distance: 190.3 miles point to point
Difficulty: Difficult
Trail surface: Using dirt footpaths and abandoned dirt roads, hike along steep ridge crests, through deep valley hollows and bogs, and across high-altitude meadows.
Nearest towns: Marion, VA (south access); Roanoke, VA (north access)
Canine compatibility: Dogs permitted
Trail contacts: Appalachian Trail Conservancy, Harpers Ferry, WV, (304) 535-6331, www.appalachiantrail.org; Roanoke ATC, www.ratc.org; Outdoor Club at Virginia Tech, www.facebook.com/OutdoorClubVT; Piedmont Appalachian Trail Hikers, www.path-at.org; Mount Rogers National Recreation Area, Marion, (276) 783-5196, www.fs.usda.gov/gwj
Maps/guides: AT Guide Set #9 Southwest Virginia covers the AT from the Virginia/Tennessee state line to Pearisburg, VA; Guide Set #8 Central Virginia covers the AT from Pearisburg, VA to Rockfish Gap (northern end of the Blue Ridge Parkway). www.atctrailstore.org

FINDING THE TRAILHEAD

To Marion Trailhead: From Marion, proceed south on VA 16 to the Mount Rogers Visitor Center (6 miles from VA 16's junction with I-81). Turn right into the visitor center parking lot and park. Follow a sidewalk to the front of the visitor center, walk to VA 16, and cross the highway. The Appalachian Trail (AT) enters the woods on the northbound side of VA 16. *DeLorme: Virginia Atlas & Gazetteer*: Page 23, B5. **To Roanoke Trailhead:** See Segment 3: Roanoke to Rockfish Gap.

THE HIKE

From the point where it leaves the Great Valley, north of the Mount Rogers National Recreation Area, the AT crosses seven mountain ridges. Little Brushy Mountain is the first. Beyond it stand Big Walker, Lynn Camp, and Garden Mountain. Each ridge rises sharply, then drops into stream valleys. Crawfish Valley, at the base of Big Walker, is secluded and overgrown. Across Big Walker, Rich Valley is wide and busy, with the North Fork Holston River and VA 42 running along its bottomland.

> **HEADS UP**
> In 2023 the Forest Service established a Special Biological Area from the Dragons Tooth parking lot to the Appalachian Trail. Visitors are asked to stay on the marked trail and camping is prohibited.

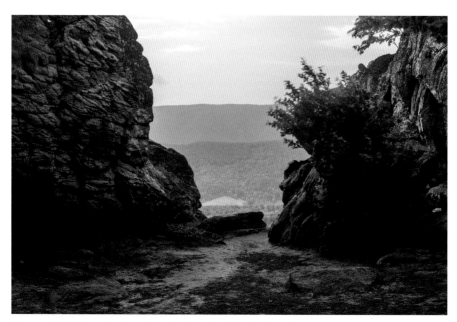

Dragons Tooth is an iconic spot on the Appalachian Trail. VTC/NATE DENNISON

AT SHELTERS/HUTS
(MILEAGE ON THE AT FROM VA 16 NORTH TO US 220)

Mile 0.0   Partnership Shelter (at Mount Rogers Visitor Center on VA 16)

Mile 7.0   Chatfield Shelter

Mile 14.2   Davis Path Campsite

Mile 25.4   Knot Maul Branch Shelter

Mile 34.4   Chestnut Knob Shelter

Mile 44.4   Jenkins Shelter

Mile 58.2   Helveys Mill Shelter

Mile 68   Jenny Knob Shelter

Mile 82.2   Wapiti Shelter

Mile 90.6   Doc's Knob Shelter

Mile 105.7   Rice Field Shelter (also called Star Haven Shelter)

Mile 118.0   Pine Swamp Branch Shelter

Mile 121.9   Bailey Gap Shelter

Mile 130.7   War Spur Shelter

Mile 136.5   Laurel Creek Shelter

Mile 142.9   Sarver Hollow Shelter

Mile 148.9   Niday Shelter

Mile 157.8   Pickle Branch Shelter

Mile 171.7   Johns Spring Shelter

Burke's Garden breaks the valley and ridge pattern in scenic fashion. Garden Mountain forms the southern boundary of this bowl-shaped valley, and the AT follows its crest for 5 miles. At Chestnut Knob and again at Davis Field Campsite, views west drop 900 feet into the valley, which formed millions of years ago when a basement rock of limestone eroded and washed away. The resulting claylike soil makes for prime farmland. Local lore says James Burke, the first white man to settle in the Garden, tossed a few potato peels on the ground during his first visit here in the mid-1700s. The next season, Burke returned and found potato plants. True or not, a small community of farmers continues a tradition that dates back centuries. They've also managed to keep the commercial world at bay, with prohibitions on billboards and neon signs.

Northwest of Burke's Garden, the AT crosses three more ridges. On the last, Pearis Mountain, an overlook called Angels Rest provides beautiful views across the New River to the slope of Peters Mountain. The AT crosses the New on a highway bridge and follows Stillhouse Branch up the steep side of Peters Mountain. On the ridgetop, the West Virginia border and AT crisscross for 12 miles through grass fields and a portion of the Peters Mountain Wilderness.

Like Catawba Mountain to the north, which derives its name from the Catawba rhododendron, Peters Mountain shares its name with a plant. Peters Mountain mallow grows only in Giles County, Virginia. The single known community of this purple-blossoming herb is protected on land owned by The Nature Conservancy. The AT is partly to blame for its earlier decline. In the late 1960s, a section of the trail ran along the mountain's sandstone outcrops, a favored habitat of the mallow. Heavy foot traffic took its toll. Virginia and the federal government now list the plant as endangered. What communities exist are fenced in and tended carefully. Trail relocation remedied encroachment by AT hikers.

The descent off Peters Mountain marks a turn in the AT. Its direction is now once again northeast, a course that will eventually intersect with the Blue Ridge Mountains, beyond Roanoke. For the intervening 74 miles, the AT crosses eight more ridges, each with a corresponding stream valley. The first, Potts Mountain, caps out at a rocky point called Wind Rocks in Mountain Lake Wilderness. The 10,753-acre federal wilderness, like Burke's Garden, is a welcome respite to the valley and ridge routine. Gently graded trail leads across two flat-topped mountains, Salt Pond and Lone Pine, and their upland bogs. The descent off Salt Pond steepens and ends at Johns Creek. In quick succession,

HEADS UP

The Appalachian Trail from Marion to Roanoke contains two major impacts for hikers. The Mountain Valley Pipeline project in Peters Mountain Wilderness Area infringes on the AT right-of-way and hikers must follow Forest Service rules as they pass (www.fs.usda.gov/alerts/gwj/alerts-notices/?aid=84178). The second impact is removal of a bridge over Craigs Creek north of VA 620 in Craig County. The creek may be forded at low water. High water levels forces hikers to use a road detour. Visit the Appalachian Trail Conservancy (www.appalachiantrail.org) for updates on these two impacts.

Rock steps on the trail to Dragons Tooth VTC/NATE DENNISON

the AT then crosses Johns Creek, Sinking Creek, Brush, and Cove Mountains. Cove Mountain makes a U shape around the headwaters of Trout Creek and rises to the pointed, skin-your-knee-rough rock on Dragons Tooth.

The wide valley east of Dragons Tooth is part of the Great Valley system that runs down the Appalachian chain from southern New Jersey into Tennessee. Views of Roanoke, the largest city in southwest Virginia, signal the approaching end of this leg of the AT.

Before leaving the valley and ridge region, the AT crosses Tinker Cliffs. Blocks of sandstone in Devils Kitchen and the overhangs at Snack Bar Rock and Rock Haven make striking formations. Tinker Cliffs itself is reminiscent of another high-mountain ridge, Pine Mountain, on the Virginia-Kentucky border. Like Pine Mountain, the edges of Tinker and Catawba Mountains were, millions of years ago, a leading edge of a thrust fault—essentially a piece of the earth's crust that slid up and over another piece of the earth. The resulting topography is steep and often sheer to the west, while more graded and sloping eastward.

The subdivisions and farms visible on the last 6.5 miles of the AT signal the descent into the Great Valley. From a final rock outcrop, Hay Rock, the view reaches west across the heavily populated valley to the Blue Ridge, and another leg of the AT.

HIKE INFORMATION

Local Information

Roanoke Valley Convention & Visitors Bureau, Roanoke, (800) 635-5535, www.visit roanokeva.com

Montgomery County Tourism, (540) 394-4470, www.gotomontva.com

SEGMENT 3. ROANOKE TO ROCKFISH GAP

The Appalachian Trail once ran the crest of the Blue Ridge from Roanoke north to Rockfish Gap, until construction of the Blue Ridge Parkway pushed sections onto outlying peaks. That's good news for hikers who like climbing. From heights of 4,000 feet atop The Priest and Cold Mountain, the trail descends to an elevation of 659 feet at the James River. The Blue Ridge, Virginia's oldest mountains, show weathered knobs of resistant bedrock at Humpback Rocks, Spy Rock, and Fullers Rocks. Views from each seem better than the last.

Start: Shoulder of US 220 west of I-81

Distance: 133.4 miles point to point

Difficulty: Difficult

Trail surface: Using dirt footpaths and abandoned dirt roads, hike along ridge crests, peaks, and rock outcrops and through open meadows, virgin hemlock, and the James River Gorge.

Nearest towns: Roanoke, VA (south access); Waynesboro, VA (north access)

Canine compatibility: Dogs permitted

Trail contacts: Appalachian Trail Conservancy, Harpers Ferry, WV, (304) 535-6331, www.appalachiantrail.org; Old Dominion ATC, https://olddominiontrailclub.wildapricot.org; Tidewater ATC, www.tidewateratc.com; Natural Bridge ATC, www.nbatc.org; Shenandoah National Park, Luray, (540) 999-3500, www.nps.gov/shen; George Washington and Jefferson National Forests, www.fs.usda.gov/gwj

Maps/guides: AT Guide Set #8 Central Virginia covers the AT from Pearisburg, VA to Rockfish Gap (northern end of the Blue Ridge Parkway). www.atctrailstore.org

FINDING THE TRAILHEAD

To Roanoke Trailhead: From Roanoke, drive north on combined I-581/US 220 to I-81 north. Drive north on the combined routes of I-81/US 220 for 6 miles and take exit 150. Turn left at the bottom of the exit ramp onto US 220. In 0.2 mile, turn left onto VA 816 and park in the park-and-ride lot. Walk the few steps back to US 220 and turn left (north). In 0.2 mile, reach the Appalachian Trail (AT) where it crosses US 220. *DeLorme: Virginia Atlas & Gazetteer*: Page 42, B3. **To Rockfish Gap Trailhead:** See Segment 4: Rockfish Gap to Chester Gap.

THE HIKE

The AT route north of Roanoke begins with a steep climb up Fullhardt Knob. In Tollhouse Gap, the main trunk of the Blue Ridge is visible slightly east. It will be another 10 miles before the trail and the mountain crest intersect at the Blue Ridge Parkway, a scenic highway that runs south into the North Carolina Smokies.

Like Skyline Drive in Shenandoah National Park to the north, construction of the Blue Ridge Parkway followed a route AT volunteers blazed decades earlier. Subsequent trail relocations moved the AT off the main Blue Ridge. On the outlying mountains, like The Priest and Three Ridges, the AT gains and loses 3,000 feet in elevation in a few miles. Bumpy terrain—AT thru-hikers call them PUDs (pointless up-and-downs)—along

The authors with their nieces, Vanessa and Sarah, at the Maupin AT Shelter on Three Ridges

Cove Mountain's ten small knobs are punishing, as are the short sprints up Spy Rock and Humpback Rocks.

The newest section of AT falls within James River Face Wilderness. The James is Virginia's longest river, running 450 miles from its mountain headwaters into Hampton Roads on the Chesapeake Bay. Between Buena Vista and Lynchburg, the river breaches the Blue Ridge in a deep gorge. Land south of the river falls inside Virginia's first and largest wilderness area, the James River Face. Inside the wilderness boundaries the AT follows tall river cliffs and a scenic stream, Matts Creek. A pedestrian footbridge across the James, opened in 2000, made the relocation possible. The footbridge honors the memory of Bill Foot, a Natural Bridge ATC president who pioneered construction of the James River Foot Bridge, but passed away before seeing it completed.

On the north bank of the James River, the AT enters the Glenwood-Pedlar district of the George Washington–Jefferson National Forest. A series of fires dating from the 1890s, including one as recently as 1963, consumed thousands of acres of woodland in this area. The 1963 fire stopped at Little Rocky Row (reached via twenty-one switchbacks out of the gorge). It's here, from a vista on Fullers Rocks, that the last—and perhaps best—view of the James and the gorge unfolds south and west. More climbing awaits for northbound hikers to Bluff Mountain (3,372 feet) and Rice Mountain (2,228 feet). Past Rice Mountain, the trail gains 2,000 feet to the summit of Bald Knob (4,059 feet), which is actually crowned with a healthy head of trees. After dipping into Cow Camp Gap, the AT climbs again to Cold Mountain (4,022 feet), a grassy peak once grazed by livestock. The Forest Service, swayed by the beautiful views from the peak, keeps it clear with controlled burns.

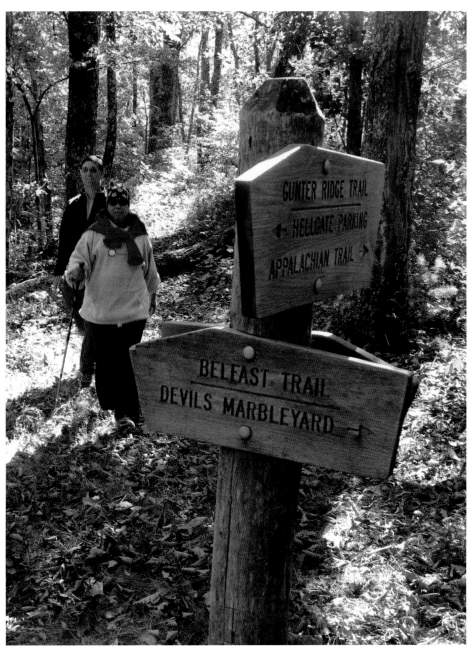

Joanne Ross and Allen Gean hiking the AT in James River Face Wilderness

AT SHELTERS/HUTS (MILEAGE ON THE AT FROM US 220 NORTH TO ROCKFISH GAP)

Mile 5.0   Fullhardt Knob Shelter

Mile 11.2   Wilson Creek Shelter

Mile 18.5   Bobbletts Gap Shelter

Mile 24.9   Cove Mountain Shelter

Mile 31.8   Bryant Ridge Shelter

Mile 36.8   Cornelius Creek Shelter

Mile 42.1   Thunder Hill Shelter

Mile 54.5   Matts Creek Shelter

Mile 58.4   Johns Hollow Shelter

Mile 67.2   Punchbowl Shelter

Mile 76.0   Brown Mountain Creek Shelter

Mile 81.6   Cow Camp Shelter

Mile 91.8   Seeley-Woodworth Shelter

Mile 99.2   The Priest Shelter

Mile 106.1 Harpers Creek Shelter

Mile 112.3 Maupin Field Shelter

Mile 128.4 Paul C. Wolfe Shelter

The view from Cold Mountain includes the Religious Range—a series of peaks named by Robert Rose, a large landowner in the area. There is The Priest and Little Priest, as well as the Friar and Cardinal Ridge. The Priest stands within Virginia's newest wilderness area, designated in 2000. Because of the prohibition on mechanical tools for trail maintenance in a wilderness, the board of the Natural Bridge ATC opposed this initiative. Instead, they sought a special management area designation, like that which covers Mount Pleasant. Special management areas offer similar protection as wilderness, but with relaxed rules that allow chainsaws. But wilderness advocates prevailed, and in November 2000, President Clinton announced creation of Virginia's seventeenth wilderness, The Priest–Three Ridges Wilderness Area.

Humpback Rocks (3,080 feet) is the AT's last hurrah before it descends to Rockfish Gap and enters the Shenandoah National Park. With views in all directions, it's a perfect spot to get a glimpse of how far you've come. And what lies ahead.

HIKE INFORMATION

Local Information

Lynchburg Tourism, (800) 732-5821, www.lynchburgvirginia.org

Roanoke Valley Convention & Visitors Bureau, Roanoke, (800) 635-5535, www.visitroanokeva.com

SEGMENT 4. ROCKFISH GAP TO CHESTER GAP

Shenandoah National Park and the Appalachian Trail grew up together. Civilian Conservation Corps crews built Skyline Drive on right-of-ways carved by AT trail volunteers. The routes stay within a half-mile of each other as they pass through mountain gaps, past old farms and orchards, and over rocky mountaintops. Iconic images of Shenandoah—autumn foliage, waterfalls, and soaring views off rocky outcrops—foster the idea of a timeless, never-changing park. A few days hiking the AT dispels this notion. Fires, floods, ice-storm damage, invasive insects, and gypsy moth infestation leave their distinctive mark on large areas of the forest in Shenandoah. In these areas, the AT gives hikers a view of the shrubby plants, small trees, wildflowers, and vines that mark early stages of reforestation.

Start: Blue Ridge Parkway south of I-64

Distance: 107.1 miles point to point

Difficulty: Moderate

Trail surface: Using dirt footpaths and abandoned dirt roads, hike along ridges and outcrops; down steep wooded slopes; and through old fields, red spruce, and balsam fir at the highest elevations.

Nearest towns: Waynesboro, VA (south access); Front Royal, VA (north access)

Canine compatibility: Dogs permitted (must be on a leash at all times)

Trail contacts: Appalachian Trail Conservancy, Harpers Ferry, WV, (304) 535-6331, www .appalachiantrail.org; Potomac Appalachian Trail Club (PATC), Vienna, (703) 242-0315, www .patc.net; Shenandoah National Park, Luray, (540) 999-3500, www .nps.gov/shen; Skyland Resort, Skyline Drive, (877) 847-1919, www .goshenandoah.com

Schedule: Open year-round. Skyline Drive may close without advance notice due to inclement weather. Portions of this road are also closed during hunting season to discourage poachers. Call (540) 999-3500 for closures.

Fees/permits: Entrance fee (honor boxes at north and south park boundaries). Appalachian Trail (AT) hikers must register for a free backcountry permit at Tom Floyd Wayside (north district) and Rockfish Gap entrance station (south district).

Maps/guides: AT Guide Set #7 covers Shenandoah National Park. www.atctrailstore.org

FINDING THE TRAILHEAD

To Rockfish Gap Trailhead: From Waynesboro, at the junction of US 340 and I-64, take I-64 east for 5.1 miles to the Afton Mountain exit 99. At the bottom of the exit ramp, turn right onto US 250. In 0.2 mile, turn right onto the Skyline Drive/Blue Ridge Parkway access road. Park at the Augusta County Visitor Center at Rockfish Gap, which is behind the Chevron gas station. The AT is located on the east side of the Blue Ridge Parkway. **Note:** If leaving a car for multiple nights, inform the visitor center staff. *DeLorme: Virginia Atlas & Gazetteer*: Page 67, D5. **To Chester Gap Trailhead:** See Segment 5: Chester Gap to Harpers Ferry.

THE HIKE

The AT just north of Rockfish Gap passes little in the way of rock formations, gorges, and waterfalls that draw millions of visitors to Shenandoah National Park. There are, instead, acres of farmland and meadow. Cattle graze and views spill off the mountains onto farms and towns of the Shenandoah Valley.

As introductions go, this pastoral entry into Shenandoah National Park feels right. The parkland was, for hundreds of years, privately owned. Much of it was farmed. Every meadow and mountain gap, every peak, pass, and hollow holds a story or mystery about the people who lived there. At Blackrock, 20 miles north of Rockfish Gap, legend says a friend of Thomas Jefferson hid Virginia colony's Great Seal and the archives of the colonial assembly in a cave during the Revolutionary War. The cave has never been identified (although the records and state seal survived the British raid that prompted the stash). Mystery aside, Blackrock commands attention on its own merits. This formation was once a cliff that collapsed after the soft limestone beneath it dissolved. Limestone, by its very nature, erodes faster than granite and greenstone. Where it underlies harder rock, erosion can result in the formation of talus, or large rock piles, at the base of cliffs.

North of Jarmans Gap, mountain laurel spreads roots into the cracks of exposed rock. Rhododendron grows tall and lush around stream headwaters near Moormans River Overlook. Taken together, these plants signal that more rugged, rocky terrain lies ahead. At Ivy Creek, the AT drops into a small canyon (2.7 miles north of Loft Mountain camp store). Briefly, it follows the hemlock-lined stream. The forest undergrowth is lush with mountain laurel, a plant that prefers the shade of pines and hemlocks. If it's been a mild winter, look for an extra spectacular spring laurel bloom. The many white, cup-shaped laurel flowers make this short stretch of the AT one of a kind in the park.

AT SHELTERS/HUTS (MILEAGE ON THE AT FROM ROCKFISH GAP NORTH TO CHESTER GAP)

Mile 7.0	Calf Mountain Shelter
Mile 20.0	Blackrock Hut
Mile 33.2	Pinefield Hut
Mile 41.4	Hightop Hut
Mile 53.8	Bearfence Hut
Mile 65.3	Rock Spring Hut
Mile 76.2	Byrds Nest Shelter #3
Mile 80.6	Pass Mountain Hut
Mile 93.7	Gravel Springs Shelter
Mile 104.2	Tom Floyd Wayside (primitive site)

On the approach to Big Meadows (17.4 miles north of Swift Run Gap), a cemetery and pieces of a pasture fence are visible from the AT. Periwinkle blooms in spring. The wildflower, with small, waxy-looking leaves that spread like a ground ivy, is not a naturally occurring mountain wildflower. Its presence usually indicates that a homesite once stood in the area. Nearby, on Tanner's Ridge, residents refused to leave their homes after

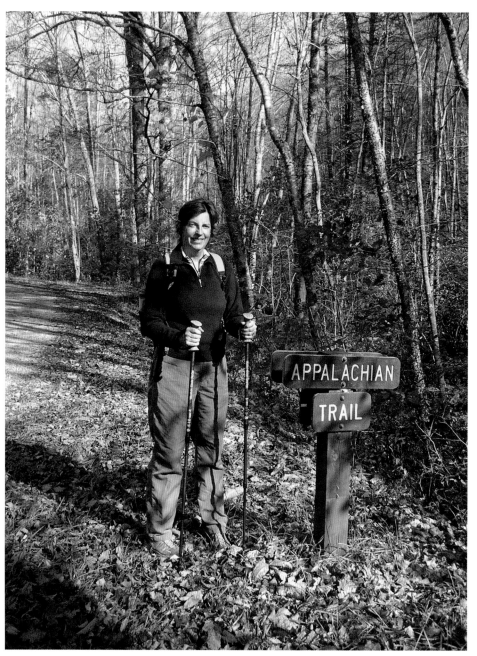

The author heading out on an AT day hike

President Franklin D. Roosevelt dedicated the park in 1936. Old pictures show sheriff deputies carrying a woman away from her house, a vivid example of forced eviction.

Not every mountain settler resisted. Some left willingly. North of Rock Spring Hut, where the AT passes beneath the cliffs of Hawksbill Mountain (4,051 feet), a view opens north onto Ida Valley. This is where the federal government built its first resettlement community for park residents in 1937. Hawksbill is the tallest mountain in Shenandoah National Park, but the AT passes below, not over, the summit. The trail reaches its highest point in this section a few miles north on Stony Mountain. Stony is followed in quick succession by the Pinnacles and Little Stony Mountain. These peaks, short on tree cover, offer great views from rock summits and cliffs. They are also within easy reach of Skyland Lodge, a hotel and restaurant that draws flocks of visitors.

Skyland is famous for its founder, George Freeman Pollack, who opened the resort in the 1880s. In 1924 Pollack helped sell the idea of making the Blue Ridge, from Front Royal to Rockfish Gap, America's first national park east of the Mississippi River. "A national park near our nation's capital" became the group's slogan. After 12 years, they succeeded. There is a story about local boys who climbed from the valley to watch tourists drive Skyline Drive and counted as many as six cars in a day. In 2016, Shenandoah National Park recorded 1.2 million visitors, making it the fifth-most visited national park in the nation.

Like periwinkle, an orchard tree—apple, pear, cherry, or other fruit—signals that a homesite or farm once stood in the area. Apples were prized for making moonshine brandy in Gravel Spring Gap (14.5 miles north of Thornton Gap). Nicholson Hollow, south of Mary's Rock, was renowned for its apple brandy. Jarmans Gap, at the southern end of the park, was known for corn whiskey. Moonshine, though illegal, offered poor mountaineers extra income. If a man had the skills, nature provided the ingredients: clean, running water, fruit or corn, and yeast. Stills were hidden and well protected from suspicious strangers who wandered nearby. This included early AT trail volunteers. Stories tell of how settlers chased Potomac Appalachian Trail Club (PATC) volunteers by setting fires.

Like a bird returning to its summer/breeding grounds, an AT thru-hiker in Shenandoah National Park is a herald of spring. Thousands of men and women begin the AT at Springer Mountain in Georgia in March. The bulk of them hit this park in May. Many have their hearts—or stomachs—set on a good meal at one of the park's three restaurants. As their thoughts wander ahead to Harpers Ferry, West Virginia—the official halfway point on the 2,173-mile trail—their feet pass over storied ground. In Shenandoah, there's a tale around every turn in the trail.

HIKE INFORMATION

Local Information

Front Royal Visitors Center, (540) 630-5788, www.discoverfrontroyal.com
   Luray-Page County Visitors Center, (540) 743-3915, www.visitluraypage.com
   Staunton Visitors Center, Staunton, (540) 332-3971, www.visitstaunton.com

SEGMENT 5. CHESTER GAP TO HARPERS FERRY

The Blue Ridge of northern Virginia has none of the 4,000-foot-plus heights so plentiful on the Appalachian Trail farther south. Still, the northern Virginia leg is one exhausting climb after another. On open mountain balds, views drop west onto the Great Valley. The bumpy spine of the Blue Ridge runs southward, and to the east lie the rolling meadows of Virginia's hunt country. Come fall and winter, the mountains here harbor quiet moments, interrupted occasionally by the thrashing of birds foraging among the hornbeam, dogwood, spicebush, and sassafras.

Start: Parking lot on the southbound side of US 522
Distance: 54.5 miles
Difficulty: Moderate
Trail surface: Using dirt footpaths and abandoned dirt roads, hike along low ridges, cliffs, and rock lookouts and through fields, meadows, and stream hollows.
Nearest towns: Front Royal, VA (south access); Harpers Ferry, WV (north access)
Canine compatibility: Dogs permitted
Trail contacts: Appalachian Trail Conservancy, Harpers Ferry, WV, (304) 535-6331, www.appalachiantrail.org; Potomac Appalachian Trail Club (PATC), Vienna, (703) 242-0315, www.patc.net; Harpers Ferry National Historical Park, Harpers Ferry, WV, (304) 535-6298, www.nps.gov/hafe
Schedule: Open year-round. Hunting season in G. R. Thompson Wildlife Management Area, mid-Nov through first week in Jan.
Maps/guides: AT Guide Set #6 covers the AT from Chester Gap, VA, to Harpers Ferry, WV. www.atctrailstore.org

FINDING THE TRAILHEAD

To Chester Gap Trailhead: From Front Royal, drive south 3.4 miles on US 522 from its intersection with VA 55. The Appalachian Trail (AT) crosses US 522 here. There's parking for several cars on the southbound side of the highway. *DeLorme: Virginia Atlas & Gazetteer:* Page 74, A3.

To Harpers Ferry Trailhead: From Harpers Ferry, WV, cross the Shenandoah River bridge and drive west 0.9 mile on US 340 to the Harpers Ferry National Historical Park Visitor Center. There's an entrance fee. A free shuttle runs every 10 to 15 minutes into Lower Town, where the AT is located. Notify park rangers if you intend on leaving the car for multiple nights. Alternate parking for day hikers is located at the junction of US 340 and VA 671 (in Virginia), at an unsecured roadside parking area near the Tri-State Amoco gas station. From the east end of the Shenandoah River bridge, proceed east 1.6 miles on US 340 to the parking area, on the left. On foot, backtrack 0.3 mile on US 340 to the Loudoun Heights Trail on the southbound side of the road. *DeLorme: Virginia Atlas & Gazetteer:* Page 79, B7.

THE HIKE

Small as it appears on a map, Chester Gap looms big on the AT. The Blue Ridge tapers suddenly into this gap, located east of Front Royal. Northward, the range becomes a chain of low, rounded ridges. After hundreds of miles of exposed ridges, mountain balds, and towering cliffs, this section shrinks into short, vigorous climbs. From Manassas Gap to Snickers Gap, it's either steep up, or steep down, with little in between. Thru-hikers nickname it the roller coaster for its many breath-stealing bumps.

The story of Chester Gap touches on the mystery of Virginia's first white explorer who crossed the Blue Ridge. John Lederer explored the mountains for Virginia's colonial government and, in 1670, wrote of the inspiring view from the mountains. Where exactly he stood is still debated. The AT passes a monument in Linden, Virginia, at Manassas Gap, in honor of his explorations. Some historians say he climbed the Swift Run Gap in Shenandoah National Park. Others say Mount Marshall, also in Shenandoah. Because Lederer's mission was to locate the headwaters of the Rappahannock River, many believe Chester Gap is where he broke through the Blue Ridge in 1670. The Rappahannock starts as a small mountain stream east of Chester Gap, eventually to become a major tributary of the Chesapeake Bay.

Wherever he stood, Lederer's first impression of the mountains speaks volumes about how early explorers and settlers viewed the Blue Ridge. It was, for the English, terra incognito. Lederer, maybe feeling lightheaded from his long climb, initially described the blue haze covering the western mountain slope as some kind of great western ocean. When the haze lifted, he moved across the Great Valley and explored present-day West Virginia.

It's nostalgic, as you hike this 54-mile stretch of the AT, to imagine how volunteers in 1927 plotted the first miles of the world-famous long trail in this region. Only a few stretches of original trail remain intact north of Chester Gap. Trail relocations peaked in the 1950s, when private landowners blocked access. With Washington, DC, only 60 miles east, and because of the many gaps that permit short hikes, the AT in this region has historically received heavy day use. Landowners' protest is now a moot point. The AT passes near homes and uses several dirt and paved roads south of Manassas Gap. But there are also long stretches through heavy forestland where the scarlet tanager's song floats down from tall treetops.

Birds make much racket in the overgrowth of spicebush, honeysuckle, and Virginia creeper along the trail. Redstarts, vireos, wood thrush, bluebirds, robins, and thrushes flit branch to branch, wavering for a second or two on a twig that can barely hold their weight. If they're lucky, the noisy forage for food ends with a prize: the grapelike fruit of Virginia creeper. Any hiker who has violently pitched forward, tripped up by a camouflaged creeper, knows this vine deserves to be pruned rather than admired. The vine grows adhesive discs on its tendrils that cement to the surfaces of trees, fence posts, and all forms of climbable surfaces. Perhaps we would all have higher regard for the creeper if Virginia's General Assembly had enshrined it as the state flower. Instead, by a one-vote margin, the vine lost to the flowering dogwood.

The climb on the AT north from Snickers Gap follows a rocky switchback ascent. After topping out, the trail drops and crosses a boulder-lined stream in Pigeon Hollow. Sounds of water bubble up from beneath the rocks. The trail will climb again, descend to another stream, and then climb once more to Crescent Rock. Beyond this folded section of Catoctin greenstone, the trail continues its roller-coaster route. Three times between Snickers Gap and Ashby Gap, the AT climbs to high points: Lookout Point, Tomblin Hill, and Buzzard Hill. Three times the trail drops, first into a valley formed by a branch of Spout Run, then into Fent Willey Hollow and Reservoir Hollow.

During the Civil War, the mountain hollows of northern Virginia sheltered a group of Confederate raiders known as Mosby's Rangers. John Singleton Mosby led the group

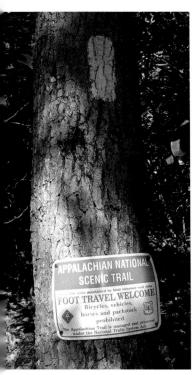
Appalachian Trail sign and white blaze. The AT is blazed white in Virginia.

and coordinated his soldiers' guerrilla-style tactics. They sprang upon Union soldiers in the mountain passes, took clothes, weapons, and money, then led prisoners into Confederate strongholds. By the end of the war, Mosby ruled a small fiefdom in Loudoun County, from Bull Run Mountain to the crest of the Blue Ridge. Ruled isn't too strong a word, either. His rangers were not allowed to leave the boundaries of the Confederacy without permission. Any man who missed two roll calls without good reason was discharged. At war's end, Mosby received a pardon (as did most Confederate soldiers), and then supported his old battlefield enemy Ulysses S. Grant in the presidential election.

Few towns are richer in Civil War history than Harpers Ferry, West Virginia. This national historical park is the end of the AT in Virginia, at the bridge crossing on US 340. The Shenandoah River thunders below this symbolic crossing. The Blue Ridge extends into Maryland and southern Pennsylvania. In that region, the chain goes by the name South Mountain. Not until the White Mountains of New Hampshire does the AT reach heights equal to Virginia's mountains. From Weaver Cliffs, north of Harpers Ferry, the AT hiker can look back south along the Blue Ridge. If conditions are right, you might see (or believe you see), if only for a whimsical moment, what John Lederer saw in 1670, an endless ocean of blue haze.

AT SHELTERS/HUTS
(MILEAGE NORTH FROM CHESTER GAP)

Mile 5.2   Jim & Molly Denton Shelter

Mile 10.7   Manassas Gap Shelter

Mile 15.1   Whiskey Gap Shelter

Mile 24.1   Rod Hollow Shelter

Mile 31.0   Sam Moore Shelter

Mile 45.1   David Lesser Shelter

HIKE INFORMATION

LOCAL INFORMATION

Loudoun Visitors Center, Leesburg, (703) 771-2170 or (800) 752-6118, www.visitloudon.org

Front Royal Visitors Center, (540) 630-5788, www.discoverfrontroyal.com

GREAT DAY HIKES ALONG THE APPALACHIAN TRAIL

Compiled here is an index of great day hikes along the Appalachian Trail (AT) in Virginia. Some are featured hikes in this book, others are Honorable Mentions, and the rest are great sections of the AT that should be hiked at one time or another.

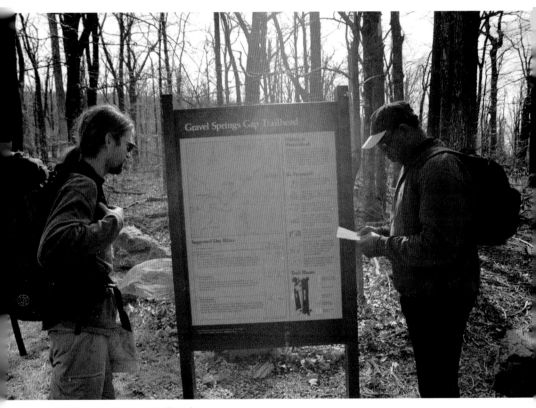

Gravel Springs Gap Trailhead

SEGMENT 1. DAMASCUS TO MARION

1. FEATHERCAMP BRANCH
See Hike 29: Feathercamp Ridge.

2. WHITETOP LAUREL CIRCUIT
For nearly 6 miles, the AT follows the ridge of Straight Mountain with overlooks onto wild Whitetop Laurel Creek. At either end, it junctions with the Virginia Creeper Trail, a multiuse trail for hikers and mountain bikers. Together, the AT and Creeper Trail make a vigorous 10-mile loop. The Creeper Trail is a model for the Rails-to-Trails effort. Its total length along the former Abingdon Branch of the Virginia-Carolina Railroad measures 34 miles. The stretch used in this loop is noted for its pathway along scenic Whitetop Laurel Creek. Begin and end the loop at a parking area on VA 728, south of US 58 near Beartree Day Use Area. Mount Rogers NRA/JNF, (276) 579-7092. *DeLorme: Virginia Atlas & Gazetteer.* Page 22, C3.

3. ELK GARDEN-MOUNT ROGERS SUMMIT
See Hike 31: Mount Rogers Summit.

4. RHODODENDRON GAP
See Hike 31: Mount Rogers Summit.

5. GRAYSON HIGHLANDS STATE PARK
There are 3 miles of the AT in this popular state park. The quickest link to the long trail is via the Highlands Horse Trail from the park ranger station at Massie Gap. From there, the AT goes north to Little Wilson Creek Wilderness and high-country meadows over-looking Scales. In the other direction, the AT ascends along Wilburn Ridge to amazing rock outcrops, deep thickets of rhododendron, and finally the Mount Rogers Spur Trail. Grayson Highlands State Park and Mount Rogers NRA/JNF, (276) 579-7092 or (276) 783-5196, www.dcr.virginia.gov/state-parks/grayson-highlands. *DeLorme: Virginia Atlas & Gazetteer.* Page 23, C5.

SEGMENT 2. MARION TO ROANOKE

6. CRAWFISH–CHANNEL ROCK LOOP

See Honorable Mention GG: Crawfish/Channel Rock.

7. BEARTOWN WILDERNESS

It's an easy 2.4-mile hike up the AT from FR 222 (an extension of VA 625) and the boundary of Beartown Wilderness. The AT skirts the south edge of this 6,375-acre federal wilderness until Chestnut Knob. From the mountain, views drop into Burke's Garden, a pocket of agricultural bliss formed when subsurface limestone eroded. Beartown Wilderness has no marked trails besides the AT, but old logging roads allow for exploring Roaring Branch and a sphagnum bog at the headwaters of Cove Branch. Eastern Divide Ranger District, (540) 552-4641. *DeLorme: Virginia Atlas & Gazetteer:* Page 39, D5.

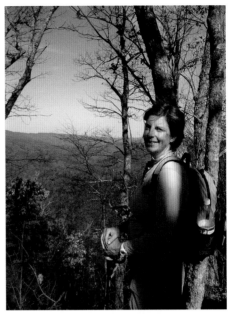

The author at Crawfish/Channel Rock

8. TRAIL BOSS–AT LOOP

Trail crews rerouted 2.1 miles of the AT to descend off Brushy Mountain as it approaches VA 615. The old section was renamed Trail Boss in honor of a dedicated volunteer. Combined, they make a 5.1-mile loop hike. The AT's route up Brushy Mountain is steep, with ten switchbacks and several overlooks. This is, however, primarily a woodland hike through an oak-hickory forest. There are mountain laurel and rhododendron. In the dark hollows, look for the bloodroot wildflower, plus many mosses and ferns. Eastern Divide Ranger District, (540) 552-4641. *DeLorme: Virginia Atlas & Gazetteer:* Page 39, C7.

9. ANGELS REST

South of the New River from Pearisburg, the AT makes a steep, switchback-heavy trip up Pearis Mountain. In 1.5 miles, a trail leads a few hundred yards to Angels Rest. This 3,550-foot perch has views into the New River's passage through the Narrows, a rock fault between Devonian shale and Cambrian limestone. The trailhead for this 3-mile in-and-out hike is on VA 634 (Morris Avenue) in Pearisburg. A turnaround at Angels Rest makes a 3-mile day hike. Eastern Divide Ranger District, (540) 552-4641. *DeLorme: Virginia Atlas & Gazetteer:* Page 40, B3.

10. THE RICE FIELDS

See Honorable Mention HH: The Rice Fields.

11. PETERS MOUNTAIN WILDERNESS

See Honorable Mention FF: Huckleberry Loop.

12. MOUNTAIN LAKE WILDERNESS

See Hike 25: Mountain Lake Wilderness.

13. KELLY KNOB

A 3.3-mile trek from Sinking Creek and VA 42 to Kelly Knob ends with views off this 3,742-foot peak. The AT crosses privately owned farmland near the trailhead. Be sure to follow all posted signs regarding parking and hiking. Past Kelly Knob, the AT dips to Big Pond; a side trail here leads 100 yards to views from White Rocks. For an 8.5-mile point-to-point hike, continue hiking up the AT and descend Johns Creek Mountain Trail. Park a shuttle at the Johns Creek trailhead on VA 658 west of Twin Oaks. Eastern Divide Ranger District, (540) 552-4641. *DeLorme: Virginia Atlas & Gazetteer.* Page 41, B6.

14. DRAGONS TOOTH

It is a steep and rugged climb on the AT for 2.6 miles to Dragons Tooth, a craggy rock that juts 35 feet above the summit of Cove Mountain. En route, the AT traces the razor edge of Tuscarora sandstone in an area called Rawies Rest. Use the blue-blazed Dragons Tooth Trail to make a loop hike that begins and ends at VA 624. There is alternate parking and trail access on VA 311 north at the Dragons Tooth parking lot past Catawba Grocery. Eastern Divide Ranger District, (540) 552-4641. *DeLorme: Virginia Atlas & Gazetteer.* Page 42, B1.

15. MCAFEE KNOB

The AT leads 3.5 miles uphill to McAfee Knob, a 3,197-foot high point on Catawba Mountain. The southern trailhead is on VA 311, west of Salem, Virginia. For a longer day hike, continue past McAfee for another 6 miles along Tinker Mountain with its gorgeous cliff overlooks. A junction with the blue-blazed Andy Lane Trail leads 2.3 miles left to VA 600. Highlights of this trip include views of Catawba Valley, boulders in the Devils Kitchen area, and a half-mile of exposed, cliff trail on Tinker Cliffs. Appalachian Trail Conservancy corridor, NPS, (540) 961-5551. *DeLorme: Virginia Atlas & Gazetteer.* Page 42, A/B2.

SEGMENT 3. ROANOKE TO ROCKFISH GAP

16. LITTLE COVE MOUNTAIN TRAIL

South of Jennings Creek, the AT rides a high ridge called Cove Mountain. In total, there are ten small knobs en route, from the trailhead on VA 614 to the blue-blazed Little Cove Mountain Trail. Cove Mountain (2,720 feet) marks the highest point. A return hike on Little Cove Mountain Trail passes through the watershed of Cove Creek and Little Cove Creek. Where the Little Cove trail ends at VA 614, turn left and walk 0.7 mile up gravel VA 614 to the trailhead. This hike features a shale barren, a rare ecosystem hosting prickly pear and other fragile plants, located off the AT near VA 614. Glenwood-Pedlar Ranger District, (540) 291-2188. *DeLorme: Virginia Atlas & Gazetteer.* Page 53, D5.

17. APPLE ORCHARD FALLS–CORNELIUS CREEK LOOP

The AT measures only 1.1 miles between Apple Orchard Falls National Recreation Trail and Cornelius Falls Trail. This short stint, however, makes possible a delight of a hike alongside two beautiful streams replete with waterfalls, pools, and thick stands of rhododendron and mountain laurel. There is considerable elevation loss and gain on this 7.6-mile loop—as much as 2,000 feet difference from the AT to FR 59, where you pick up the Cornelius Falls Trail for a return to the AT. Begin the trip at a parking area on the Sunset Field Overlook on the Blue Ridge Parkway (milepost 78.4). Glenwood-Pedlar Ranger District, (540) 291-2188. *DeLorme: Virginia Atlas & Gazetteer.* Page 53, D6.

18. JAMES RIVER FACE WILDERNESS

The AT through this mountainous, 8,903-acre wilderness area was reconstructed in 2000. It now begins at the James River Foot Bridge, on the north bank of the James on US 501/VA 130 (the bridge is named in honor of Bill Foot, a Natural Bridge ATC volunteer who passed away in 2000). After crossing, the AT passes beneath high cliff walls in the river gorge, then climbs gradually up Matts Creek to the Matts Creek Shelter. (The old AT route has been renamed.) Several trails branch off the AT in the wilderness. Belfast Trail leads to Devil's Marbleyard, an 8-acre boulder field with rocks the size of cars. From an alternate trailhead on the Blue Ridge Parkway (milepost 71), hike the AT 1.2 miles to Highcock Knob (3,073 feet). Views from the top are limited in summer. Glenwood-Pedlar Ranger District, (540) 291-2188. *DeLorme: Virginia Atlas & Gazetteer.* Page 53, D7.

19. OLD HOTEL TRAIL

See Hike 24: Mount Pleasant.

20. ROCKY MOUNTAIN/LOVINGSTON SPRING

A 5.8-mile stretch of the AT runs from Salt Log Gap on FR 63 (extension of VA 634) to the Seeley-Woodworth AT shelter. A return on Lovingston Spring Trail makes an 11.7-mile loop. Wildflowers, mosses, and ferns grow thick around the many springs on these trails. There are signs of an old apple orchard near the AT uphill from Salt Log Gap. Wolf Rocks is a scenic overlook with views of The Priest (northeast) and Rocky Mountain (west). The return trip includes a 0.8-mile side trip (0.4 mile each way) up Rocky Mountain, a summit with views west over the Shenandoah Valley. Glenwood-Pedlar Ranger District, (540) 291-2188. *DeLorme: Virginia Atlas & Gazetteer*: Page 54, B2.

21. SPY ROCK

There are two access points on the AT for this overlook, famous for its wide views of the Cardinal, The Priest, Little Priest, and the Friar. If time is short, use the 0.4 mile of the AT that links Fish Hatchery Trail (a 1.2-mile extension of VA 690 east of Montebello) with the 0.1-mile Spy Rock Trail. This makes a total loop of 3.4 miles. (Ask permission to park at the state-run fish hatchery.) For a longer trip, hike the AT for 3.2 miles between VA 826 (Crabtree Farm Road) and Spy Rock. Access to the AT is 0.5 mile uphill from Crabtree Campground on VA 826. Glenwood-Pedlar Ranger District, (540) 291-2188. *DeLorme: Virginia Atlas & Gazetteer*: Page 54, B2.

22. MAU-HAR TRAIL

See Hike 23: Three Ridges.

23. HUMPBACK ROCKS

The AT departs the Humpback Rocks parking area on the Blue Ridge Parkway (milepost 6) and in 1 mile, passes a spur trail to Humpback Rocks. This 3,080-foot outcrop offers wide views of the Blue Ridge and Shenandoah Valley. Another mile on the AT brings the summit of Humpback Mountain (3,600 feet). A return to the parking lot makes a 4-mile hike. Blue Ridge Parkway, (828) 271-4779. *DeLorme: Virginia Atlas & Gazetteer*: Page 55, A4.

SEGMENT 4. ROCKFISH GAP TO CHESTER GAP

24. RIPRAP HOLLOW–AT LOOP
There is a 2.7-mile stretch of the AT between the Riprap Trail parking area (milepost 90) and Wildcat Ridge parking (milepost 92.1). To make a 10-mile loop hike, begin at the Riprap Trail parking area and descend Riprap Trail past Chimney Rock and Calvary Rock. Climb from the hollow on Wildcat Ridge Trail. Signs of a forest fire date from a 1998 blaze that originated in the area of Calvary Rock. This a great hike for witnessing nature's regenerative powers. SNP South District, (540) 999-3500. *DeLorme: Virginia Atlas & Gazetteer.* Page 67, C5.

25. JONES RUN–DOYLES RIVER TRAIL
The AT runs for 3.5 miles alongside Skyline Drive between Jones Run Trail and the Doyles River Trail. Using all three trails makes for a nice 8.2-mile hike, with small waterfalls and rock outcrops on Jones Run and the Doyles River. Begin the hike at Doyles River parking area (milepost 81.1). Descend Jones Run and ascend Jones Run Trail to Skyline Drive, then hike north on the AT. Brown Gap Road is a cutoff for a shorter 6.6-mile loop. SNP South District, (540) 999-3500. *DeLorme: Virginia Atlas & Gazetteer.* Page 67, C6.

26. BIG RUN LOOP TRAIL
A 1.6-mile stretch of the AT links either end of Big Run Loop Trail. The hike begins at Big Run Loop Overlook (milepost 82.2), drops into the Big Run stream valley, and returns to the AT in 4.2 miles. A forest fire torched parts of the Big Run watershed. Finish the 5.8-mile loop by hiking north on the AT to the Doyles River trailhead, then uphill 200 yards to Skyline Drive. SNP South District, (540) 999-3500. *DeLorme: Virginia Atlas & Gazetteer.* Page 67, B6.

27. WHITEOAK CANYON–CEDAR RUN FALLS
This is an extremely popular hike that uses 3.3 miles of the AT. Popular, however, does not mean easy. At 11 miles, this loop takes the better part of the day. There are steep dropoffs and difficult climbs. Payoff comes with 40-foot cascades in Whiteoak Canyon, and the many falls and pools along Cedar Run. Use the Stony Man Nature Trail parking area (milepost 41.7) at Skyland as a starting point, and the Whiteoak–Cedar Run Link Trail to complete the loop. SNP Central District, (540) 999-3500. *DeLorme: Virginia Atlas & Gazetteer.* Page 74, D1.

28. LITTLE STONY MAN–STONY MAN
Stony Man (3,387 feet) is a popular site thanks to Skyland, a park resort. This route uses a northern approach from the Little Stony Man parking area (milepost 39.1). The 1.2-mile hike on the AT traces tall cliffs and intersects the 0.4-mile loop trail around Stony Man's summit. Past Stony Man, leave the AT and descend on Stony Man Horse Trail and

Furnace Spring Trail. Return via the Passamaquoddy Trail. SNP Central District, (540) 999-3500. *DeLorme: Virginia Atlas & Gazetteer.* Page 74, D2.

29. MARY'S ROCK

An easy 2-mile hike on the AT leads to a 360-degree view off Mary's Rock. From the Panorama Restaurant at Thornton Gap, the AT climbs 1.9 miles on switchbacks to the overlook spur trail. Samples of rock called granodiorite from this area were carbon dated to more than 1 billion years, making it officially the oldest rock known in the park. Retrace the AT to the Panorama for a 4-mile hike. Parking is permitted at the restaurant. SNP Central District, (540) 999-3500. *DeLorme: Virginia Atlas & Gazetteer.* Page 74, C2.

30. LITTLE DEVIL STAIRS

Three miles of AT run between Little Hogback Overlook (milepost 19.7) and Rattle-snake Point Overlook (milepost 21.9). En route, the AT crosses Hogback Mountain (3,474 feet). Begin this hike at Little Hogback Overlook and use the Piney Branch Trail and Pole Bridge Link Trail to reach Little Devil Stairs, a 2-mile route down Keyser Run under sheer cliff walls and past picturesque waterfalls. Little Devil Stairs is a popular route, but dangerous. Use caution in icy or wet weather. Hike back up Little Devil Stairs and return to the Little Hogback Overlook on Keyser Fire Road for a 10.5-mile loop. SNP Northern District, (540) 999-3500. *DeLorme: Virginia Atlas & Gazetteer.* Page 74, B2.

31. MOUNT MARSHALL

See Hike 12: Mount Marshall Loop.

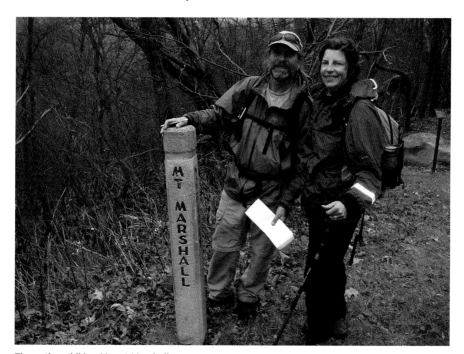

The authors hiking Mount Marshall

SEGMENT 5. CHESTER GAP TO HARPERS FERRY

32. SKY MEADOWS STATE PARK

A 3.6-mile piece of the AT runs through this beautiful Virginia state park set hard against the eastern foothills of the Blue Ridge. Large meadows lend the area a pastoral feel, but steep climbs await hikers on North Ridge Trail. Gap Run Trail follows a woodland stream, and Piedmont Overlook Trail features nice views of the meadows that sweep off the mountainside. Sky Meadows operated as a farm in the mid-1800s. A stone farmhouse now serves as a visitor center (seasonal) and there are several outbuildings, including stables for horseback riders. Entrance to the park is on US 17, 1.2 miles south of US 50. An entrance fee varies by season. Call (800) 933-PARK for camping reservations. *DeLorme: Virginia Atlas & Gazetteer.* Page 75, A5.

33. LOUDOUN HEIGHTS TRAIL

A 2.4-mile stretch of the AT joins the Loudoun Heights Trail for a moderately difficult day hike. There are views over the Potomac from Split Rock, a promontory on Loudoun Heights Trail. (The view also explains why Stonewall Jackson bombarded Harpers Ferry, West Virginia, from this hill in 1862.) This hike requires some roadside trekking on busy US 340 and navigation through Harpers Ferry National Historical Park. There are two access points: Harpers Ferry National Historical Park (fee charged for parking in a secure

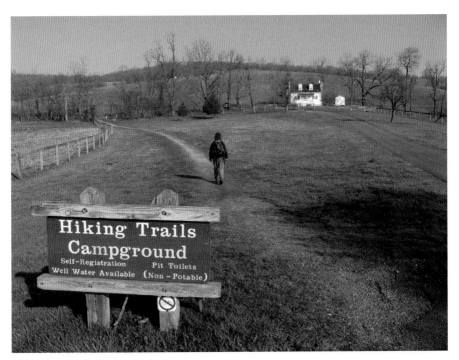

Hiking Sky Meadows State Park

overnight lot) or a roadside pull-off on US 340 at VA 671 in Virginia (unsecured and suitable for day hikes only). Call the park at (304) 535-6298 or the ATC at (304) 535-6068. In wintertime, the ATC headquarters is closed on weekends. Outfitter at Harpers Ferry, 189 High St., Harpers Ferry, WV (888-535-2087) sells maps. *DeLorme: Virginia Atlas & Gazetteer*: Page 79, B7.

CONTACT INFORMATION

STATEWIDE

Virginia Tourism Corporation, (800) VISIT-VA, www.virginia.org

Department of Conservation & Recreation (DCR), Division of State Parks, (800) 933-PARK, www.dcr.virginia.gov/state-parks. Campsite reservations: (800) 933-PARK (7275), www.reservevaparks.com

DCR, Natural Heritage Program, (804) 786-7951, www.dcr.virginia.gov/natural-heritage

Department of Wildlife Resources, (804) 367-1000, https://dwr.virginia.gov

NATIONAL FORESTS

Supervisor's Office, Roanoke, (540) 265-5100, www.fs.usda.gov/main/gwj

RANGER DISTRICTS

Clinch, Norton, (276) 679-8370

Eastern Divide, Blacksburg, (540) 552-4641

Glenwood-Pedlar, Natural Bridge Station, (540) 291-2188

James River and Warm Springs, Hot Springs, (540) 839-2521

Lee, Edinburg, (540) 984-4101

Mount Rogers, (276) 783-5196

North River, (540) 432-0187

NATIONAL PARKS

www.nps.gov

Blue Ridge Parkway, Asheville, NC, (828) 271-4779

George Washington Memorial Parkway, McLean, VA, (703) 289-2500

Great Falls Park, Great Falls, VA, (703) 285-2966

Prince William Forest Park, Triangle, VA, (703) 221-7181

Shenandoah National Park, Luray, VA, (540) 999-3500

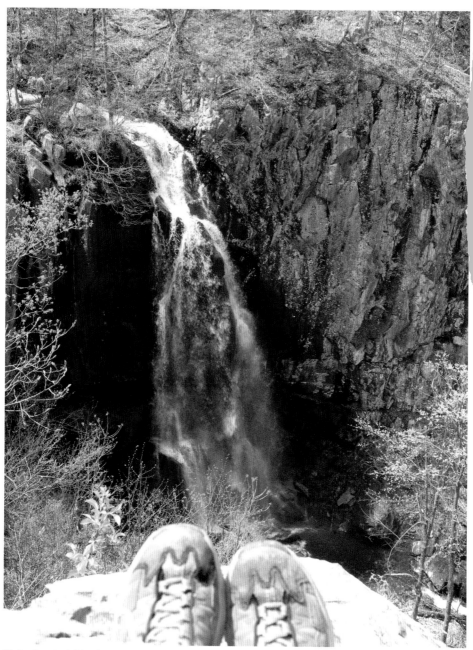

Highest waterfall in Shenandoah National Park

HIKE INDEX

THE TEN ESSENTIALS OF HIKING

American
Hiking
Society

American Hiking Society recommends you pack the "Ten Essentials" every time you head out for a hike. Whether you plan to be gone for a couple of hours or several months, make sure to pack these items. Become familiar with these items and know how to use them.

1. Appropriate Footwear
Happy feet make for pleasant hiking. Think about traction, support, and protection when selecting well-fitting shoes or boots.

2. Navigation
While phones and GPS units are handy, they aren't always reliable in the backcountry; consider carrying a paper map and compass as backups and know how to use them.

3. Water (and a way to purify it)
As a guideline, plan for half a liter of water per hour in moderate temperatures/terrain. Carry enough water for your trip and know where and how to treat water while you're out on the trail.

4. Food
Pack calorie-dense foods to help fuel your hike, and carry an extra portion in case you are out longer than expected.

5. Rain Gear & Dry-Fast Layers
The weatherman is not always right. Dress in layers to adjust to changing weather and activity levels. Wear moisture-wicking clothes and carry a warm hat.

6. Safety Items (light, fire, and a whistle)
Have means to start an emergency fire, signal for help, and see the trail and your map in the dark.

7. First Aid Kit
Supplies to treat illness or injury are only as helpful as your knowledge of how to use them. Take a class to gain the skills needed to administer first aid and CPR.

8. Knife or Multi-Tool
With countless uses, a multi-tool can help with gear repair and first aid.

9. Sun Protection
Sunscreen, sunglasses, and sun-protective clothing should be used in every season regardless of temperature or cloud cover.

10. Shelter
Protection from the elements in the event you are injured or stranded is necessary. A lightweight, inexpensive space blanket is a great option.

Find other helpful resources at AmericanHiking.org/hiking-resources